Democratization

7,8

Also by Jean Grugel

POLITICS AND DEVELOPMENT IN THE CARIBBEAN BASIN

FRANCO'S SPAIN (with T. Rees)

REGIONALISM ACROSS THE NORTH–SOUTH DIVIDE
(edited with W. Hoot)

DEMOCRACY WITHOUT BORDERS (editor)

Democratization

A Critical Introduction

Jean Grugel

palgrave

First published 2002 by
PALGRAVE
Houndmills, Basingstoke, Hampshire RG21 6XS and
175 Fifth Avenue, New York, N.Y. 10010
Companies and representatives throughout the world

PALGRAVE is the new global academic imprint of
St. Martin's Press LLC Scholarly and Reference Division and
Palgrave Publishers Ltd (formerly Macmillan Press Ltd).

ISBN 0-333-67968-7 hardback
ISBN 0-333-67969-5 paperback

This book is printed on paper suitable for recycling and made from fully
managed and sustained forest sources.

A catalogue record for this book is available from the British Library

Library of Congress Cataloging-in-Publication Data

Grugel, Jean.
    Democratization : a critical introduction / Jean Grugel.
        p.cm.
    Includes bibliographical references and index
    ISBN 0-333-67968-7 – ISBN 0-333-67969-5 (pbk)
    1. Democratization. 2. Democracy. I. Title

JC423 .G78 2001
321.8–dc21   2001036990

10   9   8   7   6   5   4   3   4   1
11   10   09   08   07   06   05   04   03   02

Printed in China

To Martin

Contents

List of Boxes

Acknowledgements

I would like to acknowledge the support of a number of people in writing this book. In the first place, thanks to my publisher Steven Kennedy for his help, support and cheerful demeanour in the face of missed deadlines, to two anonymous readers who made very useful suggestions for improving the manuscript and to Francesca Gains, Gillian Beard and Tony Heron who provided valuable research assistance. Thanks also to my students, undergraduate and postgraduate, who helped me clarify some of the ideas in the book. The Department of Politics at the University of Sheffield is a very congenial environment to work in and I would like to thank all my colleagues for their support. I would particularly like to acknowledge Petr Kopecky and Georgina Waylen, who are probably as relieved to see the end of this book as I am, and Sarah Cooke, Christine Whittaker, Sue Kelk and Katie Middleton for cheering me up while I was writing it. Jenny Pearce and Hazel Smith provided much appreciated encouragment at moments when I needed it. I owe an enormous debt of gratitude to Valerie Atkinson for her care and friendship over many years and I would like to take this opportunity to publicly acknowledge her support – a small thank-you for so very much help. A very special thanks to Martin Smith, who not only discussed the project, read the manuscript and made useful suggestions for improving it, but, more important, put up with me while I finished it. Our daughter contributed nothing to the manuscript and offered only endless distractions from it, but nonetheless I owe her everything, so, finally, thank you to Anna.

JEAN GRUGEL

Introduction

This book analyzes one of the most exciting developments in contemporary politics: the sustained attempts, which have gradually gathered pace since the 1970s, to subject government to popular control and to make states work in ways that favour the broad mass of the people. Struggles to establish democracy have their roots in the belief that everyone deserves to live in conditions of dignity, tolerance and respect. This book explains how a range of global pressures and events combined to open a political opportunity for democratization at the end of the twentieth century. It also analyzes the fate of some experiments in democratization. In brief, it presents the view that, despite the range of global pressures for democratization, the consolidation of democratization is nationally determined. Where democratization is successful, it is due to two factors, namely the emergence of strong, dense and vibrant civil societies that work consistently to democratize politics and to hold the state accountable, and the existence of a capable and flexible state. This book, therefore, takes issue with the hyper-globalizationist view that national politics and states no longer matter.

It is sometimes mistakenly assumed that there are 'recipes' for successful democratization, as if it were somehow possible to choose paths to, or models of, democracy from a menu of options. In fact, as this book shows, democratization is a slow and painful business. Elite commitment to democracy can weaken and is often contingent; structural factors frequently impede the deepening of democratization; and globalization can be as much an obstacle as an assistance. It should be no surprise that the number of successful democratizations is outweighed numerically by either failed or stalled experiments, for the creation of democracy is a radical and challenging business, during which groups with interests embedded in the maintenance of the non-democratic status quo have to be either defeated or reformed. Neat theories of democratization contrast with the real world experiences of partial, ambiguous, fuzzy – and frequently disappointing – democratization.

Contemporary Democratization

In the middle of the 1980s, observers of world politics became convinced that they were witnessing a new era in global politics: a third

1

wave of democratization. This followed two earlier periods of democratic expansion, first in the nineteenth century, and then in the years after the Second World War. By 1990, governments committed to building democracy had taken office in a range of apparently unconnected countries, including Portugal, Spain, Argentina, the Philippines, Poland and South Korea. The collapse of Communism in 1989 and the pro-democracy demonstrations in China the same year led to the belief that liberal democracy was fast becoming the only legitimate political ideology. Only a few Marxist authors (see, for example, Callinicos 1991) continued to argue that socialist democracy remains a viable political goal for humanity, the Soviet debacle notwithstanding, although a critical view that the spread of *liberal* democracy (rather than participatory or community-focused democracies) would not provide sufficiently for human needs was expressed from the beginning (Guehenno 1993; Robinson 1996).

Nevertheless, democratization, coming as it did in the wake of the collapse of the Soviet empire, was generally taken as an indication of the triumph of the West in political, economic and geopolitical terms. Fukuyama (1992) famously interpreted these events to signify 'the end of history'. After the fall of the Berlin Wall in 1989, Fukuyama thought that it would no longer be possible to posit a real alternative to either capitalism or democracy. World history, he argued, had been dominated since the nineteenth century by material and ideological conflicts between capitalism and democracy and socialism and communism. The defeat of communism signified the closure of this long-running contest and, with it, the end of grand questions concerning the best way to organize human society. History, in the sense of competing ideologies, had been brought to a close.

Others, however, were far less sure that democracy would emerge painlessly after 1989. After all, until the 1980s, it had been generally expected that democracy would only emerge under very particular circumstances. This meant, in practice, that democratic government would be confined either to the West or to advanced capitalist countries. Yet a distinguishing feature of the third wave is that democracy has become a global aspiration, irrespective of religion, culture and levels of development. It is possible to speak of democratization in Nicaragua, Sri Lanka, Nigeria, China, and Russia. Democracy has achieved, quite simply, 'global primacy' (McGrew 1997: 21). Whether we conceive of democratization as functional for global capitalism, as an imposition of global capitalist institutions, the introduction of formal structures of accountability or as social struggles to invest citizenship with meaning, democratization has become a key tool for the analysis of the contemporary world. Why democracy has gone global – and what this suggests for the meaning of democracy – is the subject of much debate.

Two features of the global order in particular have been important for understanding contemporary processes of democratization: the creation of a global political economy and the end of the Cold War. Together, these events have created opportunities for democratization. But they also signify the ascendancy of the capitalist, already-democratic West and, as such, constitute the foundations of an international order predicated upon Western dominance. This context renders democratization profoundly ambiguous. It means that while democratization is made up of real struggles to establish 'a mode of decision-making about collectively binding rules and policies over which the people exercise control (Beetham 1992: 40) it is also a reflection of an unequal global order predicated upon Western political, cultural and economic supremacy.

The Meaning of Democratization

Initial studies of democratization in the 1970s and 1980s presumed that the meaning of democratization was self-evident: it meant simply a transformation of the political system from non-democracy towards accountable and representative government. These studies adopted a process-oriented approach, concentrating on identifying the mechanisms or paths that lead to democratization. An important distinction was made between transition, or the beginning of the building of a democracy, during which politics is fluid and democracy not assured, and consolidation, when democracy becomes 'the only game in town' (Linz and Stepan 1996: 5). In a pioneering article, Stepan (1986) identified eight distinctive paths leading to the end of authoritarianism and the onset of democratization. These are set out in Box I.1.

As democratization developed, it became evident that although some countries successfully made a transition to democracy, others collapsed and many more fell – and remain – in the category of problematic democracies. The result was a shift in academic interest towards identifying those factors that make new democracies endure and those that, conversely, make for fragility or weakness. Consolidation of democracy became the principal focus for research in the 1990s. This represented a shift in the democratization debate, from a primary interest in structure and agency and their respective roles in causation, towards a focus

---

Box I.1   Stepan's Paths to Democratization

Internal restoration after external reconquest	Netherlands, Belgium, Norway and Denmark (all after 1945)
Internal reformulation	France (after 1945)
Externally monitored installation	West Germany and Japan (after 1945)
Democratization initiated from within authoritarian regime	Spain (1977) Brazil (1982) Portugal (1974)
Society-led termination	Argentina (1969) Peru (1977)
Party pact	Colombia (1958) Venezuela (1958)
Organized violent revolt (led by democratic parties)	Costa Rica (1948)
Marxist-led revolutionary war	Nicaragua (1979)

---

on how political culture (Diamond 1999), political economy (Haggard and Kaufman 1995) and institutionalism (Remmer 1997) shape outcomes. These theoretical debates are examined in detail in Chapter 3.

Whether the focus was on transition or consolidation, process-oriented scholarship failed to engage with the first-order question of what 'democratization' meant. A glance at the vast literature on democratization reveals that, far from consensus, there are significantly different ways of understanding the term. Democratization has been conceptualized as a discourse, a demand, a set of institutional changes, a form of elite domination, a political system dependent on popular control, an exercise in power politics and a demand for global solidarity – and this is by no means an exhaustive list. It has been analyzed from the perspective of political theory, comparative politics, international relations, sociology, cultural studies and political economy. It has been thought of as a discrete set of sequential changes achieved in a few years, as a series of open-ended struggles and a transformation of deep structures or as an unobtainable utopia. In short, democratization is as 'essentially contested' (Gallie 1964) a concept as democracy itself.

From the perspective of political studies, democratization has been understood along a continuum from a minimal to a maximalist position, with most commentators positioning themselves at different points in the middle. The basic minimalist definition sees democratization as the regular holding of clean elections and the introduction of basic norms (e.g. an absence of intimidation, competition from at least two political parties, and an inclusive suffrage) that make free elections possible. A slightly more inclusive definition demands the introduction of liberal individual rights (freedom of assembly, religious freedom, a free press, freedom to stand for public office, etc.) or the creation of a polyarchic order. Nevertheless this definition still remains quite limited because it fails to take either the issue of power or the importance of structural obstacles to participation seriously. This book favours a broader definition, in which democratization is the introduction and extension of citizenship rights and the creation of a democratic state. Another way to think of this is as rights-based or 'substantive' democratization, in contrast to 'formal' democratization. The litmus-test for democracy is not whether rights exist on paper but, rather, whether they have real meaning for people. Inevitably, this implies a redistribution of power.

A more difficult question is to what extent democratization should include the elimination of the most extreme forms of socio-economic inequality. Democracy is a political, not an economic, order. However, economic entitlements (or the lack of them) affect political entitlements. In developing countries in particular, poverty and social exclusion operate as real barriers to citizenship. Even in developed countries such as the US and Britain, poverty means reduced access and influence in the public sphere. Moreover, women are everywhere economically disadvantaged compared with their male counterparts and consequently participate less in politics and have less influence over policy-making. In practice, a full democratization cannot take place without either socio-economic reform, cultural and social change and a transformation of gender relations. However, it is not practical to use too utopian a definition of democratization. This would mean excluding established and accepted democracies and limiting the use of the term to idealized versions of the 'good society'. No country, in fact, could then be termed a democracy since inequalities, political and economic, persist in all societies. Nevertheless, it is important to remember that inequalities inevitably shape the politics of democracies. Where they are so great as to prevent sections of the population, be they women, ethnic groups, or the poor, from exercising meaningful political citizenship, it is difficult to speak of democratization. It is more accurate to categorize political systems in these cases as limited, facade, pseudo or illiberal democratizations.

Democratization and Democracy

The assumption that democracy means liberal democracy was the normative underpinning of most studies of democratization until the mid-1990s. This was generally taken to mean the holding of elections, the existence of a multi-party political system and a set of procedures for government. But, as Holden (1993) argues, this is to mistake the necessary conditions for liberal democracy for its defining characteristics. Neither the creation of political parties nor the holding of elections, in themselves, guarantee the existence of key democratic freedoms and rights, such as tolerance, respect for civil liberties and equality before the law.

Instead of defining democracy through the trappings of liberalism, it is more useful to adopt Beetham's (1992) approach. He suggests that the core meaning of democracy is straightforward. It is 'a mode of decision-making about collectively binding rules and policies over which the people exercise control' (Beetham 1992: 40). Democracy is, in its literal sense, rule by the people. However, confusion arises not over meaning but as a result of normative judgements about how much democracy is appropriate in any given society:

> Disputes about the meaning of democracy which purport to be conceptual disagreements are generally disputes about how much democracy is either desirable or practicable; that is about where the trade-off should come between democratic and other values, or at what point along the spectrum a given set of institutional arrangements for realizing the principle of control by equal citizens is in practice sustainable. (Beetham 1992: 40)

The main dispute is between those who insist on a minimal definition of democracy and those who, in contrast, argue that democracy implies not only procedures for government but also substantive rights. The difference between minimal (or formal) and substantive democracy is captured neatly by Kaldor and Vejvoda:

> Formal democracy is a set of rules, procedures and institutions ... substantive democracy [is] a process that has to be continually reproduced, a way of regulating power relations in such a way as to maximize the opportunities for individuals to influence the conditions in which they live, to participate in and influence debates about the key decisions which affect society. (Kaldor and Vejvoda 1997: 67)

Przeworski (1986; 1999) provides the most thought-out of contemporary justifications for a minimalist understanding of democracy. He argues that minimal democracy is a means of processing conflict, and, as such, is 'nothing short of miraculous' (Przeworski 1999). Far from being a second-best option, it is the only democracy possible due to the constraints of capitalism. For Przeworski, the structural power of capital is such that it can veto distributional democracy (Przeworski 1986). Any attempt, in fact, at redistribution may well provoke a capitalist backlash and put an end to even minimal democracy.

Nevertheless, democracy, as a theory and an ideology, has normally been understood to mean more than the introduction of procedures for changing governments peacefully. Furthermore, the institutions of government, and the state more broadly, can only be fully democratic when they enjoy popular legitimacy and represent the political community. It is therefore difficult to separate democratic government from the concept of citizenship. According to Jelin (1996: 104), citizenship 'refers to a conflictive practice related to power – that is, to a struggle about who is entitled to say what in the process of defining common problems and deciding how they will be faced'. Democracy is a political system which contains and resolves these power struggles. It can be said to exist when there is popular consent, popular participation, accountability and a practice of rights, tolerance and pluralism. Understanding democracy in this way should not be taken to imply that the state or government institutions do not matter; they do – very much. They are the resources through which citizenship can be made real, guaranteed and reproduced. Ideally, the state should provide the framework which allows daily lives to be lived out democratically.

Democratization and Globalization

The context of contemporary democratization is globalization, or the growth of ever deeper forms of interconnectedness between societies, citizens and organizations across state boundaries (McGrew 1997). It is therefore pertinent to ask how democratization is related to globalization. The original debates about the causes of democracy (Lipset 1959; Moore 1966; Therborn 1978) presumed that main forces for democratization were all rooted in particular nation states. Even at the start of the third wave, international factors were seen as secondary factors in what were essentially domestically-bound processes (Whitehead 1986). Huntington's (1991) seminal study of the third wave was path-breaking in this regard, for it identified global factors as the principal cause of contemporary democratization.

There are three main ways through which globalization shapes democratization processes:

- culturally, though the creation of a global communications network and a global culture (Robertson 1992);
- economically, through the establishment of a global capitalist economy (Strange 1992); and
- politically, through the establishment of institutions of global governance (Scholte 2000).

All three encourage the penetration or diffusion of values generated at the global level into previously insulated national politics. Under conditions of globalization, state sovereignty is eroded and the state is internationalized (Cox 1987; Cerny 1990). Domestic politics, in other words, becomes subject to global trends and global constraints. According to Cox (1997), globalization means the creation of a *nebuleuse*, a loose pro-Western elite that shapes global values and influences global policy. So, in the period after 1989 especially, democracy became a central value of the new global order. However, globalization favours a particular variant of restricted liberal democracy which allows for the generation of conformity in economic terms. Democratization, in other words, is a means to establish a capitalist global market that serves global capitalists (Robinson 1996). Since globalization is inherently an uneven process (Holm and Sorensen 1995), its impact is much greater on developing states than on developed ones. This means that it is possible for global forces to push this form of restricted democratization more strongly in the underdeveloped world.

However, states, even developing states, remain much stronger than the hyper-globalizationists suppose (Evans 1997; Weiss 1998). National politics matters. Globalization creates opportunities for political change, but global forces cannot impose democracy from outside. In some cases, they can provide support. But in other instances, globalization creates false expectations or distorts the very processes that governance institutions or Western states claim to favour. Institutions of global governance have encouraged power holders towards more open government, but this does not lead to democratization where there are insufficient pro-democracy pressures inside nation states. Indeed, in some cases the actions of governance institutions have served to re-legitimize authoritarianism by creating for it a veneer of accountability.

Since the 1980s, Western governments and governance institutions have had greater opportuinites than ever before to play a significant role in the internal affairs of developing countries. Global institutions make assumptions about the relationship between the political order and the economic order. They operate with a belief that the development of the market automatically favours democratization. As a result, they encourage, or even demand, the introduction of market mechanisms in previously statist economies. These policies frequently come under the rubric of support for democratization. How far, in fact, market deepening actually works to encourage genuine (i.e. substantive) democracy is open to doubt. It may be, even, that it acts as an impediment to the expansion of citizenship, especially where marketization proceeds too rapidly or without compensatory measures to protect the most vulnerable.

The relationship between democratization and globalization is, in sum, complex. Globalization is not an unambiguous support for democratization, as it has sometimes been assumed.

The Structure and Purpose of This Book

The main purpose of this book is to provide a comprehensive introduction to democratization. It offers a conceptually rigorous study of democratization by linking it to a normative understanding of democracy. It situates democratization studies within more general theories of social and political change and it provides informed case studies across a broad geographical range of areas which draw out the reasons for the successes and failures of democratization experiments. It identifies the key dimensions of democratization necessary for its explanation and analysis. These key dimensions are the state, civil society, and the global order, or globalization. It is hoped that it will provide readers with a starting point towards a deeper analysis of particular democratizations than it is possible for this book to provide.

Secondly, the book aims to provide an introduction to the main theoretical debates in democratization studies and to offer examples of how they have shaped our understanding of particular cases. The study of democratization is a vast and interdisciplinary field. Trying to understand why democracy happens, why it is sometimes successful and why it fails in other cases has led scholars to range across the disciplinary boundaries between political science, international relations, political philosophy, sociology, history and economics. Scholars have posited explanations that depend on individuals, leaders, classes or nation states;

or on structures such as institutions, cultures, mentalities or economic practices. Inevitably, it is impossible to pay due attention to all the important work in this area. There are bound to be omissions. However, I have tried to identify the main contributions to contemporary debates and to point out their strengths and their weaknesses.

One of my motivations in writing the book has been to highlight and question the sometimes facile assumptions about democratization that are made by politicians and international agencies. There is a tendency to believe that if democracy is presented as an unproblematic and uncontested trend, then it must, perforce, be real. In fact, democratization is an extremely difficult enterprise. Legacies from the past – cultural, political, social – condition, shape and constrain how (and whether) democratization happens and the perceptions of key actors about what is, and is not, possible. Democratization is, in other words, path-dependent. Furthermore, democracy and capitalism co-exist uneasily, in relations of ambiguity and tension. Capitalist development, globally and nationally, may create opportunities for democratization but it also generates structural inequality, which operates as a barrier to the realization of democracy. Finally, it should also be remembered that democratization is a profoundly *human* affair. By this, I mean that it is full of unforeseen obstacles, unintended consequences, human errors and human failures; experiments sometimes go wrong not because the people guiding the project are bad or cynical but because they are not all-seeing and all-knowing. Nor are they always and fully committed to the public good. Private and partial interests get in the way. It is rarely possible to know what the 'right' course of action is until after the fact. Democratization, like politics generally, is a flawed art, not a science.

The first three chapters of the book provide an overview of – and explore the relationship between – democracy and democratization. Chapter 1 discusses the different ways democracy has been conceptualized over time, and examines the tensions between liberal and participatory theories of democracy. It explains why empirical democratic theory was initially dominant in democratization studies and suggests a more fruitful approach, combining citizenship theories and state-centred approaches. Chapter 2 explains democratization in historical perspective. Chapter 3 analyzes the main theoretical approaches to democratization: modernization studies, historical sociology and agency (or transitology). It offers an alternative approach, building on the key dimensions of democratization, namely the state, civil society and the global order.

The next three chapters are thematic chapters which build on the approach outlined in Chapter 3. Chapter 4 focuses on the role of the state. It discusses democratization as institutional change, stresses the role of state capacity for successful democratization and identifies the main obstacles to democratization in terms of the state. Chapter 5 concentrates on the role of civil society in democratization. The chapter adopts Tarrow's (1998) political opportunity structure as a way into a discussion of the influence of particular civil society actors in democratization, including labour, women's movements, environmental groups, community organizations and indigenous groups. It closes with a discussion of the role of civil society after the transition. Chapter 6 identifies the role of globalization and the global political economy in democratization. It looks at ways to conceptualize the role of the global in what remain essentially national processes and it contrasts the different strategies of a range of global actors committed to democratization.

Chapters 7, 8, 9 and 10 analyze democratization in countries and regions where it has taken off since the 1970s: Southern Europe, Latin America, Africa, the post-communist countries of Europe, Russia and Asia. Written to a common format, they outline attempts at democratization, analyze the successes and failures of democratization in terms of the state and civil society, and explain the ambiguous role globalization plays within democratization processes.

The conclusion draws on the case studies to suggest a framework to explain the different outcomes from democratization and the relationship between the three key dimensions which shape democratization processes: the state, civil society and the global order.

1
Democracy

Democratization studies examine and explain processes whereby governments, states and societies attempt to move away from some form of authoritarianism towards some form of democracy. But there is considerable debate regarding the meaning of democracy, the type of democracy and the level of democracy that can realistically be expected within the public sphere. This first chapter explores the trajectory of the concept of democracy and examines the changing meanings of the term. One aim of the chapter is to show how liberal democracy gradually came to be constructed as the only acceptable form of democracy, and was justified in the Cold War period by empirical democratic theory. Secondly, the chapter identifies a rich tradition of alternative understandings of democracy that draw in different ways on direct or communitarian traditions of democracy. These, it is argued, provide a more rigorous theoretical underpinning for the analysis of democratization than the empirical tradition.

Democracy: A Simple Concept?

Democracy can be understood as an ideology, a concept or a theory. It is an ideology in so far as 'it embod[ies] a set of political ideas that detail the best possible form of social organization' (MacKensie 1994). It can therefore be understood as an ideal. To be a democrat is to have faith in people, to believe that people have inalienable rights to make decisions for themselves, and to be committed to the notion that all people are equal in some fundamental and essential way.

The meaning of democracy can be summarized as

> a mode of decision-making about collectively binding rules and policies over which the people exercise control, and the most democratic arrangement [is] that where all members of the collectivity enjoy effective equal rights to take part in such decision-making directly – one, that is to say, which realises to the greatest conceivable degree the principles of popular control and equality in its exercise. (Beetham 1992: 40)

Democratic theory is concerned with philosphical and political disputes about how to put this apparently simple concept into practice. Some of the key questions it addresses are:

- Who, precisely, make up the 'people'?
- What is the best process through which the wants and preferences of the 'people' can be made known?
- How can the democratic rights of the 'people' best be understood and safeguarded?
- Who sets the agenda to which the 'people' respond?
- Can the 'people' be expected to come to a shared preference, given competing material interests and normative preferences, and what are the most democratic mechanisms for taking decisions which protect the rights of everyone?

Twentieth-century democratic theory has also addressed the following fundamental questions:

- How much democracy is appropriate – in particular, is there a trade-off between democracy and other rights?
- Should democracy be confined to the political sphere or should it include the system of economic production?
- How can the tension between the rights of the individual and the rights of the community be resolved?
- What are the arenas of human interaction for which democracy is appropriate? Should democracy refer strictly to procedures for government, should it apply to the interactions between society and the state, or should it also extend to arenas traditionally regarded as the sphere of private relations, such as the family, and the international order, traditionally seen as 'beyond' the reach of democracy?

From Direct to Liberal Democracy

It is possible to trace two principal strands of democratic theorizing: direct and representative democracy. The tradition of direct democracy draws on the Athenian legacy of popular government within a small city state and the Renaissance republican tradition. It was championed by Rousseau in the eighteenth century who argued for unmediated popular government, by which he meant that citizens should decide laws and make public policy without the mediation of political representatives (Weale 1999: 24–5).

Direct democracy is principally concerned with ensuring democratic rights for the *community* as a whole. As a result, the tradition of direct democracy influenced the later developments of Marxism and anarchism. The alternative tradition of representation draws instead on the liberal idea of the *individual*, who has a right, but not an obligation, to participate in politics. By infusing the traditions of liberalism into democracy, it suggest that the goals of democracy were best served by protecting the autonomy of the individual. Moreover, liberalism seeks to justify, but limit, the sovereign power of the state (Held 1992). This is to be achieved through the political representation of those individuals deemed mature enough to be granted political equality. The role of the state is to safeguard the individual's right to self-fulfilment and development. Liberal or representative democracy thus becomes the aggregation of individual preferences.

In its origins, democracy meant direct popular control over government. It emerged for the first time in Athenian society in the fifth century BC. Building a state responsive to popular authority in Athens at this time was relatively easy. The 'people' was understood to be made up of relatively few men and these were able to form an Assembly, the deliberative body of government. Of course, it should be remembered that, in contemporary terms, Athenian democracy was highly exclusive. Those who could potentially be regarded as dangerous by Athenian-born men – women, slaves and foreigners, for example – were excluded from citizenship and thereby were rendered powerless. The number of citizens, in other words, was small (Held 1996: 23). Moreover, Arblaster (1994: 22–3) points out the apparent paradox that freedom for Athenian citizens was built upon the revenues of empire and the subjugation of the rights of others. Slavery, then, was not only ignored by Athenian democrats: it was the other side of the coin.

Despite – or in some cases, perhaps because of – its shortcomings, Athenian democracy exercised an important influence in Western conceptions of the 'good society'. Democracy was rediscovered in the republican and communitarian traditions of the European Middle Ages, and later reformulated in the seventeenth and eighteenth centuries in England and North America (Dunn 1992; Held 1996; Black 1997). Both the American and the French Revolutions were carried out in the name of democracy. But what was meant by democracy changed over time. By the eighteenth century, with the shift from city state to nation state, direct democracy no longer seemed feasible because of the size of the polity. Liberal notions of representation, equality before the law, and accountability were eventually grafted onto democracy, although they were at odds with the more radical democratic traditions of republicanism and communitarianism.

Democratic theory in the eighteenth century and nineteenth century was intimately tied in with broader trends in European and North American societies at the time: the development of liberalism, the emergence of socialism, the spread of revolutionary ideals and the expansion of capitalism. New social actors, and in particular the increasing power of big business compared to the aristocracy, and the growth of an organized labouring class, forced theorists to rethink the nature of government, institutions, rights and citizenship. There were divisions between, for example, proponents of protective democracy and advocates of developmental democracy. These divisions encompassed the question of the most suitable way of organizing the state, the boundaries of the political and the role of 'the people' in decision-making (Macpherson 1977). Madison, Bentham and James Mill argued that democracy must be tempered with respect for authority and understood that one purpose of political institutions was to safeguard the state and the community from the 'excesses' of democracy. In contrast, John Stuart Mill, writing in the 1860s, foresaw that the limited suffrage they accepted would not survive the challenge of an increasingly organized working-class movement:

> Of the working men, at least in the more advanced countries of Europe, it may be pronounced certain, that the patriarchal or paternal system of government is one to which they will not again be subject. ... That question was decided when ... they were brought together in numbers, to work socially under the same roof; when railways enabled them to shift from place to place and change their patrons and employers as easily as their coats; when they were encouraged to seek a share in government, by means of the electoral franchise. The working classes have taken their interests into their own hands, and are perpetually showing that they think the interests of their employers not identical with their own, but opposite to them.
> (Mill, quoted in Macpherson 1977: 45)

John Stuart Mill thus challenged the classic liberal view that an inclusive citizenship would undermine the stability of the capitalist order. He suggested instead that, properly handled, democracy offered 'a moral vision of the possibility of the improvement of mankind' (Macpherson 1977: 47), meaning that working people could 'learn' how to be citizens. Even Mill, however, argued that democracy was not 'right' for all peoples; some lacked the necessary levels of 'civilization' or displayed 'positive defects of national character' (Mill, quoted in Macpherson, 1977: 48).

As we can see, throughout the nineteenth century and into the twentieth, the key problem for liberal democracy was specifying who should be included in the polity, identifying the rights and duties that citizenship entailed and establishing the form that democracy should take. It was perfectly possible to lay claim to democracy and still argue for a limited citizenship. Indeed, even by the end of the nineteenth century, the expansion of the electorate was a concession, introduced with the aim of circumventing popular control. It was not conceived of as a way necessarily to extend or deepen participation. In the nineteenth century, liberal democracy, where it existed, was compatible with elite or aristocratic government. Property or income qualifications determined citizenship and women everywhere were judged unworthy of the franchise. This persisted well into the twentieth century. In some countries, race or colour were the determinants of citizenship until after the Second World War, and in some cases such as the US and South Africa, well beyond 1945. Nevertheless, democracy with a limited citizenship always required a sleight of hand by which it could be argued that parliament represented the whole community, even though it had been elected with a restricted suffrage. In this way, parliamentary sovereignty became a substitute for democratic sovereignty.

With all this in mind, it is not surprising that the liberal democracy was under challenge from alternative ideologies, and alternative visions of democracy, by the early twentieth century. Marxists developed the concept of socialist democracy. Bourgeois democracy, they argued, was a cover for the economic and cultural exploitation of the majority in order to increase the profits of the few. The liberating potential of democracy was curtailed by the fact that liberal democracy was, in practice, a system created to uphold the market. Democracy was stunted by its marriage to capitalism, and political rights without economic equality were meaningless because they could never become real. At the same time, the exploitation and alienation generated by capitalism prevented people from realizing their potential and society as a whole from living in harmony. Since capitalism was establishing itself as a global order, socialists proposed revolution and class solidarity as vehicles that would further their dream of a genuine or socialist democracy.

The Second World War constituted a watershed in the history of democratic theory. Within Europe and the US the Second World War led to a mass mobilization of 'ordinary' people, men and women, and weakened the bonds of social deference. As a result, after 1945 it became difficult to legitimize political exclusion on the grounds of birth, occupation or sex, although racial exclusion persisted in the US until the

1960s. As democracy was re-legitimized in a less exclusive mould, so the space for dissent from liberal democracy gradually narrowed. Fascism had been defeated and, what is more, discredited in moral terms. Although socialism survived rather more intact, Western European socialists came to terms with capitalism and liberal democracy and focused instead on extending and deepening patterns of representation and promoting social and economic reform. Communists gradually focused their attention of the supposed achievements of the Soviet bloc. It was only outside Europe that socialists and communists remained committed to creating genuinely alternative utopias through revolution. Here Marxist and other revolutionary movements tended to invoke the direct or participatory democratic traditions in opposition to liberal democracy. But these movements gradually came to be seen as outside the democratic mainstream and the thrust of Cold War propaganda was to present anti-liberal movements as essentially undemocratic. In short, after 1945 democracy was successfully married to liberalism. Liberal democracy was no longer seen as one strand of democracy: it was presented as the only version there was. Liberal democracy was presented in opposition to both Communism (seen as an ideology and a geopolitical force) and Fascism over which democracy was thought to have triumphed.

Empirical Democratic Theory

After the onset of the Cold War, the meanings and the usages of democracy shifted in a highly significant way. It became a part of the vocabulary of real politics as a way of distinguishing between 'the free world' and Communism. As a result, democracy was more and more equated with the political arrangements current in Western Europe and the US. Democracy came to mean almost exclusively liberal or representative democracy and to imply a particular set of arrangements for government and, more generally, the empirical 'reality' of the West. Empirical democratic theorizing was thus bound up with the Cold War and with the need to justify liberal democracy.

This trend was strengthened by developments within the discipline of politics. The study of politics was moving towards developing a vocabulary for describing and analyzing the processes of modern systems of power and organized rule and was less interested in abstract notions of the 'good society'. This coincided with the rise of behaviouralism within political science in the 1950s and 1960s.

Behaviouralism radically changed the way in which democracy was understood and researched. According to Lijphart (1984), democracy was a reality that existed in 'the real world'. By this, he meant the political systems existing in the US and Western Europe, or the 'free world'. Democracy, in other words, ceased to be an explicitly normative concept and was presented, instead, as a descriptive one. Dahl (1956: 63) explained:

> One way [to define democracy] ... is to specify a set of goals to be maximized; democracy can then be defined in terms of the specific governmental processes necessary to maximize these goals ... A second way – this might be called the descriptive method – is to consider as a single class of phenomena all those nation states and social organizations that are commonly called democratic by political scientists and ... discover first the necessary and sufficient conditions they have in common and second, the necessary and sufficient conditions for social organizations possessing these characteristics.

Behaviouralists ostensibly worked in the second way, justifying in the process a division between empirical and what were termed 'normative' or 'philosophical' traditions of democracy.

Empirical democratic theory found its most important inspiration in the work of the economist Joseph Schumpeter. Schumpeter saw democracy as a form of government and in particular as a mechanism for the election of leaders. He stressed the importance of limiting popular expectations of the democratic system (see Box 1.1). Underlying Schumpeter's approach was an assumption that the majority of the population could not be entrusted with the important task of decision-making. Democracy, in other words, became a way of institutionalizing competition for power (Shapiro and Hacker-Cordon 1999: 4). Schumpeter focused on the conditions that would allow competition between elites. These include: high-quality leadership in political parties; autonomy of political elites from the state; an independent bureaucracy; an opposition and civil society that accept the rules of the game; and a political culture of tolerance and compromise. Narrow and minimalist, a Schumpeterian understanding of democracy nevertheless provides clear and transparent criteria for measuring democracy; this is, in fact, its chief attraction and explains why its influence has been so extensive (Sartori 1987).

This needs to be contrasted with the rather different approach pioneered by Dahl. He was careful not to confuse the practices within actually existing democracies with 'democracy' as a political ideal.

Box 1.1   Schumpeterian Democracy

'The classical theory [of democracy] ... attributed to the electorate an altogether unrealistic degree of initiative which practically amounted to ignoring leadership. But collectives act almost exclusively by accepting leadership – that is the dominant mechanism of practically any collective action which is more than a reflex ... Our theory is of course no more definite than is the concept of leadership. This concept presents similar difficulties as the concept of competition in the economic sphere, with which it may usefully be compared ... in political life there is always some competition, though perhaps only as a potential one, for the allegiance of the people. To simplify matters, we have restricted the kind of competition for leadership which is to define democracy to free competition for a free vote. ... According to the view we have taken, democracy does not mean and cannot mean that the people actually rule in any obvious sense of the term "people" and "rule". Democracy means only that the people have the opportunity of accepting or refusing the men who are to rule them.'

Source: Schumpeter (1976: 268–70).

Instead, he suggested the use of the term 'polyarchy' since he recognized that there were conditions for democracy which the Western 'democracies' did not actually meet. The institutions of polyarchy may, normatively, be far more desirable than authoritarianism but, he argued, 'typical of democrats who live in countries long governed by polyarchy

---

Box 1.2   The Institutions of Polyarchy

Polyarchy rests on a combination of elected government and civil liberties, which should ensure that different groups in society have access to the political system. The main institutions are:

- the election of government officials.
- free and fair elections.
- an inclusive suffrage.
- the right of all citizens to run for public office.
- freedom of expression.
- citizens have a right to source of information other than official ones. *Free Media*
- associational autonomy, and the right to form independent associations or organizations, including political parties and interest groups.

Civil Society

Source: Dahl (1989: 221).

---

is a belief that polyarchy is insufficiently democratic and should be made more so' (Dahl 1989: 222). Dahl's concept of polyarchy has grad-ually became the basis for describing the empirical characteristics of liberal democracy since the 1970s (see Box 1.2).

Essentially, polyarchy is consensual government by competing elites. With no single centre of power, polyarchy works through the pluralist representation of different and conflicting social interests (Dahl 1961). Institutions matter, but, their operation depends on an almost unspoken 'consensus on the rules of procedure; consensus on the range of policy options; [and] consensus on the legitimate scope of political activity' (Held 1996: 207).

Critiques of Empirical Democratic Theory

Empirical democratic theory proved useful both to academics working within the behavouralist tradition and to Western policy-makers. But it was, in fact, inadequate as a description of the operation of Western political systems. It falsely assumed, for example, that Western societies were pluralist – that is, that it was possible for all groups in society to be heard equally. It ignored the structured privilege that was generated and sustained by capitalism. This was a very serious flaw. For, if empir-ical theory did not accurately capture the reality of Western systems of government, its utility had ceased in its own terms. How could it serve as the standard by which to measure movements towards democracy in other parts of the world or, indeed, claim to replace other kinds of dem-ocratic theory?

Where empirical democratic theory sees democracy as more than a set of procedures for electing leaders, its emphasis is on pluralism. It is assumed that power is distributed through society; democracy is merely the political order reflecting this social reality. Pluralism implies that socially-constituted groups (labour organizations, business groups, farmers' groups, grassroots movements, neighbourhood committees, women's organizations, gay and lesbian movements, religious pressure groups, etc.) operate within a level playing field. Finer (1966), for example, maintained that any interest group with 'a good case' will, in a democracy, eventually get a hearing. But pluralism is an inadequate tool for understanding Western societies because it ignores the question of power. Lukes (1974) argued that pluralism ignored the structural, ideological and 'hidden' dimensions of power that rendered these poli-ties fundamentally undemocratic.

Hidden or structural privilege prevents a level playing field and groups cannot compete equally for access to government, as pluralism assumes. Capitalists, for example, have more structural power than does labour. Neo-pluralists like Lindblom (1977) and Marxists (Jessop 1990) identified the structural power of capital and of business over decision-making as a violation of the very principle of democracy. Structural power explains why policy-making is not democratic, even where elections are free and fair and civil liberties are respected. Secrecy and elitism in government are also important mechanisms for the reproduction of non-democratic forms of policy-making. Furthermore, non-democratic policy communities form around specific policy areas and, although unelected, unrepresentative and unaccountable, become the key actors rather than government or parliament (Rhodes and Marsh 1992; Smith 1993). Even Dahl (1985) modified his earlier view of pluralism. Instead of conceptualizing Western society as made up of groups competing within a neutral arena, and power as fluid and dispersed between social actors, he recognized that the inequalities generated by capitalism affect political decision-making and shape the state. Weir and Beetham (1999) suggest that it makes no sense to imagine that any political system is wholly democratic. As a result, it is misleading to equate democracy with actually existing Western systems of government.

A further problem for empirical theory is its evident Western bias. Empirical democratic theory deduces its core understanding of democracy from an ideal model of the operation of Western politics. Democracy is reduced to what is thought to exist in the West. The normative assumptions implicit in understanding democracy in this way become evident once this paradigm is applied to the developing countries of Africa, Asia and Latin America, or the South. Democratization becomes highly prescriptive process in which the South is supposed to learn from the developed countries – it becomes the reproduction of the procedures for government which have been developed in Western Europe and the US. Democratization thus runs into the danger of becoming an exercise in colonization.

At the same time, empirical democratic theory promotes an electoralist or procedural understanding of democracy. It concentrates on the observable behaviour of political actors. But, as was noted above, it takes no account of the hidden structures of power. As a result, it is an inappropriate model for the analysis of politics in the South and ignores the gulf between the formal structures of the political system and the cultures and practices which shape political activity on the ground. Hawthorne (1991: 27) argues that a cultural divide separates the developing world from the developed and that a number of important political repercussions flow from this:

> All these countries [the Third World] display a combination of characters which has been ... perplexing, at the very least paradoxical, to Western observers: the combination, as one might describe it, of an incipiently modern economy and (behind a curtain of modern constitutions) an archaic politics; the co-existence of the economics of separate interests and a politics which is more like that of ancient liberty ... This explains why the liberal paradigms, extrapolated from the imagined facts of Western experience and suggesting an even, equitable and eventually self-equilibrating modernity, do not capture the facts of the present Third World.

In particular, then, empirical democratic theory misses the political reality behind the formal and observable structures of government. This can lead to an assumption that systems are democratic because elections are relatively free, parties exist and liberal freedoms are enshrined in a constitution, even though violence, exclusion and repression may be the daily realities for the majority of the population.

Finally, the failure of empirical democratic theory to address how economic resources (or a lack of them) impinge upon the operation of the political system has particular consequences when applied to the developing world. In fact, liberal democratic theory in general has little to say about socio-economic or other forms of structural inequalities either within states or globally because it presumes that they are unimportant for the exercise of citizenship. But the experiences of the Third World suggest that equal citizenship cannot take root alongside extreme income inequalities.

In most developing countries, poverty and privilege operate as barriers to democratic incorporation. This explains the appeal in developing countries for theories of democracy that take into account issues of cultural, social and economic empowerment, beyond the formal creation of liberal rights, and prioritize the common good alongside, or in some cases instead of, the individual.

Contemporary Theories of Democracy

The very evident intellectual problems with empirical democracy theory focused attention on the failures and problems with liberal democracy more generally. At the same time, the fact that liberal democratic theorizing in the 1960s and 1970s was so normatively bound up with the West, the defence of capitalism and the Cold War provoked an interest in exploring alternative approaches to democracy. The result was a renewed interest in democracy as a vehicle for human emancipation and as a means for promoting the good of the community as a whole, rather than the individual. Since the 1960s, new theories of democracy have emerged, including participatory democracy, feminism, associationalism, citizenship theories, and cosmopolitanism. All consciously evoke the notion of democracy as a utopian project and draw in different ways on the traditions of communitarianism.

Participatory Democracy

According to Pateman (1970), participatory theories of democracy challenge the myth that there is one 'classical' theory of democracy – liberal democracy. Instead, she points to a long lineage of theorists for whom participation, not representation, was the core of democracy. Participatory theories of democracy start from an assumption about the importance of freedom and activism and a belief that the existence of voting rights and alternation in government do not, in themselves, guarantee the existence of democracy. They envisage democracy through the development of reciprocal relations of trust between individuals. For Macpherson (1977), participatory democracy constitutes a categorical rejection of the Schumpeterian model of democracy and its negative view of humanity.

In Europe, demands for a participatory democracy emerged from the 'New Left' and student movement in the 1960s and 1970s. But it also found expression in 'the rise of movements for workers' control in industry' (Macpherson 1977: 93). It was, then, a critique of the way 'actually existing democracies' operated, focusing in particular on the role of the state, state–society relations and the impact of economic production on citizenship. Participationism is characterized by a highly ambiguous view of the state. Participationists sometimes reject the statism and welfarism of the Western 'democracies' after 1945, which they see as stifling individual and community initiatives. But they are far from being *laissez-faire* liberals, rejecting all forms of state intervention. Keane (1988), for example, argues that the state must move beyond paternalism towards embracing social organizations in active participation in decision-making.

A problem with participatory democracy is the difficulty of applying it to large communities such as the nation state. Macpherson (1977: 93–100), one of the earliest of its contemporary proponents, recognized this, but added that the more serious problem was

> not how to run it but how to reach it. ... What roadblocks have to be removed i.e. what changes in our present society and the now prevailing ideology are prerequisite or co-requisite conditions for reaching participatory democracy? ... One is a change in people's consciousness (or unconsciousness) from seeing themselves and acting essentially as consumers to seeing themselves and acting as exerters and enjoyers of the exertion and development of their own capacities. This is requisite not only to the emergence but also to the operation of a participatory democracy. For the latter self-image brings with it a sense of community which the former does not ... the operation of a participatory democracy would require a stronger sense of community than now prevails. The other prerequisite is a great reduction of the present social and economic inequality, since that inequality ... requires a non-participatory political system to hold the society together. And as long as inequality is accepted, the non-participatory political system is also likely to be accepted by all those in classes who prefer stability to the prospect of complete social breakdown.

Participatory democracy requires, in other words, a transformation in how goods are produced and shared in capitalist societies. Moreover, it takes a maximalist position in terms of its understanding of democracy in that it suggests that equality and a search for the communal good are possible. It has been suggested that increasing representation throughout society, decentralization of power and creating participatory forms of local government would represent real steps forward towards more participatory systems of government (Judge 1999).

Feminism

Feminism has systematically sought to uncover the relationship between social, economic and political gender inequalities and the ways in which Western 'democracies' are, in fact, systematically undemocratic since they treat women as inferior to men, thereby violating the first principle of democracy, that all citizens have equal rights (Pateman 1989). By revealing the gendered structural bias within liberal democracy, feminism pioneered a review of democratic theory itself and suggested that addressing structural inequality is an essential part of building a genuine democracy.

Feminists have identified 'a deep gender-bias in democratic theory itself' (Mendus 1992). Pateman (1988) argues that the categories of the 'individual' and the 'citizen' are themselves male and cannot reflect either the needs or the desires of women. She insists that women have never consented to the democratic system because they have never been consulted. If the needs of women are not met by liberalism; if, in fact, the liberal democratic state is not gender-neutral (Waylen 1998); and if the abstract individual, so beloved of liberal theory, does not encompass the experiences of women (Phillips 1993), can liberal democracy even be said to be a desirable goal or a stable form of government?

Feminism has thus become associated with the quest to liberate democracy from the straitjacket of liberalism through emphasizing participation and a need to redefine the boundaries of the 'political'. Feminist scholarship stresses the importance of the day-to-day and of the mundane tasks which preoccupy most people; it has identified the family and interpersonal relationships as sites for democratization with the claim that 'the personal is political'; and, by stressing that social and political attitudes are formed within the private sphere, it has brought under scrutiny the liberal separation of the private from the public. Feminism has therefore challenged the implicit assumption of liberal democracy that what is important for humanity occurs in the public realm and, in the process, pointed out that to regard democracy simply as a system for government (meaning institutions) is absurd. Moreover, by revealing the schizophrenic split that lies with Western liberal democratic polities between the public – the arena of government in which all are equal – and the private – sets of family and interpersonal relationships which are based on exploitation and structured inequality – feminism has provoked an important intellectual debate centring on the extent to which *liberal* democracy can be regarded as properly democratic at all. For feminists, the charge is 'not simply that democratic *states* are, as a matter of fact, ones in which women are disadvantaged (though they are) but rather that democratic *theory* is, as a matter of principle, committed to ideals which guarantee that that will remain so' (Mendus 1992). Feminism is, therefore, an essential strand of contemporary theories that take an emancipatory approach to democracy.

Furthermore, by challenging the liberal preoccupation with the (supposedly) neutral individual, stripped of her or his class, race, ethnicity

and history, feminists have drawn attention to the importance of
collectives, communities and groups:

> Among the issues that have emerged in feminist theory, the most
> provocative centre around universality ... there *is* no gender-neutral
> individual and when liberals try to deal with us only in our capacity
> as abstract citizens, they are wishing away not only differences of
> class but what may be even more intransigent differences of sex.
> Liberal democracy wants to ignore (and civic republicanism tran-
> scend) all more local identities and difference; in reality both tradi-
> tions have insulated the male body and male identity into their
> definitions of the norm. Liberal democrats, in particular, believed
> they had extended all necessary rights and freedoms to women when
> they allowed them to vote on the same terms as men. This is quite
> simply inadequate as even the crudest of indicators (like the number
> of women in politics) will show. Democracy cannot stand above
> sexual difference but has to be reconceptualized with difference
> firmly in mind. One obvious implication is that democracy must deal
> with us not just as individuals but groups. (Phillips 1991: 149)

Associationalism

For Hirst (1997), associationalism offers a more democratic system than
the present one for advanced capitalist societies, at least. His concern
lies with the failure of the state to protect working people and the poor.
Recognizing both the intrinsic capitalist bias of Western states, and the
decline in the state's capacity to provide welfare, he suggests building
upon the traditions of associationalism within nineteenth-century
working-class movements. Hirst thus advances a theory of society the
central claim of which is that human welfare and liberty are both best
served when as many of the affairs of society as possible are managed
by voluntary and democratically self-governing associations.
Associationalism gives priority to freedom in its scale of values, but
suggests that freedom can only be pursued effectively if individuals participate in the community. Hirst's argument, therefore, is that associational
democracy is a remedy for the malaise of post-industrial societies and the
deep dissatisfaction with their economic performance. It offers a renewal
of Western democracy, which has been reduced to 'choosing and legitimizing the rulers of a big governmental machine that is out of control'
(Hirst 1997: 42). How far associationalism constitutes a valid model for
developing societies or post-communist societies is more doubtful. But

associationalism is undoubtedly part of the demands for a renewal of democracy through increasing society's control over policy-making.

Citizenship

Citizenship theories of democracy draw upon the renewed interest in civil society in politics. Stressing the importance of civil society for democracy is a way of drawing attention to the role of political culture, civic virtues, the network of associations within and across societies and the importance of contestation in the practice of democracy.

In the eighteenth and nineteenth centuries, the term 'civil society' was used to

> imply a form of universal citizenship within the nation state based on the one hand on the principles of individualism and on the other on the participation of those individuals in public life, a participation that was in turn based on the mutuality of citizens in the form of compacts, contracts and the moral, economic, social and political ties binding those individuals. (Seligman 1992: 111)

However in practice, access to citizenship was severely limited for women and working-class men. Thus civil society was simultaneously an artifice covering a network of relationships that were based on domination and exclusion and a set of values about the need for incorporation. Today, civil society retains the sense of democracy through inclusion. But it has been extended to become a conceptual tool for the analysis of associations, networks, agency and resistance to the state (Havel, Klaus and Pithart 1996). Identifying a central role for civil society in politics has led to the development of civil society theory which points to the necessity of examining the role of ordinary people and their associations in the process of social and political change (Bobbio 1989). According to Fine (1997: 9),

> the distinguishing mark [of civil society theory] is that it *privileges* civil society over all other moments or spheres of social life, on the grounds that civil society furnishes the fundamental conditions of liberty in the modern world.

Within citizenship and civil society approaches there is a divide between theorists who see citizenship as an eminently *political* affair, and those that argue that citizenship must be understood to encompass social and economic components as well. Phillips (1999) argues that citizenship can only be exercised once certain inequalities are addressed. Similarly, for Marshall (1973: 71–2) democracy only works when some basic rights are guaranteed for all. These include 'the right to a modicum of economic welfare and security ... the right to a share ... to the full in the social heritage and to live the life of a civilized being according to the standards prevailing in society'. Democracy, in other words, requires social and economic inclusion. The justification of democracy thus becomes the fact that it deepens and protects a range of political, economic and social rights. Democracy is legitimized because most citizens experience material, social or psychological benefit from it and because it confers the possibility of making rights real (Hall 1995: 26).

Cosmopolitanism

The idea that the source of democracy lies in civil society, rather than the state, has been reinforced by the trends towards globalization and the transnationalization of politics (see Chapter 6). According to Strange, the state has become defective or simply 'evaporated' under pressure from globalization (Strange 1995: 56). As a result, the significance of non-state actors for national and international politics has expanded while the capacities of state actors are ever more reduced. Even sceptics of globalization recognize that states and citizens are now affected by decisions outside their own nation state. It is from these assumptions that the theory of cosmopolitan democracy has emerged, the core idea of which is that how we conceive of democracy must change so as to fit a globalizing world.

The backdrop to cosmopolitan democracy, then, is the process of globalization, or increased interconnectedness between states and citizens and the stretching and deepening of links between institutions, social organizations and citizens (Giddens 1990). This leads to what Held (1996: 343) has termed a number of disjunctures in the world order. The first, and perhaps the most directly significant, is the disjuncture between the formal authority of states to manage economic policy-making inside national territories and their actual capacity to do so, given that the main players in the global economy are no longer either states themselves or organizations within the control of states. They are multinational corporations (MNCs) and financial capital which is not tied to any particular state formation. MNCs and financial organizations no longer control simply wealth but also what creates wealth – knowledge and technology. The second disjuncture is 'the vast array of international regimes and organizations that have been established to manage whole areas of transnational activity (trade, transportation, the uses of the oceans and so on) and collective policy problems'. This has led to changes in the decision-making structures of world politics and a shift away from state control towards 'new and novel forms of geo-governance'(Held 1996: 345–7). Thirdly, international law is developing powers which challenge the sovereign immunity of the state. And finally globalization undermines the state as 'an autonomous culture centre'with the result that national cultures are no longer distinct.

In view of the challenges to the state posed by these changes, Held suggests that democracy needs to be posited at the global level. This would involve empowering old political institutions such as regional assemblies with new and greater powers and the creation of an authoritative assembly of all democratic states and societies at the global level (Held 1996: 355). Alongside this, there would be the elaboration of a set of rights for all global citizens. The power of representative non-state actors (social movements and organizations) would be enhanced at the expense of states and the new global order would be based on extending citizenship rights and redistributing resources (see Archibugi, Held and Kohler 1998).

Doubts have been expressed about the 'hyper globalization thesis' – the idea that globalization leads ineluctably to the collapse of the state (Hirst and Thompson 1996). The current preoccupation with globalization and the eclipse of the state has even been attributed to 'changes in the global ideological climate', rather than material changes in the distribution of political and economic resources away from states, and the 'growing global hegemony of Anglo-American ideology' (Evans 1997). Nevertheless, a recognition that new forms of production and global finance bring in their train state transformation and an acknowledgment of the rise of global governance implies the need to reflect upon how they impinge upon the practice of global democracy.

An important number of global organizations are committed to the globalization of democracy. In particular, a growing number of transnationally active social movements argue that democratization can only occur through global activism (Keck and Sikkink 1998). Non state actors increasingly engage in operations across state borders as a way of effecting changes within states and of pressurizing international agencies to take charge of issues which were once regarded as the domain of the state (Clark, Friedman and Hochstetler 1998). So, even if cosmopolitan democracy appears as a utopian project which ignores the continuing strength of the state, it nonetheless is important in drawing attention to the increasing role of international advocacy movements in global and domestic politics and of the international arena for the study of democracy.

Conclusion

The chapter has outlined how theories of democracy have changed over time. It has traced the development of the idea of democracy from direct self-government, through to the emergence of the liberal project and the struggles between competing models of democracy in the twentieth century. Ideas of democracy adapted to the development of the modern state, industrialization and the rise of the middle and working classes, as well as to the changing demands of government. After 1945, history, in the shape of the Cold War, and the demands of an expanding political science establishment combined to create the influential tradition of empirical democratic theory. In so doing, theories of socialist democracy were not only wiped out from the Western mainstream but, at the same time theories of participatory or communitarian democracy were marginalized. By tying democracy conceptually to actually existing democracies, empirical democratic theory managed both to establish the idea that there was a dichotomous distinction between democracy and other forms of government, and to set out transparent criteria for measuring democracy. Despite its clarity, empirical democratic theory came under sustained criticism for failing to catch the essence of democracy, which was variously attributed to participation, citizenship or inclusion, and for offering a misleading analysis of the nature of the state in supposedly democratic societies. As a result, since the 1970s, there has been a revival of explicitly normative theories of democracy. In particular, theories of feminism, associationalism, cosmopolitanism, participation and civil society have sought to articulate alternative approaches to democracy that place notions of active social citizenship at its core.

In view of the vitality of newer theories of democracy just as the third wave was beginning to occur, it is worth pausing to ask why, initially at least, democratization studies preferred the empirical approach. The explanation is twofold. First, despite the criticisms, empirical democratic theory exercised an important influence within the study of politics, especially within the study of comparative politics. Secondly, empirical democratic theory set clear and transparent standards which could be used to measure democracy, to evaluate progress away from authoritarian forms of government and to generate wide-ranging comparisons between countries and regions. Democracy was taken to mean simply the creation of procedures for free and fair elections and the alternation of political leadership. For those who rejected Schumpeter's exclusive focus on leaders and elites, Dahl's concept of polyarchy, with its assumptions of pluralism, was the preferred alternative. As a result, democratization came to be perceived as essentially an exercise in creating institutions for government. Culture, society and the economy were, by and large, ignored.

However, as democratization got under way, it gradually became evident that while some new democracies would succeed in establishing free, fair elections and creating new institutions for government which have gradually allowed for the development of a democratic polity, others have ended in failure. In many, the introduction of elections has made no difference to the essentially undemocratic cultures and practices of politics and policy-making. So, whilst in Spain, authoritarianism gave way to a system that, if not fully democratic by citizenship or participatory standards, is in many ways a match with other Western polities, in most of sub-Saharan Africa, elections and formally democratic institutions are covers for elitist, exclusionary and arbitrary rule. As a result, democratization studies began to embrace more complex, if more fuzzy, notions of what actually constitutes democracy (Collier and Levtisky 1997).

This has heralded a growing interest in citizenship, in particular, as the bedrock of democratization. Creating democracy means not only the elimination of authoritarian institutions and the establishment of formal institutions for the election of leaders and the creation of political parties but, just as important, legitimizing on-going struggles to eliminate authoritarian social practices. At the same time, the processes of democratization must go beyond establishing formal citizenship rights towards making them meaningful even for groups traditionally excluded from the polity, such as ethnic or racial minorities, women and the very poor. Emphasizing the role of civil society and participation is no substitute, however, for the role of the state in democracy. The state remains both the key arena for policy-making and the principal site for the creation of welfare politics. As Iris Marion Young (1999: 161) argues, democracy requires 'strong regulative and coordinating programs mandated through state institutions, strongly linked to participatory and critical civic organizations'. Democracy, in other words, is not achieved either through citizenship or through state institutions; it rests on and requires both.

2

Democratization in Historical Perspective

Democracy has unfolded gradually across the globe since the nineteenth century. This process has not been linear or uncontested, however. Moreover, the causes of democratization have varied over time and space. So, whilst the motor of democratization in the nineteenth century was class, by the 1980s and 1990s it was driven by a complex mix of social conflict, state-building and external influence. One way to explain the expansion of democratization over time is to group experiences together in distinct 'waves'. This suggests that democratization in the countries linked together in the 'wave' at least have common causes. In 1991, Samuel Huntington suggested that waves of democratization have been followed by reverse of authoritarianism, as some societies failed to consolidate democracy and others experienced democratic collapse. The wave theory has now become a conventional part of the story of democratization. This chapter examines the history of democratization, beginning with the idea of the wave. It argues that, despite its utility as a metaphor, the wave theory does not provide an explanation of democratization. It is necessary to move beyond the idea of the wave in order to understand more fully democratization both in historical perspective and in the present day.

The Wave Theory

Huntington (1991: 15–16) describes a wave of democratization in the following way:

> A wave of democratization is a group of transitions from nondemocratic to democratic regimes that occur within a specified period of time and that significantly outnumber transitions in the opposite direction during that period of time. A wave also involves liberalization or partial democratization in political systems that do not become fully

32

democratic. Each of the first two waves of democratization was followed by a reverse wave in which some but not all of the countries that had previously made the transition to democracy reverted to non-democratic rule.

For Huntington, the long first wave started at the beginning of the nineteenth century and the number of democratic governments grew gradually until around 1930. Liberal democracy was in a process of expansion during this time, although it was challenged by the alternative notion of socialist democracy, which linked the concept of popular rule to a socialist organization of society and the economy. Communism, in other words, was a persuasive anti-capitalist ideology. But the most substantive challenge to liberal democracy, and indeed to Communism, came from Fascism. The rise of Fascist movements across Europe and the Fascist seizures of power in Italy and Germany brought the first wave to a close. A reverse wave followed, which, according to Huntington, lasted from 1926 until 1942. During this period, democratic political systems collapsed in Italy, Germany, Spain, Argentina and some of the fledgling democracies in Eastern Europe. Fascism formed the ideological core of the dictatorships that spread across Europe in the 1920s and 1930s. Although it was eventually defeated in Italy and Germany, the dictatorships that emerged in Portugal and Spain in the 1930s survived into the 1970s.

The second wave identified by Huntington was considerably shorter. Its beginning was signalled by the physical defeat of the Axis powers in 1945. The American, British and French allies were the chief architects of democratization in the occupied territories of Germany, Japan and Austria. Democracy also took off around this time in parts of Latin America. Decolonization after the Second World War further enlarged the number of democracies, initially at least, although democracy in much of Africa was both unstable and formalistic. Democratic consolidation was patchy through the 1960s and by the 1970s the developing world in particular was in the grip of harsher dictatorships than had ever before been the case. The dictatorships in Argentina and Guatemala, for example, were as violent and repressive as the Fascist regimes in Europe thirty or forty years earlier.

Huntington identifies a third wave beginning with democratization in Portugal in 1974, followed quickly by Greece and Spain. In the 1980s, a number of Latin American countries began to democratize. Democratization began in 1989 in East and Central Europe, the former Soviet Union and parts of Africa. Democratic movements also emerged at this time in Asia and transitions away from entrenched authoritarian rule began in Taiwan and South Korea.

Huntington argued that waves of democracy could be distinguished with sufficient clarity in time and space to suggest common causes both for the spread of democracy and for its reversal. He also suggested that the existence of waves meant that trends to democracy were global, and that therefore global factors were at work. He did not imply that there was one single global cause of democratization, however, either historically or in the present era. So, while the first wave was associated with expanding capitalism and the creation of global markets, coupled with the diffusion of the idea of democracy, the second wave was a consequence of the defeat of Fascism, the global authority of the Allies after the Second World War, the influence of the West in decolonization, and the Cold War, which suggested the ideological triumph of liberal democracy within the capitalist 'free' world.

The third wave, he argues, is the product of five key factors (Huntington 1991: 45–6):

- the deepening legitimacy problems of authoritarian systems. This was made worse by the fact that non-democratic regimes tend to depend excessively on performance legitimacy. A number of non-democratic regimes were undermined either by poor economic performance in the wake of oil-price rises in the 1970s or by military defeat;
- rising expectations following the economic boom of the 1960s, leading to demands for raised living standards and education, especially on the part of the middle classes;
- the liberalization of the Catholic Church following the Second Vatican Council of 1963–5, assisting the transformation of national churches (and individual church leaders) and making it possible for them to act as proponents of reform;
- the changing policies of global organizations such as the European Union, and of actors such as Gorbachev and the shift in US policy towards endorsing an agenda of democratization and human rights; and
- demonstration effects, or snowballing, the result of the global growth of communication networks.

Strengths and Weaknesses of the Wave Approach

The wave theory points to the importance of grouping democratizations in time. This is its strength. It forces us to look for commonality in democratization processes in countries that, at first sight, may be very different. It directs our attention to the big picture, beyond national experiences. It indicates the cyclical way in which democracy has waxed and waned as a organizing principle for government and as a popular aspiration. But there are also limitations to the wave theory.

First, there are some empirical problems with the wave approach. ①
Used as a metaphor, the idea of the wave captures quite graphically how
democracy spreads spatially and over time. But on closer examination
the waves turn out to be rather indistinct and even overlapping. Why, for
example, Portugal, Greece and Spain should form part of the third wave
of democratization, alongside East and Central Europe, South Africa
and the former Soviet Union, rather than the second wave, is not really
very clear. After all, in terms of time, barely twenty years separate the
beginning of democratization in Portugal and the end of democratization in West Germany. Furthermore, it could be argued that democratization was not completed in Germany until its reunification, suggesting
that the distinction between the second and third wave is quite blurred.

Secondly, Huntington adopts an excessively narrow understanding of ②
democracy. He comes close, in fact, to seeing democracy simply as relatively clean elections, independent of the size of the electorate, the
nature of the party system or the state of civil liberties. This can easily
give rise to the 'fallacy of electoralism' (Karl 1995: 72–86). So, for
example, he puts Italy and Argentina in the first wave, although governments were undemocratic until the time of the First World War.
Thereafter democracy was limited, unstable, elitist, contested and of
short duration – barely democratic, in fact – before collapsing completely, in 1926 in Italy and in 1930 in Argentina. It makes more sense
to date the beginning of the democratic order in Italy from the time of
the Second World War, while recognizing at the same time that Italy has
a long history of democratic struggle. Meanwhile, the period Huntington
describes as the first wave of democracy in Argentina is better seen as
part of the long-running conflict between unstable and unconsolidated
elite politics, military intervention and populism, which remained, in
fact, the mould of Argentine politics throughout most of the twentieth
century. The construction of democracy in Argentina can only be said
to have begun in the 1980s and it remains troubled and incomplete still.

Finally, by overemphasizing the global aspects of democratization, ③
the wave approach misleads as to the causes of democracy. Even though
Huntington argues that global factors are crucial in democratization, he
is unable to specify chains of causality or identify the mechanisms that
bring democracy into being. He assumes that globalization provides a
sufficient explanation. In fact, while global factors can be significant in
allowing democracies to emerge, they are not enough to explain why
democracy does (and does not) take root. In short, the wave approach

overstates the role of globalization. Huntington shows that there have been transnational trends towards democratization, although where they begin and end is actually quite fuzzy; but this not the same as proving that the success and failure of democratization can be attributed to globalization. Furthermore, Huntington assumes that globalization is always positive for democracy, despite evidence that deepening integration into global markets can sometimes intensify or re-legitimize authoritarianism. And because he overemphasizes the role of globalization, he underestimates the importance of factors within nation states, such as class structure, civil society and the state. Consequently, the wave approach runs the risk of oversimplifying complex historical processes.

Rethinking the Third Wave

Contemporary democratization processes are far more complex than Huntington's model assumes. The wave approach fails to capture the very different explanations for democratization. In the first place, then, it is important to disentangle the causes of democratization. Secondly, the wave approach assumes that there is now a global movement to democracy – the third wave. But, in fact, as Diamond (1999: 24–5) notes, the number of stable liberal democracies is actually growing very slowly. Huntington assumed that more democracies were emerging because more elections were being held. But elections, as we noted above, do not necessarily indicate the beginning of democracy. Contemporary experiments in democratization encompass the creation of some liberal democracy in some countries, the introduction of limited electoral change in others, the manufacturing of cosmetic changes masking continued authoritarianism in still more, and on-going and unresolved struggles between pro-democracy forces and authoritarians in a final set of countries. It is important to distinguish between psuedodemocracies, problematic or partial democracies and consolidated democracies. In sum, contemporary democratizations encompass failures as well as successes. Why some democratization experiments succeed and others fail is currently the most salient question in democratization studies.

Democracies are political systems comprising institutions that translate citizens' preferences into policy, have effective states that act to protect and deepen democratic rights, and count on a strong participatory and critical civil society. A consolidated democracy is one in which this political order is routinized and accepted. Consolidation, then, implies both the deepening and stabilizing of democracy. This book argues that the chances for consolidation are greatest in cases where favourable international circumstances are allied with state capacity and a growing, vocal and effective civil society. This framework is explained in more detail in Chapter 3. The rest of the present chapter will briefly explain the expansion of democracy from the nineteenth century to the present, drawing on this approach.

Democratization in History

For Dahl (1989: 234), the history of democracy begins in 1776, when the American Revolution took place. Dahl dates democratization from the triumph of the idea of representation, which led to the American revolution and the creation of the USA. For Huntington (1991), who equates democracy with individualism, the first wave began in 1828. Strictly speaking, however, democratization does not really begin until after 1870. Before then, the suffrage was so profoundly restricted, and politics the exclusive preserve of elites, that no country could be said to have begun to democratize. Moreover, even at the end of the nineteenth century, democracy was fiercely resisted by elites and its operation in practice was limited by the poor development of the state. As Dahl (1989: 234) notes, in no country did the *demos* become inclusive until the twentieth century, and 'in most countries ... institutions were often defective, by present standards, until the last third of the nineteenth century or later'.

Democratization began in Britain, some parts of Western Europe, the US and some of colonies settled by the British, namely Canada, Australia and New Zealand. It was aided by the existence of clearly defined territorial borders allowing for the development of consolidated nation-states and the gradual expansion of the functions and capacities of the state. Just as important, however, was that capitalism advanced rapidly in these countries. Capitalism generated structures that allowed the gradual empowerment of non-elites or subaltern classes – often constructed as 'the people' – leading ultimately to a recognition of their political rights (see Box 2.1). It unleashed fierce social struggles and introduced new conflicts, which were sometimes violent, to society. Democracy emerged as a consequence of those social disputes. In addition, capitalism and social conflict led, in some cases, to the emergence of a modern and relatively autonomous state, capable of playing a role in politics independent of market forces. This new state made possible the implementation of the economic and social reforms that, in Europe, constitute the foundations of democracy. In other words, democracy was

---

Box 2.1 Capitalism, Democracy and the Role of Classes

Capitalism radically transforms class structures. For Lipset (1959) and
Huntington (1991) capitalism leads to the development of a bourgeoisie and
middle-class professionals who are the key to democratization. However, the
relationship between classes, capitalism and democracy is complex. In particular, the industrial bourgeoisie is not always democratically minded.
Furthermore, since democracy requires an inclusive citizenship, it can only
be said to come into existence when the working class and other subaltern
groups have effective rights and representation. Rueschmeyer, Stephens and
Stephens (1992: 7–8) explain this in the following way:

> [C]apitalist development is associated with democracy because it
> transforms the class structure, strengthening the working and middle
> classes and weakening the landed class. It was not the capitalist market
> nor capitalists as the new dominant force, but rather the contradictions
> of capitalism that advanced the cause of democracy. ... The working
> class was the most consistently pro-democratic force [in history]. The
> class had a strong interest in effecting its political inclusion and it was
> more insulated from the hegemony of the dominant classes than the rural
> lower classes. ... The bourgeoisie [was] generally supportive of the
> installation of constitutional and representative government, but opposed
> to extending political inclusion to the lower classes. ... The middle
> classes played an ambiguous role in the installation and consolidation of
> democracy. They pushed for their own inclusion but their attitude
> towards inclusion of the lower classes depended on the need and possi-
> bilities for an alliance with the working class.

---

the result of social pressure, combined with the development of a
reformist state that was to some degree autonomous of society, in the
context of capitalist economic expansion.

The relationship between capitalism, class structures, the state and
democracy becomes clearer if we look at particular examples. We turn
now, therefore, to the development of democracy in Britain.
Democratization in Britain is the result of a gradual process of electoral
expansion and social and economic reform. Throughout the nineteenth
and twentieth centuries, democracy was extended by degrees as a result
of pressure from below.

The origins of democracy in Britain lie in the Industrial Revolution
which revolutionized production and led to the development of capitalism early in the nineteenth century. The resulting social and economic
transformation in the countryside and the town gave rise to demands

from society for change. Capitalists and the professional middle classes pressed for changes to the political order that would reflect their growing power vis-à-vis agriculture. They wanted influence over policy-making so as to ensure a suitable climate for continued capitalist growth. Popular social movements also emerged and demanded changes that would benefit the mass of working people. These included the extension of the suffrage and citizenship rights, the development of welfare politics and the creation of an equal society. In their original state, the popular movements were revolutionary, in that their aim was to challenge the established order. However, a gradual process of social, economic and political reform took place, starting especially in the last third of the nineteenth century and continuing throughout the twentieth. This improved living standards at the same time as a gradual political incorporation of the working class, especially working-class men, took place. Furthermore, the transformation of the British state, as it gradually took on the role of protecting and deepening industrialization, meant that the number of political elites increased and their social origins widened. Gradually, the introduction of representative democracy came to be seen as a consensual and reformist project, rather than a revolutionary option. The development of democracy in Britain, then, was in some senses paradoxical. Mobilization for and against democracy generated bitter social conflicts and it was initially viewed as a very radical, even revolutionary, project. But liberal democracy became possible because class compromise and social reforms reduced popular support for more radical demands.

Democracy in Britain emerged from two different class compromises. The first comprised an agreement between the aristocracy and bourgeoisie in the eighteenth and nineteenth centuries to put an end to the hostility that had led to a civil war (1640–1649) and the establishment of a republic in the seventeenth century. As Moore (1966: 30) points out, the rapprochement between the landed elite and industrial interests was made possible by 'the strong commercial tone in the life of the landed upper classes, both gentry and nobility' which prevented the development of a 'solid phalanx of aristocratic opposition to the advance of industry'. The alliance was cemented through parliamentary reform. The 1832 Reform Act established the principle of political influence (or the vote) in accordance with the ownership of property, in contravention of the aristocratic principle of inherited power. As a result, parliament gradually came to represent and defend Britain's expanding capitalist economy. So, although politics remained chiefly an occupation for the aristocracy and the House of Lords guaranteed a voice in politics for inherited wealth, after 1832, governments could no longer ignore the political, as well as the economic, power of capitalists and the growing middle class.

A second class compromise took place later in the nineteenth century, between the bourgeoisie and the organized (male) working class. After 1832, there was a gradual expansion of the suffrage, and by 1885 a significant number of working-class men could also vote. This was achieved largely as a result of popular agitation. Britain was shaken by mobilization from below from 1838 to 1848 in the shape of the Chartist movement. The Charter included the very radical demand of one-man-one-vote. Following the demise of Chartism, the trade union movement demanded political reform. Parallel to the changes in the electoral system, Britain also witnessed the gradual legalization and protection of the union movement. The agreement was based not only on extending political representation but also on the introduction of social reforms and state intervention to establish minimum welfare rights. After 1870, public health reforms led to the provision of clean water, the creation of sewerage systems, minimum housing standards, and the introduction of some basic social reforms such as the regulation of the working day and the establishment of minimal employment conditions. By the beginning of the twentieth century, the state's role in the provision of welfare had increased still more. For Peden (1991) the reforms introduced after 1906 were a direct response to trade union pressure and the rise of a working-class party, the Labour Party. Organized labour was strong enough to push the state gradually towards social reform, including the introduction of a welfare state after 1945. Social and economic reform thus lay at the heart of this second, and far more fragile, compromise between capital and labour. It legitimized democracy and made political cooperation possible.

Consequently, the British state became not only a coercive instrument for the extraction of human and material resources but also a tool for social and economic redistribution. Public health legislation, social reform and the creation of a welfare state meant expanding the role of the state. Until the establishment of the welfare state, in fact, state infrastructure was less developed in Britain than in many other European countries, such as Germany and France. The expansion and the increasing sophistication of the state therefore made democracy possible in Britain. Indeed, the growth of the state is an essential precondition for democratization everywhere (see Box 2.2).

Box 2.2   State Power and Democracy

According to Mann (1993), feudal or pre-modern states enjoyed little capacity to act in society. After the sixteenth century, European states gradually increased their capacity to penetrate society and to carry out an increased range of functions. Mann refers to this as increased 'despotic power'. States with despotic power act without negotiations with civil society. A state with despotic power is strong, in the sense that it has the capacity to do things (taxation, protection of borders, etc.), but it is not accountable. The state acts either autonomously or through multiple but autonomous elites. Mann (1993: 59) contrasts despotic power with 'infrastructural power', that is 'collective power, "power through" society, coordinating social life through state infrastructures. ... Infrastructural power is a two-way street: It also enables civil society to control the state. ... Effective infrastructural powers ... increase collective state power.' Modern states combine despotic and infrastructural power to different degrees. High levels of despotic power are incompatible with democracy. Infrastructural power is essential for, but not exclusive to, democracies. Nevertheless, the development of infrastructural capacities makes democracy possible. The state is forced to establish close relationships with civil society and can no longer easily or permanently exclude entire sectors of society. At the same time, the increased visibility and expansion of the state contributes to the politicization of society. Finally, infrastructural power makes the distribution of public goods and the creation of welfare politics possible.

As capitalism spread, liberal democracy was gradually established in more countries, including the US, France, Sweden, Denmark, Norway, Belgium and Switzerland. By the beginning of the twentieth century, democracy was taking root in overseas British settler countries as well. Nevertheless, important authoritarian enclaves remained in these countries and elites were not always fully subject to democratic control. In the case of Britain, for example, an unelected House of Lords persisted as did an elitist culture within the state (Judge 1999). In the US, citizenship was denied to significant numbers of the population because of colour. By the beginning of the twentieth century, democratic movements were also visible in a number of other countries, as they were pulled into the global economy or as elites sought to learn the lessons of class compromise as a way of avoiding revolution. Democracy movements emerged in Italy, Spain, Chile and Argentina and the successor states to the Hapsburg and Hohenzollern empires, including Germany,

Austria, and Czechoslovakia. In some cases, the First World War acted as catalyst to democratization because it politicized vast numbers of people and reduced the hold of landed elites over the state.

However, democracy was weakly established in a number of these countries. As a result, the crisis of capitalism in the late 1920s and early 1930s and the fact that the landed elites still retained considerable economic and political power, as well as social prestige, combined to undermine commitment to democracy in many countries (Bessel 1997: 74). The collapse of democracy was most spectacular in Germany, where the failure of democracy led to the triumph of Nazism. In Italy, a fascist dictatorship emerged as early as 1926. In Spain, the civil war of 1936–9 led to the establishment of the Francoist dictatorship. Portugal and Greece also succumbed to authoritarian rule and Poland's fragile democracy collapsed. These unstable and contested democracies came to an end, ultimately, because elites rejected democracy and preferred dictatorship. In Germany, Italy, Spain, Portugal and Greece, class structures made authoritarianism a more likely outcome than democracy to class conflict, in that the landed class was still large and an alliance of the aristocracy with the bourgeoisie was possible, as a way of disciplining the working class.

In Europe, the defeat of the Axis powers undoubtedly created opportunities for democratization. In some cases, this was because the horror of the Nazi period persuaded Europeans of the value of consensus and individual rights. The spread of liberal democracy after 1945, however, is at least as much to do with the authority of the Allied liberal democracies, the US, Britain, and France. Their capacity to impose political systems ultimately lay behind the democratization in West Germany (following the division of Germany by the Soviet Union and the West), Italy and Austria. Outside Europe, the Allies pushed democratic forms of government in Japan, the Philippines and Korea. So, for the first time, democratization after 1945 was partially externally driven. Nevertheless, in all these cases, Allied powers took care to build relationships with domestic elites, many of whom were also convinced of the value of liberal democracy. After a period of careful vigilance, Allied powers gradually withdrew from the occupied territories, leaving liberal democratic institutions behind. In some cases, the withdrawal was very gradual indeed: in West Germany, for example, sovereignty in military and foreign policy was not achieved until 1955.

What of the democracy outside its European heartland or territories directly controlled by Western powers? Democratic movements had emerged in Latin America as early as the beginning of the twentieth century. But, with the partial exception of Chile, elites were consistently able to reject pressure from below. In some cases, dictatorships and repression were the result. After 1945, democracy took off to some extent, partly due to US pressure and a need on the part of Latin America elites not to be seen to go against the grain of global trends. As a result, new liberal democratic systems were set up in Uruguay, Brazil and Costa Rica. In some countries, such as Guatemala, democratization was also a response to growing popular pressure for change. Throughout the region, however, democracy was difficult to consolidate, not least because the introduction of liberal democratic institutions was rarely accompanied by social or economic reform, active policies of political enfranchisement or the elimination of vote-rigging or corruption. And where democratization was driven by strong popular organizations it frequently encountered opposition from elites and the Armed Forces. Furthermore, as the Cold War got under way in the late 1940s, the US preferred to support dictatorships in Latin America, rather than democracies that might allow Communist or other left movements to operate freely. As a result, US governments largely threw their weight behind anti-democratic movements, supporting the military coup in 1954 in Guatemala, for example. By the 1960s, particularly harsh military bureaucratic-authoritarian regimes in which active state intervention was aimed at deepening capitalism and disciplining labour had emerged in Chile, Argentina and Brazil. In Central America, the systematic repression of democratic movements peaked in the 1970s and early 1980s. The overall result was that democratization was limited and partial, until the mid-1980s.

In Africa, decolonization in the 1950s and early 1960s led for a short while to the creation of new states, most of which were initially created in the liberal democratic mould. The adoption of liberal democratic institutions was decided chiefly by the withdrawing ex-colonial powers. Democracy was not, in most cases, a result of domestic pressures or elite decisions. In view of this, it comes as little surprise that these institutions gradually collapsed, leaving authoritarian regimes in place for the most part by the 1970s. Moreover, authoritarian governments emerged in parts of Asia, including South Korea and the Philippines, in the 1970s. The failure of the democratic experiments in developing countries was indicative of the difficulties of sustaining democracy without economic development or the introduction of social and economic reform that could mediate the costs of capitalism. Elites were powerful enough to resist democracy and social reform. At times of political mobilization, they tended to resort to authoritarian rule. The failure of democracy in the developing world in the 1960s and 1970s was such that it raised doubts about whether democracy would ever be possible outside the core capitalist countries.

Contemporary Democratization

The failure of democracies in the 1960s led to a generalized pessimism about the chances for further democratization. The emergence of democracy in Southern Europe in the 1970s, therefore, took observers somewhat by surprise. First Portugal, then Greece and Spain moved towards democracy, despite being economically relatively backward countries. Furthermore, Spanish democratization was successful against a background of violent separatism. This was followed by democratization in Latin America and moves to dismantle authoritarian regimes in parts of Asia. But it was the collapse of the Berlin Wall in 1989 that really sparked the view that the world was in the grip of a period of rapid global change, with democratization at its core. The early 1990s seemed a heady combination of democratic government in Latin America, the emergence of democratic pressure in sub-Saharan Africa, democratic change in South Africa with the end of apartheid and the holding of the first non-racial elections, the emergence of democratic struggles in China and the break-up of the Soviet empire.

The emergence of pro-democracy movements in countries where capitalism was not fully developed challenged many of the assumptions about democracy. In particular, it raised doubts as to whether democratization still depended on class conflict. As we have seen, globalization was posited as an alternative explanation. But class and other forms of social conflict within societies still matter for explaining democratization. For Tilly (1997: 276), contemporary democratizations indicate that 'proletarianization constitutes the crucial conditions for democratization'. Nevertheless, he argues that the term 'proletariat' should now be broadened to include subaltern social forces whose existence is not due solely to capitalism. In other words, the agents of democratization are no longer only the organized working class. Other groups located in civil society – the peasantry, women's movements, environmental networks, and so on – can now equally play an important role in promoting and sustaining democratic change. Moreover, state capacity remains crucial in determining how far democracy movements can succeed.

These issues are discussed in detail in Chapters 7, 8, 9 and 10, which deal with particular cases of contemporary democratization. However, it is worthwhile here drawing out the implications of past attempts at democratization for the contemporary experiments. Democratization took off most strongly in the most economically developed states, in general. But democracy was contested in capitalist countries and, in some, authoritarian regimes replaced early and fragile democracies. This suggests that capitalism is important, but that it does not guarantee the emergence of democracy. Meanwhile, democratic forms of government survived in some countries for considerable periods, even though economic development was slow and elitism entrenched. In these cases, the role of the state and the activism of civil society groups were important factors in explaining the survival of democracy. We can conclude that the chances for democratization are greater when:

- capitalism is the dominant national mode of production;
- civil society groups are active and politicized;
- class and other social conflicts are resolved through political enfranchisement and the incorporation of new social groups into the polity rather than through their exclusion;
- the state is relatively autonomous and has not been captured exclusively by a small elite;
- the state has sufficient resources for redistribution and to enforce the rule of law; and
- the international order promotes and encourages democratization and ostracizes non-democratic regimes.

Conclusion

The 'wave' constitutes a useful metaphor for situating democratization in its global context. It points to the importance of recognizing that the chances for democratic outcomes to social conflict are greater at particular moments of global history. Some global conjunctures have proved especially favourable to democracy. However, the wave metaphor has only a limited utility. It allows us to make cross-national and cross-regional connections but it tells us little about how democracy actually comes about in national societies – who are the agents or the bearers of democracy; and under what conditions can democracy thrive? To understand these issues, we have to embrace theories of social and economic change and political action. These theories are rooted in the political and social dynamics particular to nation states. In other words, we need to complement the global focus with an attention to domestic politics. We have briefly looked at democratization in historical context in this way. The next chapter looks more closely at theories that explain the development of democracy.

3
Theories of Democratization

Theories of democratization have been concerned chiefly with causation and the identification of the main factors that lead to the emergence of democracies. Most explanations of democratization draw upon elements of three distinct approaches: modernization theory; historical sociology (sometimes called structuralism); and transition theory (also known as agency theory). Sometimes a distinction is made simply between structuralist theories (modernization and historical sociology) and agency approaches (transition theory) because of their very different positions regarding structure and agency. This chapter explains these different approaches and examines how they have been used in the literature on contemporary democratization. It should be remembered that all theories are attempts to impose order and find patterns in the messy and complex reality of human life; to some extent, therefore, theories are bound to be parsimonious and partial explanations. On its own, no single theory will explain completely a particular case. But the theories are useful in that they ask important questions about democratization in general and contribute to particular explanations.

As more democracies were created in the 1990s, a focus on consolidation, or the factors that make democracy endure, also crept into the debate. All three approaches have something different to contribute to the debate about consolidation. However, they all also have very significant limitations in this regard. Consequently, the chapter proposes an alternative focus, which analyzes democratizations through three key dimensions, namely the state, civil society and globalization.

Modernization Theory

For Giddens (1990), modernity is inherently globalizing, that is it spreads across the world, creating one uniform culture. Modernization theory, in other words, implicitly links democratization with globaliza-

46

tion. It links the spread of democracy to modernity and the Enlightenment idea of the universality of progress. It was codified within democratization studies by Seymour Martin Lipset (1959) and draws on a mix of Weberian notions of the 'modern' state and the pre-occupation of classical sociology with describing the social transitions – from feudalism to capitalism, from traditional to modern, from ascription to achievement – which occurred in the nineteenth and twentieth centuries. Talcott Parsons's (1951) work is a modern expression of classical sociology's tendency to classify societies in terms of simple oppositions. He identified modernity as a passage from diffuseness to specificity and from particularism to universalism. In modernization theory, the characteristics he identifies as those of modernity are generally laid down as benchmarks for all developing or non-democratic societies to achieve.

Modernity is equated with the processes of change which had occurred in the nineteenth century in the Atlantic societies of Britain and the US and, to a lesser extent, within Western Europe generally. A modern society, then, is essentially a product of capitalism. Lipset presumed that modernity was a single universal experience, leading to essentially similar societies and states. As a theory of change, modernization is functionalist and economistic, in that it sees democracy as an outcome of capitalism. It associates economic growth in a causal relationship with progress. Modernization is also predictive: democracy appears in those societies that are able to 'replicate the original transition' to capitalism (Roxborough 1979) and become enmeshed in global economic structures.

According to Lipset, capitalism is the heart of democracy because it produced wealth (which he unproblematically assumed would trickle down and lead to higher levels of mass consumption), led to an educated middle class and produced a number of cultural changes favourable to democracy, such as increased secularism and a diminution in ascriptive and primordial identities. He suggested that one link between capitalism and democracy was that capitalism diminished class conflict:

> For the lower strata, economic development, which means increased income, greater economic security and higher education, permits those in this status to develop longer time perspectives and more complex and gradualist views of politics. A belief in secular reformist gradualism can only be the ideology of a relatively well-to-do lower class. Increased wealth and education also serve democracy by increasing the extent to which the lower strata are exposed to cross

pressures which will reduce the intensity of their commitment to given ideologies and make them less receptive to supporting extremist ones. ... Increased wealth is not only related causally to the development of democracy by changing the social conditions of the workers, but it also affects the political role of the middle class through changing the shape of the stratification structure so that it shifts from an elongated pyramid with a large lower-class base, to a diamond with a growing middle class. A large middle class plays a mitigating role in moderating conflict since it is able to reward moderate and democratic parties and penalize extremist groups. (Lipset 1959: 78)

Lipset's notion of capitalism as the source of democracy was strengthened by the work of some development economists such as Walt Rostow in the 1960s. Rostow (1960) identified a lineal path for economic development along defined 'stages', as they were termed, until capitalism was achieved. These 'stages' were: the traditional society; the pre-take-off society; take-off; the road to maturity; and the mass consumption society. They thus parallel the classic sociological tradition of conceptualizing political and social change as part of a transition from traditionalism to modernity.

Lipset's work was also contemporaneous with theory-building efforts by a number of scholars around the relationship between political culture and democratization (Pye and Verba 1965; Almond and Verba 1963). Modernization was frequently associated with this work, which linked democracy to a particular political culture – one which channelled mass participation in an orderly, non-mobilizing and low-key fashion and encouraged secular and elite-led government. While the emphasis of the political culture school was somewhat different from that of Lipset – it sought to explain the difficulties societies encountered in becoming 'modern' – the work of political development scholars increased the acceptability of Lipset's thesis by linking material progress and democracy to modernity. This emphasis on culture has re-emerged in studies of contemporary democratization.

Evaluating Modernization Theory

Modernization is an attempt to theorize the fact that democracies have emerged in the modern world under capitalism. It has tried to specify the particular components of capitalism that make for democracy. That is its strength. However, it assumes an overly simple and lineal relationship between capitalism and democracy. As a result, it has been suggested that modernization theory is ahistorical, ethnocentric and overly structural. Doubts have also been expressed about the typical methodology employed within modernization studies.

Modernization is ahistorical in that it presumes that all societies can replicate a transition which actually occurred at a particular moment in space and time. It does not recognize the difficulties – indeed the impossibility – of one society copying what occurred in a different society at a different time, nor the changes which have taken place globally which mean that capitalism is now a global order rather than an economic system confined within the territorial boundaries of particular nation states. Critics of modernization have suggested that late development has in fact led to a malign version of modernity marked by authoritian capitalism rather than democracy (Frank 1971; Cardoso and Faletto 1979). O'Donnell 's (1973) influential theory of bureaucratic authoritarianism identifies the deepening of capitalism in developing countries with the emergence not of democracies but of dictatorships. He suggests that a numerically small but politically powerful bourgeoisie uses the state to maximize profit through repression. For these critics, modernization's assumption that capitalism was the source of democracy was empirically invalid and theoretically facile. From a rather different perspective, Beetham (1997) has also suggested that the idea that the market is inevitably supportive of democracy, as modernization assumes, is unsustainable. Markets can both support and undermine democracy. Finally, because modernization ignores the particular development processes of the third world and has extrapolated out of the experiences of the Western world a 'rule' for the entire planet, modernization is also inherently ethnocentric.

The idea that modernization is an overly structural explanation of political change is a critique of a different order. Rather than attacking the fundamental assumptions of modernization, it is suggested that the role of structure (that is, capitalism) is exaggerated at the expense of human action. In other words, modernization leaves politics out and should be criticized 'for being overly concerned with structures and therefore assuming that the behaviour of people – whether classes, groups or individuals – is epiphenomenal and ultimately reducible to material or other conditions' (Schmitz and Sell 1999: 24).

Finally, modernization theory has also been subject to a methodological critique. Lipset's method was to categorize all countries in terms of being 'more or less democratic'. He tested this by using two variables, wealth and education, and found that the average wealth … and level of education was much higher for the democratic countries (Lipset 1959). He then used this to suggest causation. Put simply, Lipset claimed to have proved that more telephones, more cars, more consumption – in sum, more capitalism – leads to more democracy. Even scholars broadly sympathetic to modernization's underlying thesis have found themselves forced to reduce these sweeping claims. Diamond (1992), for example, points out that Lipset's own data indicated higher levels of economic development within European non-democracies than in Latin American democracies, suggesting that democracy required the presence of factors other than economic growth. Vanhanen (1990) and Hadenius (1992) have also modified Lipset's claim, from causality to one of correlation. Przeworski and Limongi (1997) suggest that the evidence supports the thesis that democracy survives better in wealthier nations but not the original proposition that democracy is a simple consequence of economic growth.

Modernization Theory Today

Leftwich (1996) offers the most forceful contemporary restatement of modernization. He applies it, logically enough, only to developing states. He argues that economic development, whether in a democratic political setting or not, will inevitably produce democracy in the long term. As a result he recommends that: 'the West should ... support only those dedicated and determined developmental elites which are seriously bent on promoting economic growth, *whether democratic or not.* For by helping them to raise the level of economic development it will help them also to establish or consolidate the real internal conditions for lasting democracy' (Leftwich 1996: 329; italics in the orginal).

It is rare, however, for modernization to have survived in such an unreformed way. Generally, today's modernizationists do not claim direct causality between capitalism and democracy. Diamond has been particularly influential in updating modernization theory. He has picked up the 1960s concern with mass participation and political culture in newly 'modernized' states and emphasizes, in particular, the role of political culture and a dynamic civil society for democratization. In the process, he has shifted modernization away from a discussion on the causes of democracy towards a focus on consolidation. He argues that long-term democratic consolidation must encompass a shift in political culture (Diamond 1999). Emphasizing the role of civil society and civic freedoms means, in fact, that he is pessimistic about the chances for sustained democratization in much of the developing world because civil society is frequently poorly articulated and weak, and the political culture of institutions and electoral regimes is 'shallow, exclusive, unaccountable and abusive of individual and group rights' (Diamond 1996: 34). Diamond's work is of considerable academic importance. But this new version of modernization theory is just as profoundly embedded in Western policy-making circles.

For Cammack (1994), its success is due to the fact that it addresses a major issue in global politics, namely the difficulties of governance in an era of mass participation, and, furthermore, it does so from the perspective of conservative global elites. Not surprisingly, then, modernization remains the vision behind a number of democracy-promoting initiatives, especially those emerging from US governmental circles. In sum, modernization theory retains vitality and influence through its ability to identify the apparent link between capitalism and democracy. However it is unable to explain why trends to democratization are so often contradictory and partial.

Historical Sociology

Historical sociology is a kind of 'macrohistory' in which history is 'the instrument by which structures are discovered invisible to the unaided eye' (Collins 1999: 1). It is because of this emphasis on structures that the approach is sometimes termed 'structuralism'. 'Historical sociology' and 'structuralism' are often used interchangeably in democratization studies. An important strand of historical sociology has been the search to identify different trajectories of state development or paths to modernity, through, for example, war or revolution (Skocpol 1979; Tilly 1990). The historical/sociological approach to democratization has two particular intellectual origins. In part, it arose out of a reaction to the excessively society-based accounts of political change implicit in behaviouralism in the 1960s, and offers instead a state-centred view. It is therefore part of the intellectual labour of 'bringing the state back in' to politics (Evans , Rueschmeyer and Skocpol 1985). It also drew explicitly on a critique of the short-termism and causal simplicity of modernization as an explanation of democratization (Rueschmeyer, Stephens and Stephens 1992). It is, inevitably, a much more diffuse approach to democratization than modernization theory, with a primary interest in explaining, not predicting, outcomes.

Structuralists are interested in how the changing relationship between the state, understood in the Weberian sense of 'a human community that (successfully) claims the *monopoly of the legitimate use of physical force* within a given territory' (Skocpol 1985: 7; italics in the original), and classes shapes the political system. As such, they admit an important role for collective actors. They are agreed that democracies do not come into being overnight; nor does democracy happen simply because some people (individuals, groups, or classes) will it into existence. Structuralists trace the transformation of the state through class conflict over time, in order to explain how democracy – which they see as state transformation – has sometimes emerged. Structuralism also contains elements of a political economy of democratization in that it emphasizes how changes in the economy – for example the expansion of production for the market – lead to social or class conflict, although economic change is not, on its own, regarded as determining political outcomes. Unlike the wave approach of modernization theory, historical sociology identifies factors that are distinctive to particular cases.

Barrington Moore's (1966) major study of political change constitutes a significant milestone for historical/sociological understanding of democratization. His comparative analysis of eight 'big' countries, Britain, France, the US, Germany, Russia, Japan, China and India, through the nineteenth century and into the twentieth, identified the different historical trajectories that each had travelled to reach modernity. Fascism and Communism simply constituted a different version of modernity, resulting from very different sets of relationships between collective actors and states. For Moore, outcomes depended on the interactions between three important classes – the peasantry, the landed upper class and the bourgeoisie. Essentially, democracy occurred when

- the 'peasant question' was solved by the gradual elimination of peasant agriculture and the rise of opportunities for transforming the peasantry into urban workers through the expansion of towns and industrial employment opportunities; and
- the landed class was defeated and transformed in its struggles for control of the state by the rising bourgeoisie.

This latter was crucial in determining whether democracy or a form of dictatorship emerged (see Box 3.1).

Moore's work concentrated on the emergence of the first democracies. It was modified by Rueschmeyer, Stephens and Stephens (1992) in the light of later history and the expansion of the number of parliamentary and stable democracies. They describe their theoretical framework as part of the 'new comparative political economy' (Rueschmeyer, Stephens and Stephens 1992: 40). By this, they mean that they view the

Box 3.1 Routes to Modernity

Barrington Moore identified three routes to modernity: a bourgeois revolution, leading to capitalism and democracy; revolution from above, leading to industrialization and fascism; and revolution from below, leading to communism.

The Bourgeois Revolution
Moore's understanding of the bourgeois path was based on the historical experiences of Britain, France and the US. He conceptualized the transformation of the pre-modern state into a democracy as a result of two stages:

- the reduction in the overall size of the peasantry and an end to its organic dependence on the landed class; and
- a realignment of upper-class interests around the dominance of commercial and industrial interests.

Revolution from Above
This is the path of conservative modernization. Exemplified most clearly by Germany and Japan, it combines the development of capitalism in agriculture and industry, alongside state-directed change. In both Germany and Japan, the tension between economic modernization and attempts to prevent social change led to the rise of militarism and ultimately to fascism. Revolution from above was a result of:

- the survival of a large small and middle peasantry, despite the rise of the market;
- the emergence of commercially-minded landed classes; and
- the development of a centralized and strong state.

Revolution from Below
This is the path to modernity through communism and peasant revolution. It occurred in the twentieth century in Russia and China. Commercial agriculture failed to emerge in either country, although there were attempts at modernization and a significant increase in labour repression in the nineteenth century. The social institutions of the peasantry survived intact into the modern era at the same time as the strength of royal bureaucracies prevented the emergence of commercially-minded landed classes. Revolution from below thus depended on:

- the survival, numerically and culturally, of the peasantry;
- a weak landed class; and
- an absolutist state.

political system of a particular country in relationship to broader questions of social power. Their work draws on a synthesis of scholarship from classical sociology and Marxism. It was ground-breaking because of its stress on the impact of what they termed 'three power structures': relative class power, the role of the state and the impact of transnational power structures.

They draw from Marxism a view that social class and class conflict constitute the starting point for an analysis of power and the state. They add to Moore's three-class schema, with its emphasis on rural change, a discussion of other subordinate classes, and of the urban working class in particular. But their emphasis on class divisions and class struggle is modified by a recognition of the role of the state and the role of the state system. In particular, they argue that whilst states have a special dependence upon capitalists under capitalism this has not always prevented working-class organizations from reforming the state. In other words, they see democratization as the imposition of reforms on a capitalist state, not as an automatic outcome from the development of capitalist relations of production. Without successful and self-conscious reformist strategies on the part of the subordinated classes, capitalist states will, in fact, almost inevitably be authoritarian (see Box 3.2). Furthermore, they suggest that a third dimension influences the nature of the state: the transnational context. This is particularly so in the case of the under-

---

Box 3.2   The Role of the Working Class in Democratization

Rueschmeyer, Stephens and Stephens (1992) assert the central importance of urban working classes for democratization:

> The organized working class appeared everywhere as a key actor in the development of full democracy ... In most cases, organized workers played an important role in the development of restricted democracy as well. The Latin American ... working class played a lesser role in the historical events there: the relative weakness of the working class certainly has contributed to the infrequence of full democracy in the region and to the instability of democracy where it did emerge. ... In all regions, however, pressure from the organized working class alone was insufficient to bring about the introduction of democracy; the working class needed allies. ... Democracy could only be established if (1) landlords were an insignificant force, or (2) they were not dependent on a large supply of cheap labor, or (3) they did not control the state. (Rueschmeyer, Stephens and Stephens 1992: 270)

developed and dependent countries. In any analysis of democratization struggles, therefore, the role of geo-political factors will be important. However, they remain agnostic as to 'the overall relationship between democracy and political/economic dependence in transnational relations' (Rueschmeyer, Stephens and Stephens 1992: 73). In other words, it is unclear whether external dependence supports or hinders democratization.

Evaluating Historical Sociology

The strength of historical sociology is that it is richly grounded and explanatory; and that it provides the possibility of comparison across time as well as across countries or regions. However, historical and structural approaches have been the subject of a number of criticisms. Historical sociology has become largely unfashionable, like all structuralist explanations of social change. Structuralism has, in general, fallen foul of the rediscovery of individual agency and volition in politics, of the questioning of Marxian class analysis and of the post-modern suggestion that power is too diffuse a concept to be understood in any static way; it is, instead, located in changing and fluid relationships. The major critiques of structuralism have therefore been both ontological and epistemological: its view of the world is too simple or simply wrong. As Przeworski (1991: 96) put it: 'in this formulation the outcome is uniquely determined by conditions, and history goes on without anyone ever doing anything'. In fact, however, historical sociology does recognize a considerable role for agency in processes of political transformation. The main agents of change are classes, or even the state. But thise notion of collective action is not sufficient to satisfy critics who only accept individuals as agents.

Other, more empirically-based, criticisms have also been forthcoming. Structuralism, with its emphasis on long-term historical change, seemed unable to account for the onset of sudden democratization in societies such as East and Central Europe and the countries of the ex-Soviet Union, where there was apparently little evidence of class agitation or struggle for democracy, except shortly before the collapse of authoritarianism. It was logical, therefore, especially in the light of the rise of agency-based theories of political behaviour through the 1980s, that dissatisfaction with structuralism would lead directly to a new agency-centred paradigm of democratization. Before analyzing the rise of 'transition studies', however, we examine the utility of historical sociology for analysis of contemporary democratizations.

Historical Sociology Today

An analysis of structures has particularly fed into the debate surrounding the consolidation of democracy. The idea that struggle and confrontation after the immediate transition can be symptoms of democratization comes from structuralism. It is therefore an appropriate tool for the analysis of post-transition systems. Structural analysis recognizes the fundamental class antagonisms of capitalist societies and suggests that conflict is a 'normal' part of democracy. It provides the researcher with the tools to question the idea that democratization requires the subordination of sectional and class interests for democracy to take root. By linking democracy with conflict, structuralism sees confrontation as a normal part of the pattern of the emerging democratic order. A structuralist perspective, with its emphasis on history, conflict, class and the state can also contribute to explanations of partial or incomplete democratizations. Gariorowski and Power (1998) argue that the chances for democratic consolidation are affected by 'development-related socio-economic factors, the contagion effect of democratic neighbors and high inflation'. They therefore draw the conclusion that all explanations of democratization should be placed within a broader structural perspective in order to fully understand the process of political change. Finally, structuralism is important in contextualizing and situating the debate about democratization. It allows for the identification of global structures that condition and shape the environment in which democratization takes place and points to the importance of 'underlying economic conditions and social forces' in democratization (Haggard and Kaufman 1997).

We return to the salience of historical sociology for understanding contemporary democratizations below.

Transition Studies

The transition approach, or, as it is sometimes termed, the agency approach, sees democracy as created by conscious, committed actors, providing that they possess a degree of luck and show a willingness to compromise. Democracy is not, therefore, a question of waiting for economic conditions to mature or the political struggles unleashed by economic change to be won. The divide between agency-centred scholars, on the one hand, and structuralists and modernization theorists, on the other, turns on the roles of actors, structure, culture and class relations in democratization and regime change. The transition school argues that both modernizationists and structuralists see the economy, history and development as overdetermining political outcomes.

For structuralists and the modernization school, democracy is an exceptional outcome which has occurred in only a few areas of the globe. It cannot be reproduced in countries where either the required levels of development are absent or where the class or social structure is unfavourable to it. By contrast, the attractions of the transition approach lie precisely in the fact that it questions these rather pessimistic assumptions. Agency perspectives suggest that democracy can be created independent of the structural context. The optimism of transitology accounts in large measure for its success, politically and academically, for this seemed to be precisely what was happening at the end of the 1980s. By implication, therefore, the transition approach presumes that the chances for spreading democracy in the contemporary world order are good. It hypothesizes successful outcomes for democracy if elites can learn the 'right' way to proceed.

The intellectual starting point for transition approaches is Rustow's (1970) critique of modernization. Rustow argues that the flaw of modernization theory is that it mistakes the 'functional' features of mature democracies – what makes them flourish – for 'genetic' causes of new democracies – what brings them into being. In contrast, he suggests that the only condition for democracy is a unified national state: 'the vast majority of citizens in a democracy-to-be must have no doubt or mental reservations as to which political community they belong to' (Rustow 1970: 350). He then hypothesizes that the creation of democracy is a dynamic process in the context of 'a prolonged and inconclusive political struggle' (Rustow 1970: 352), which passes through three stages – a preparatory phase, a decision phase, in which the choices and negotiations of 'a small circle of leaders' play a particularly crucial role (Rustow 1970: 356), and a habituation phase in which citizens and leaders fully adapt to the new system. These stages were later transformed into liberalization, transition and consolidation.

In 1986, Schmitter, O'Donnell and Whitehead edited the seminal transitologist analysis of democratization, *Transitions from Authoritarian Rule* which became the key reference for transition studies. It marked the beginning of a massive literature which focused on the processes of democratization by examining the interactions, pacts and bargains struck between authoritarian leaders and the democratic opposition. These deals led to a 'transition', a kind of half-way house between authoritarianism and consolidated democracy, in which the institutional rules are laid down for the practice of democracy. Successful transitions, it was emphasized, depend upon agreements between elites, including generally the outgoing authoritarian leaders. In none of their cases did democracy appear predetermined by the structural situation in which the struggles take place and pacts are made. They concluded that skilful leadership, aided by luck, was the key to outcomes which lead to the establishment of democratic procedures for government.

The transition approach thus pioneered a separation of *political* negotiations from *economic* circumstances. This was partly due to the insistence on contingency and negotiations and the rejection of functional determinism; but a normative note also crept in, and some transition studies warned would-be democratizers of the dangers of mixing transition with economic redistribution. This was evident in the influential work of Adam Przeworski, who argued:

> we cannot avoid the possibility that a transition to democracy can be made only at the cost of leaving economic relations intact, not only the structure of production but even the distribution of income. ... Democracy in the political realm has historically co-existed with exploitation and oppression at the workplace, within the schools, within bureaucracies and within families. (Przeworski 1986: 63)

By 1995, Schmitter was offering the following as advice for would-be democratizers:

> to the extent that it is possible, political choices should be give priority over economic ones. Incentives for the restructuring of national political institutions should precede, temporally and functionally, those aimed at reforming national systems of production and distribution. (Schmitter 1995: 33)

Agency-centred theories of democratization have the virtue that they situate the study of democracy within mainstream political science methodologies and epistemologies. By drawing on theories of political action – and by implication abandoning either sociological or historical approaches – transition studies offer a 'political' explanation of democratization. Democratization is seen as a *process.* For process-oriented scholars, 'choices are caught up in a continuous redefinition of actors' perceptions of preferences and constraints' (Kitschelt 1992: 1028). The task is to trace and explain these processes. Przeworski (1991: 19) pioneered a rational choice explanation of transition processes, which ran parallel with the rise to prominence of rational choice in other areas of the study of politics. He argued that '[w]hat matters for the stability of any regime is not the legitimacy of this particular system of domination but the presence of preferable alternatives' (Przeworski 1986: 51–2).The strategies adopted by key actors are dictated by cost – benefit calculations:

> If the expected gains for the opposition (more freedoms, material well-being and political participation) are higher than the risks (danger to life, imprisonment etc.) then it will continue to press for change. In turn, the regime elite is most likely to split into hard- and soft-liners along the two basic alternatives, either to suppress the opposition or to regain legitimacy by using a strategy of liberalization. Successful transition is most likely when soft-liners ally with the opposition and are transformed in this process into reformers. (Schmitz and Sell 1999: 31–2)

Above all, transition studies emphasize the agency and interactions of elites. They have thus made an important contribution by detailing how elite pacts, formal or informal, or compromises shape new democracies in the first place and contribute to their institutionalization (see Box 3.3). Elite-led democratization is viewed as positive for post-transition stability. But there are also some problems that result from pact-making. Karl (1990: 11) argues that foundational pacts can be a means through which economic elites assure themselves of the 'right' to continue to exploit a majority of the population and are therefore essentially 'anti-democratic mechanisms'. Hagopian (1992) is similarly critical: she argues that it has been precisely the behaviour of the 'political class' during the Brazilian transition that has prevented democracy taking root, leading to what she terms a 'compromised consolidation'. Przeworksi (1995: 54) recognizes that while pact-making creates stability, it can also lead to the institutionalization of forms of political exclusion. In other words, pacts shape the terms of transition and those terms may not be conducive to democratization in the long term.

Because of the emphasis on elites, agency-centred perspectives have devoted relatively little time to the analysis of civil society, associational life, social and political struggles and citizenship in the construction of democracy. As a result, the transition perspective takes a rather ambiguous attitude to the role of civil society in democratization. Some agency scholars have seen an active civil society or social activism as unimportant for democratic consolidation. Przeworski (1991) suggested that in some cases popular mobilization has been detrimental to democratization since it threatened the interests of powerful elites who then went to considerable lengths to close down tentative experiments in political liberalization. This position was modified later, by a recognition of the

---

Box 3.3   Pact-Making and Democratization

The importance of pact-making has been a dominant theme of transition studies. Pact-making is a way of describing the 'establishment of substantial consensus among elites concerning the rules of the democratic game and the worth of democratic institutions' (Burton, Gunther and Higley 1992: 3). According to O'Donnell and Schmitter (1986: 37), elite pacts are 'an explicit, but not always publicly explicated or justified, agreement between a select set of actors which seeks to define (or better to redefine) rules governing the exercise of power on the basis of mutual guarantees for the "vital interests" of those entering into it.' They claim that elite pacts facilitate 'an institutional breakthrough' and make negotiations over the institutional format of the new democracy possible. The main benefit identified with pact-making is creating a stable environment and limiting uncertainty during the transition.

The literature on pact-making has generally stressed the role of 'the political class': politicians, important party officials, bureaucrats, and office-holders. But Di Palma (1990) argues that accommodating business and labour, as well as the state, is important. The Spanish transition provided an important example for understanding pact-making. The defining moment of the Spanish transition was the establishment of an elite agreement through the creation of a new democratic constitution, but the transition was aided by the creation of a tripartite economic agreement, the Moncloa Pacts. The Spanish case is thus frequently taken as the paradigmatic example of transition through pact-making and to some extent its success led to imitative pact-making in Poland, Hungary and Czechoslovakia.

---

difficulties that weak civil societies pose in new democracies (Przeworski 1995).

Evaluating Transition Studies

Transition perspectives have shed light on the micro-processes of regime breakdown, the opening of transitions and the mechanisms of democratic construction. But they have also been criticized for being overly elitist, excessively empirical and voluntaristic. Furthermore, they have tended to apply theories constructed out of the experiences of Southern Europe and Latin America to regions which are culturally, politically and economically different, such as East and Central Europe, the territories of the ex-Soviet Union, Africa and China.

Remmer (1991) has articulated most clearly the view that transition theory is a 'retreat into voluntarism' or 'barefoot empiricism'. This and its other problems, it could be argued, stem from its excessively narrow understanding of democracy. Democracy is visualized as a set of procedures for government negotiated by and between political leaders. Thus the transition approach separates democracy from its essential meaning as rule by the people and conceptualizes it principally as the establishment of a set of governing institutions. At the same time, the perspective's elitism consigns the mass of the people to a bystander role in the creation of new regimes. This ignores empirical evidence which points to the role of popular struggles in some transitions as the determining element in unleashing democratization in the first place. It also ignores the importance of civil society in democratization or at best confines it to a purely instrumental role (Baker 1999).

Typically, the transitology literature sets out a straightforwardly institutionalist and electoralist definition of democracy, then quickly passes on to identifying mechanisms of regime change as the more interesting phenomenon. In an important article, Schmitter and Karl (1993) attempt to describe what 'democracy is ... and is not'. Although they recognize that democracy is contingent upon socioeconomic performance and entrenched state structures and policy practices and reject electoralism in favour of arguing that democracy must offer a variety of competitive processes and channels for the expression of interest apart from elections, they ultimately prefer to concentrate on democracy as a set of procedures for creating institutions and the government (Schmitter and Karl 1993). They argue that democracy is too abstract a concept to tie down in any useful way. Instead, they suggest that it makes more sense to establish a 'procedural minimum' for a functioning 'democracy' and work from this.

By focusing mainly on short-term changes, transitologists fail to examine deep-rooted obstacles to democratization over the long term. When democratizations go wrong it is, by implication, because individuals 'get it wrong'. The transitology approach does not explain adequately why outcomes are different, except by presuming inadequate leadership styles or the adoption of incorrect policies. It does not distinguish between outcomes – they are all 'democratic' in some way once elections are held and authoritarian office holders are forced out – or explain why apparently democratic institutions can operate in nondemocratic ways. And finally, it omits to analyze in any depth the roles of culture, development, history or the internationalization of politics in democratization. In sum, it does not pay sufficient attention to structural contexts and constraints. Yet as more authoritarian regimes collapsed in different parts of the globe, the understanding of democracy had to be stretched, confused and weakened in order to fit regimes that sometimes barely appeared to qualify for the label. At the same time, a number of 'transitions to democracy', for which hope was initially expressed, have ended very far indeed from the democratic ideal, indicating that the 'catch-all' definition of democracy was rather too loose.

Transition studies offered a general approach to democratization based on an interpretation of experiences of Southern Europe and Latin America. Its relevance elsewhere has been questioned. For Pei (1994: 1) it was possible to 'treat the process of regime transition from communism as identical to the regime transitions from authoritarianism that occurred between the mid-1970s and mid-1980s in southern Europe, Latin America and East Asia', with the proviso that Russia and China experienced a '*dual* transition' (author's italics) to democracy and to market capitalism. Bunce (1995a) and Parrott (1997), however, strongly disagree. According to Parrott (1997: 2)

> the relevance of the paradigms of democratization ... is far from self-evident. Just as some economists have challenged the applicability of models drawn from non-communist societies to the dilemmas of economic reform in postcommunist states, some political scientists have questioned whether paradigms of democratizations drawn from non-communist countries are relevant to the study of postcommunist political change.

He argues that, in particular, transition theory pays insufficient attention to the problems of ethnicity, the 'legacy of large internal ethnic "diasporas" and the emergence of ultranationalism in internal ethnic "homelands"' in the East (Parrott 1997: 10). We return to this important issue in Chapter 9.

Transition Studies Today

Transitology is largely responsible for the suggestion that democratization constitutes the most appropriate paradigm through which to analyze the complex process of regime decay and political change in apparently dissimilar countries such as Spain, Portugal, South Africa, Mozambique, Nigeria, El Salvador, Mexico, Turkey, Poland the ex-Soviet Union and China since the 1970s. For, by divesting democracy of its structural context, the transition perspective suggests that democracy can take root outside Western Europe and the US and that the global upheavals of the 1980s and 1990s were, in fact, struggles for democracy. Thus transitology is inherently responsible for the global scope of democratization studies.

Transition studies havegenerated an important literature on the state and transition. According to Przeworski (1986: 59), the emergence of democracy does not necessarily signify that all key political actors have become democrats; rather it means that the opposition and the soft-liners in government have persuaded hard-liners that there is more to gain from cooperating with change than from opposing it. Hence a democratic transition is only a 'contingent institutional compromise' (Prezworski 1986: 59). Consequently, the new institutions take on an important role in their own right. The design of the new institutions is paramount for the success of the transition:

> if a peaceful transition to democracy is to be possible, the first problem to be solved is how to institutionalize uncertainty without threatening the interests of those who can still reverse the process. The solutions to the democratic compromise consist of institutions. (Przeworski 1986: 60)

Transitology is therefore responsible for the emphasis in contemporary studies on the creation of institutions, the writing of constitutions and the choice of electoral systems.

Furthermore, transition studies have shaped academic perceptions that the micro-politics of democratization are significant. Studies of transition have emphasized agency, negotiation, compromise and the *politics* of change. They have also emphasized the importance of distinguishing different stages of democratization – liberalization, transition and consolidation. In some of his work, in fact, O'Donnell (1992: 18) goes further and talks of 'two transitions', the first an empirically verifiable transition from authoritarianism, and the second, the creation of a 'political democracy (or polyarchy according to Dahl), which may coexist with varying degrees of democratization in the economic, social and cultural spheres'. The result of this approach has been to allow the disaggragation of research into different moments, with the ultimate aim, according to O'Donnell, of specifying the relationship between political change on the one hand and socio-economic and cultural change on the other. In practice, however, transition research has emphasized political factors and democracy as a set of institutional practices which do not transform social, economic or cultural power relations. Not surprisingly, therefore, transition studies offer a vision of democracy stripped of its revolutionary potential: 'the wider picture that emerges is of a near-consensus ... that actually existing liberal democracy is the only form of democracy on offer' (Baker 1999).

An Alternative Approach: The State, Civil Society and Globalization

The theories of democratization that we have identified so far vary in terms of the importance they allocate to rationality, culture, individual and collective action, economic development, social conflict and transnational factors. They draw on different epistemologies and explanations of social change. Taken together, these studies have generated a rich body of literature and have established the study of democratization as a core area of social sciences. They have shed light on different aspects of regime breakdown, transition and the nature of immediate post-transition politics. In some cases, they also illuminate aspects of why some systems are able to move on towards consolidation and others do not, although their main focus has generally not been on consolidation but on causation.

This was an appropriate focus for research during the first phase of democratization. However, some contemporary experiments in democracy are now more than twenty-five years old. Logically enough, academic interest now centres on the survivability of new democracies and the quality of democracy, not the number of transitions that are taking place. Democratization is a risky enterprise and experiments that begin with transition do not always end in consolidation. Yet why democracy succeeds in some cases and not in others is not always clear. Theory has not yet quite caught up with this changing research agenda. New approaches, that explain what happens after the initial transition as well as during it, are needed.

There is therefore a need to explain democratization holistically. In order to do so, this book draws on a framework that builds on the insights garnered from the historical sociology approach in particular. Structures, in other words, are vitally important for explaining outcomes. But the key contribution made by the transition perspective to the democratization debate – namely that democratization is a dynamic process, shaped by human behaviour and choices – is also centrally important. Actors, whether collective or individual, engage in struggles to transform authoritarian states and to build democracy. But they operate within structured environments. The options that are open to them are crucially shaped by the weight of structures such as the patterns of interaction between the state and society, traditions of organization and mobilization, state capacity and the global order. This is not to say that outcomes are predetermined in any way. Democratization is not inevitable in some countries; nor are attempts at democracy condemned to failure in others. But the chances for democracy are certainly greater in some societies than others. Our framework suggests that the chances for democratization are furthered by economic development, the development of a complex state and the emergence of a strong, working class or other subaltern groups that organize to promote political change. Democratization, in short, requires collective action – that of classes or social movements – more than the agency of particular individuals.

Democratization became a global movements at the same time as the new global political economy of marketization and liberalization emerged. This points both to the salience of the transnational context for understanding democratization and the importance of adopting a comparative economy focus similar to that pioneered by Rueschmeyer, Stephens and Stephens (1992) in order to explain outcomes. The shift to more open models of economic development, especially in post-communist and developing countries, has led to increased pressure for political change, has transformed the capabilities and ideology of the state and has created very different opportunities for state-society interaction. These inevitably shape the democratization process. It is important, however, not to assume that globalization is inevitably a positive force for democratization. In fact, the evidence that is presented through the case studies points to the ambiguous role of globalization and liberalization in democratization. Like Rueschmeyer, Stephens and Stephens (1992), we are therefore agnostic as to whether increased transnationalization leads to democratization and this is reflected in our framework.

Our alternative framework makes use of three key concepts, namely the state, civil society and globalization or the global order. This framework can be used for the analysis of the *problematique* of consolidation as well as of transition and has the advantage that it incorporates within it a substantive understanding of democracy. The aim is to shed light not only on the onset of democratization but also to explain the very different trajectories, processes and outcomes that are grouped together under the banner of 'democratization'. In reality, of course, these three dimensions, state, civil society and global order, are to some extent overlapping and interactive because they are structures through which power is deployed. Why each of these three dimensions is so central to democratization is explained below.

The state is the embodiment and essence of political power (Mann 1993). The state is central to democratization in a number of crucial ways. First, and above all, democratization means building a democratic state. This requires *institutional change* (the form of the state), *representative change* (who has influence or control over state policies) and *functional transformation* (what the state does or the range of state responsibilities). For democratization to occur, the state has to experience a substantive transformation in its operations and its representativeness. Secondly, states are actors and have interests. It is logical to assume that, at moments of democratization, states include actors with interests in impeding the process or in subverting it. So states can also act as impediments to democratization. Thirdly, state capacity plays a role in determining the success or failure of democratization. Democratization implies that states make promises – that people will live more secure lives, that the judicial system will work impartially, that people will have the chance of a better standard of living, etc. For this to happen, states need to be able to carry out complex functions. Finally, states need generally to enjoy uncontested sovereignty. So a solution to the 'stateness problem' (Linz and Stepan 1996) is essential for democratization.

Democracy describes a particular set of relationships between the state and society. Democratization in the first wave was achieved in the nineteenth and twentieth centuries by the mobilization of subordinate classes and other social groups in the search for equality, security, protection and rights. While the formation of a mass polity does not, in itself, create a democracy, it is impossible to envisage democracy without it. Rueschmeyer, Stephens and Stephens (1992) see democracy as the imposition of reform on a capitalist state. In other words, they argue that democracy occurs when subordinated social groups achieve sufficient access to the state so as to transform it. As a result, the state is no longer, in any straightforward sense, simply an instrument to protect the dominant class. Democracy represents, then, a shift in the power balance within civil society. As a result, any explanation of democratization must pay attention to the role of mass participation and the struggles for rights and citizenship.

For Huntington (1991) the most distinctive feature of the third wave is that it is global in scope. It could be argued, in fact, that democratization emerged as a global trend in large part due to international pressure. International factors are also shaping the outcomes and the political struggles that are taking place as democracy is – or fails to be – consolidated. Even amongst those who argue that politics inside countries still matters more anything beyond the nation state, there is a recognition that the international or the global level is more significant than ever. For Schmitter (1995: 19), for example, '[a]t this time in history almost without exception, democracy of one type of another is the only legitimate form of political domination'. Contemporary models of democracy, as well as the fate of democratization experiments, are largely bound up with globalization. At the same time, the rise in global communications networks, and transnational advocacy coalitions and social movements has meant the creation of global pro-democracy networks. These have inevitably become important actors in some processes of democratization. Because globalization is the expression of a power relationship, it affects states and actors very differently. The impact of the global, therefore, varies considerably from democratization to democratization.

Conclusion

The traditional theories of democratization, especially modernization, have generally been concerned with understanding why democratization begins. Along with historical sociology, modernization also tended to take a long-term perspective on political change, looking for underlying transformations in society and the economy. Transition studies, in contrast, have centred their attention on the politics of building a democracy, concentrating on the period immediately following the authoritarian breakdown and on elite behaviour. While the influence of the mode of transition on later politics has been noted, transition studies have not on the whole generated a holistic approach to democratization, understood as consolidation as well as transition. Instead, this chapter has proposed an analysis of democratization experiments by identifying three core dimensions of change: the state, society and the global order. The task now is to analyze in detail why the state, civil society and the global order are so vital to contemporary democratization. That is the subject of the following three thematic chapters. Since the role of the state, civil society and the global order varies from country to country, the final four chapters analyze the differing patterns of interaction between the three dimensions of change in five geographic areas of contemporary democratization, namely Southern Europe, Latin Ameirca, Africa, the post-Communist world and Asia.

4

Democratization and the State

Democratization means, above all, building a democratic state. It is not always clear, however, what this entails or how it can be brought about. There is a general agreement that it means more than just the introduction of elections, but there is no academic consensus about what reforms, precisely, are required. This chapter begins by explaining the range of institutional reform that democratization should entail. It argues that the reforms that have been introduced in contemporary democratizations so far have generally stopped short at the introduction of minimal democracy and have therefore failed to produce fully democratic states. The chapter analyzes why this should be so. It suggests that the reasons include the institutional arrangements generated during transitions, problems of diminished or contested sovereignty, poor state capacity, elite opposition, authoritarian legacies which block reform and the imperative of economic reform and integration into global markets.

Democratization of the State

The state is, ultimately, an instrument of social domination. All states, whether 'democratic' or not, have at their core a capacity for coercion and violence. The rise of the state historically is associated with the growing capacity of individuals and groups to force people to acquiesce to its power (Goverde, Cerny, Haugaard and Lentner 2000: 15). But the violence associated with democratic states is (usually) legitimate in the eyes of its citizens. It is also distinguished from authoritarian state violence by the fact that it is violence of last resort, at least in terms of its deployment against its own citizens. Non-democratic states depend on a range of techniques for rule, including the use of naked force, the manipulation of fear, the marginalization of dissidents, the creation of apathy or the forced mobilization and psychological brainwashing of people. In democracies, by contrast, the state is far less present in

people's lives as a force for coerci‹
ordered, rational and predictable, at lea‹
of governments is limited by constitition‹
Some chief characteristics of democratic‹

Democratic states tend to rule throu‹
combine legitimate power, persuasion an‹
distance or mediation between the state ‹
bureaucratic structures inevitably diffuse ‹
So, another characteristic of democratic sta‹
tiple sources of authority and decision-maki‹
racies are hedged in by competing agencies, ‹_ ‹entres and the
existence of alternative power contenders. The legitimacy of democratic
governments rests on the fact that they can plausibly lay claim to be representative and accountable to the people. In fact, precisely because
democratic states can be held accountable, they need to be seen to be
acting in the people's interest – however that is defined. This means that
although democratic states under capitalism have a bias for business,
they are more likely to be responsive to demands for social and economic justice. In sum, democratic states contain channels for the representation of subordinate social groups.

A full democratization of the state, then, combines *institutional
change* (the form of the state), *representative change* (who has influence
over policies? and to whom is the state responsible?) and *functional*

Box 4.1   Some Characteristics of a Democratic State

- Territorial integrity, either as a result of the belief that the state
  represents a nation or through negotiations and legitimate and binding
  agreements that make a multi-national state possible
- The rule of law; that is, minimal rights and duties of citizens are legally
  encoded and the parameters of state activity legally defined
- A minimal use of legally sanctioned violence against its own citizens
- Popularly elected and representative government that is formally
  controlled by constitutional channels of accountability
- A complex bureaucracy that can make claims to impartiality
- The existence of multiple centres of power
- The formal existence of channels of access to decision-making, even for
  subordinated social groups, which are operational to some degree
- Some commitment to social and economic justice, however defined.

what the state does or the range of state responsibility, no state is fully democratic.

temporary democratizations, most attention has focused on
eering institutional changes to the state, rather than bringing about
presentative or functional transformation. It has been generally
assumed that some degree of representative change and functional transformation will follow on automatically, although there may be a time-
lag. Furthermore, functional and representative change, because they
are more radical, tend to be blocked by elites. So it is not safe to assume
that substantive transformation will necessarily follow on from the introduction of new institutions. The evidence so far is that states can experience some institutional change but still resist a deeper democratization.

Institutional Transformation

The state comprises the visible institutions of the state and the invisible
rules which govern the behaviour of officials and policies of the state. Of
course, it is easier to reform the visible institutions of the state because
these are amenable to legal and constitutional reform and these reforms
constitute a *sine qua non* of democratization. If heads of government are
unelected or the elections are unfree or seriously corrupt, for example,
or if political parties are not independent of the state, then it is impossible to argue that democratization has even begun. This is one reason
why scholars of democratization, and indeed actors in democratization
processes, have focused most attention on these kinds of changes.

For Di Palma (1990), democratization can essentially be reduced to
the business of 'crafting' these new institutions. An important body of
scholarship has grown up examining this craft, identifying the mechanisms by which formal democratic institutions are brought into being.
Attention has been paid in particular to the design of new constitutions,
the holding of elections, the establishment of new party systems and
executive–legislative relations. The importance of these institutions is
explained in more detail in Box 4.2. According to Przeworski (1986:
60), a successful transition is essentially about the creation of new institutions that can 'institutionalize uncertainty without threatening the
interests of those who can still reverse this process'. He argues that
'solutions to democratic compromise consist of institutions'.

Some of the most important institutional changes involve the setting-
up of elections, the development of a party system, and the nature of
executive and legislature relations.

Box 4.2   The Role of Institutions in Democratization

For Przeworski (1995) the most important institutional issues are:

- the relationship between the executive and the legislature;
- the nature of the electoral system;
- whether the legislature is uni- or bicameral;
- the role and number of legislative committees;
- whether the new system is unitary or federal;
- the limits, if any, to majority rule;
- the role of judicial review; and
- the role of interest groups.

Insitutional design affects the efficiency of government. But, more important, institutional arrangements have distributional consequences. So the institutional decisions made during the transition tend to reflect the balance of power between groups at that time. As a result, the new insititutions frequently protect the interests of ex-authoritarians or economic and social elites to a disproportionate extent. Because the new institutional arrangements are the essence of the transitional pact, they are difficult to reform later. As a result, the institutional formula adopted at the start of the process of democratization shapes the mould of post-transition politics, often creating a barrier to deeper democratization in the process.

Elections

Holding democratic elections has come to be seen as the beginning of democratization. Influential international organizations, such as the US-based Carter Foundation, have helped define democratization as the introduction of free, competitive multi-party elections. International assistance for democratization concentrates resources on creating free elections (van Cranenburg 1999). Moreover, free and democratic elections has often proved an important rallying point for very disparate opposition movements to authoritarianism.

Elections matter, then. They provide the first signs of democratization, and in some cases are the first step in the creation of a new democracy. The most obvious example of this is Spain. The elections for the Constituent Assembly provided a mechanism for popular representation in the elite task of writing the constitution and signified the transitional government's commitment to a fuller democratization. Elections throughout the transition period (1977–82) were important in crystallizing and deepening democratization and in isolating the authoritarian rump of Francoism. They provided opportunities for popular participation, organization and genuine debate. They also furnished ex-authoritarians with the chance to work within democracy and offered the head of state, the King, a framework through which to convince the people of his own democratic credentials.

But the holding of elections cannot be taken, by itself, to signify democratization. Elections have been used to sustain non-democratic regimes, from Soviet-style regimes to personalist dictatorships. Furthermore, the tendency of the international community to try and promote democratization through aid leverage has led authoritarian office-holders to introduce electoral procedures for completely cynical motives. In these cases, elections simply provide a cloak to hide dictatorships. The elections in Ghana and Tanzania in 1992 and 1995 respectively, are examples of this. They were held simply because of international pressure (Sandbrook 1996). In both cases, election procedures were unfair and corrupt. In Ghana, furthermore, the elections caused other problems. The incumbent president, Jerry Rawlings, used government funds to dispense patronage and gave civil servants pay rises in order to win votes, with the result that the elections pushed the government into budgetary deficit.

Furthermore, Bratton (1998: 65) argues that Ghana and Tanzania are by no means exceptional. In general 'the quality of multiparty elections in Africa is far from perfect – and getting worse'. Elections are becoming a cynical staging-post in the round of aid negotiations between African states and the international community and a tool of legitimation for the 'big men'. With few exceptions, incumbents are able to manipulate the electoral process in order to remain in power. In the 1997 elections in Mali, for example, polling stations did not open, voting materials ran out and inaccurate electoral lists excluded significant numbers of people from casting a vote. Not surprisingly, turnout was extremely low – 28 per cent. Perhaps even more worrying is that the incumbent, Alpha Oumar Konare, won 96 per cent of the vote (Bratton 1998: 60).

If the record of elections in sub-Saharan Africa is depressing, what of the other areas where transition to democracy is recent? The introduction of elections in the post-Communist countries, Asia and Latin America have rather better records overall, although the picture is mixed. In the Czech Republic, Hungary and Poland, post-transition elections have been carried out fairly and freely, although participation is sometimes low. Nevertheless, the elections are genuine contests between different candidates and parties. In contrast, White's (2000) account on the elections of 1999 and 2000 suggests that, in Russia, they are not. He argues that the elections simply signified a 'dynastic succession that made clear that the president and his entourage were now in a position to organize elections that satisfied formal requirements but which would also give them the results they wanted' (White 2000: 303). In Latin America, meanwhile, participation in elections is dropping amid popular perceptions that they serve only to rotate a small elite in power and that voting makes no difference to policies or government direction.

Parties

Elections are more likely to be manipulated by the incumbent regime in cases where the system of political parties, is weak or government-controlled. Democratic elections require genuine competition between effective political parties, and a strong, healthy, dynamic, competitive party system is one way to ensure that elections become arenas for genuine change. It makes sense, therefore, to pay great attention to the nature of political parties in new democracies since these are a means to ensure that elections work democratically. Furthermore, parties have traditionally been regarded as the classic intermediary organization of liberal democracy, linking citizens with the state. The party system, for many years, was thought of as the main vehicle for political participation.

The third wave has thrown up a range of experiences in terms of party development. Box 4.3 summarizes the factors which affect the new party system. Parties have re-emerged relatively easily in cases where there has been a past tradition of strong parties. So Chile, Uruguay and Brazil, for example, have experienced few difficulties in re-establishing party systems, although that is not to say that the systems work perfectly democratically. In Spain, where party activity was all-but-suspended during forty years under Franco, parties nevertheless re-emerged quickly in the 1970s, partly because they had existed before 1939 and because some of the post-1977 parties had formed as clandestine organizations as early as the 1960s. The formation of the party system in Southern Europe generally was assisted by proximity to Western Europe and the processes of European integration.

Successful cases such as these are relatively few in number, however. Most new democracies have experienced considerable trouble in establishing stable and democratic party systems. Party systems – and particularly party systems that are supportive of democracy – are difficult to create quickly. For Mainwaring (1999), one of the greatest problems

---

Box 4.3   Party Systems and Democratization

The emergence of a system of democratic political parties is contingent upon a number of factors. These include:

• the regional context. The closer to North and West Europe, the more likely party development is to be relatively successful. Western Europe exercises a democratic 'pull' to which elites respond, as well as providing training and resources for the development of political parties.
• institutional memory. The existence of a party system in the past is positive for the development of a strong party system during democratization.
• parliamentary regimes, by giving a greater institutional role to parties, are more supportive of the development of a stable party system than presidential regimes.
• the socio-economic context. Relative prosperity and social stratification typical of developed capitalism favour the emergence of a strong party system. It is hard to imagine a strong and stable party system in a society where class is unimportant.

---

facing party systems in new democracies is their lack of institutionalization; they enjoy low levels of legitimacy, have weak roots in society, and are poorly organized, and there are few opportunities for structured interaction between parties. As a result, they frequently work to a different logic from what the academic literature on parties, garnered from the experience of Western European systems in particular, would suggest. In East and Central Europe, the ex-communist parties have tended to dominate the political scene due to their organizational strength, leaving little chance for other parties to grow. Parties are also markedly hierarchical and enjoy little internal democracy. Agh (1996) shows that East and Central European parties have built few linkages into society. Instead, parties look to the state. Furthermore, they come into existence and disappear with remarkable rapidity. The Russian system is particularly unstable. Thirteen electoral blocs contested the 1993 elections; only four existed with the same name a year later (White, Rose and McAllister 1997).

   In Latin America, post-transition parties have returned to their historic patterns of behaviour which derive from traditions of personalism, clientelism, elitism and, in some cases at least, corruption. The party systems have failed to catch up with the changing political and social landscape wrought by economic change, migration, and citizen withdrawal and

distrust of the state (Hoskin 1997). The return to democracy has promoted a kind of hyper-electoralism, in which the parties engage in
debate with each other, with society increasingly disconnected from
political events. In sub-Saharan Africa, meanwhile, parties are distant
from the electorate, ephemeral and operate as personalist vehicles or
tools of the state. In Asia, parties remain strongholds of elitism.

Political Leadership, Presidentialism and Parliamentary Systems

Democracy implies establishing constitutional limitations on the power
of political leaders. Democratic constitutions codify the mechanisms for
electing new leaders and the range of powers they should enjoy. They
create channels through which to review executive authority. The terms
of transition or the negotiations or agreements between different political groupings, past traditions and current fashions shape the new mechanisms for electing leaders, executive powers and executive – legislative
relations. New democracies have thus ended up with a wide variety of
political systems.

An important strand of the literature on institutional design focuses
on the relative merits of presidentialism or parliamentarianism. Linz
(1994) and Lijphart (1994)have both argued that democracy is stronger
where elites opt for a parliamentary rather than a presidential system.
Shugart and Mainwaring (1997) suggest that presidentialism creates a
'dual legitimacy problem' wherein both presidents and parliaments lay
claim to popular legitimacy, that presidentialism is less flexible and that
it aggravates problems of exclusion from politics because of a 'winner-
take-all' approach. Presidentialism has also been criticized for skewing
the party system towards a one-party dominant system and away from
a multiparty system, thereby rendering it unstable and prone to breakdown. The arguments for parliamentary systems draw strength from the
fact that the successful Southern European countries are parliamentary
democracies, while the post-Communist systems show a mix of presidential and parliamentary regimes and the more problematic Latin
American and African cases generally have presidential systems.

However, parliamentary government is no guarantee that politics will
not be personalized. Politics in Spain revolved around *felipismo* or the
charisma of Prime Minister Felipe Gonzalez throughout the 1980s. By the
same token, presidentialism is not always unstable, as the experience of the
US shows. Philip (1999) argues that, in Latin America at least, the presidency is the focal point for political action simply because it is the only
dynamic institution in the system; strong presidencies emerge because the

rest of the architecture of the state is inadequate. In Sandbrook's (1996) view, it is the prevalence of personalism, clientelism and corruption that undermine the institutionalization of democracy in sub-Saharan Africa, not the nature of the constitutional settlement. So, how far either presidential or parliamentary systems are, in themselves, central to democratic stability and development is open to doubt. Research by Power and Gasiorowski (1997) supports this. In a study of 56 democratizations, they found that the choice of institutional design was not significantly related to the likelihood of democratic survival. In short, either presidentialism or parliamentarian systems can work democratically; but both must be underpinned by democratic norms as well as clear constitutional procedures in order to do so.

The Limitations of Institutional Change

Democratization requires a transformation to the visible structures of the state. The visible institutions of the state were initially thought to be the principal force shaping the invisible world of state cultures and social relationships that underpin state institutions. It was therefore assumed that cultures would change once the institutions themselves were reformed. In other words, it was expected that the creation of democratic institutions would lead slowly but inexorably to a fuller democratization of the state. But in fact pre-democratic or authoritarian cultures also shape the institutions. As Kaldor and Vejvoda (1997: 70) note, 'in the search for democratic institutions, rules and procedures, the main internal obstacle remains the absence of a democratic political culture'. In other words, institutions only work as well as the setting they are in.

Furthermore, the creation of new systems of deciding governments, does not, in itself, address the key question of who has power and the extent to which those who act on behalf of the state are accountable to the people. Karl (1995) has suggested that an overemphasis on changing government structures has contributed to the fallacy whereby elected governments are assumed to be fully democratic. There is, in sum, a growing recognition that reform of the visible institutions of government is only part of the process of democratic transformation (Diamond 1999).

If institutional change is to lead to a more substantial democratization of the state, it needs to encompass broader and deeper reforms to the state, as well as, in some cases at least, reforming aspects of the transtitional pact. Reform has to be extended to include a democratization of non-elected bodies of the state, such as the bureaucracy, the police, the security forces, and the judicial system. Featherstone (1994), for example, points out that Greek democratization, more than twenty-five years after its initiation, is compromised by the fact that the party in government remains able to dominate appointments to the state bureaucracy, reducing its independence, efficiency and accountability. Similarly, the Czech and Slovak governing parties retain considerable control over the state bureaucracy, a reflection of the party-state tradition which they inherited. As a result, the judiciary and the legal system are democratically compromised (Kopecky 2001).

Reforming the police and the judicial system is particularly important in order to strengthen a culture of democratic rights. Failure to do so weakens democracy, as examples from Latin America show. Throughout the region, the police have proved resistant to reform even where they have been shown to be active in illegal and violent vigilante groups, such as in Brazil where they have been responsible for shooting and disappearing considerable numbers of street children. In Argentina, human rights groups have expressed concern about the rising tide of state repression and violence that is directed againts gay activists. Yet little has been done to challenge the way-law-and-order policies are being carried out. At the same time, there is uneven access to the law. The judicial system works only for the rich and the well-connected and, as such, is an instrument of domination. Failure to reform the system is due to the weakness of the new states vis-à-vis elites who support tough policing and see the legal system as a way to reproduce their own privileges. Consequently, the state is left unable to 'enforce its own legality' (O'Donnell 1993: 1361). The result is democracy with low-intensity citizenship.

Obstacles to the Democratization of the State

Deepening democracy is blocked partly by the difficulties of institutional reform, the prevalence of non-democratic cultures and elite opposition. But there are other problems that account for the democratic deficits in post-transitional states. These include nationality problems, diminished sovereignty, poor state capacity, authoritarian legacies embedded in state practices, and the problems that result from economic reform.

Nationality Problems

At the very least, the survival of sub-state nationalism in nation states presents a considerable challenge to democracy. It may take the form of an armed threat to the state. Unequal political, economic, social and cultural rights, legally enshrined or the result of custom, however, corrode the chances for democracy almost as much. Linz and Stepan explain (1996: 25):

> In many countries that are not yet consolidated democracies, a nation-state often has a different logic than a democratic polity...the leaders of the state pursue ... nationalizing state policies aimed at increasing cultural homogeneity. Consciously or unconsciously, the leaders send messages that the state should be 'of and for' the nation. In the constitutions they write, therefore, and in the politics they practice, the dominant nation's language becomes the only official language for state business and for public (and possibly private) schooling, the religion of the nation is privileged in all state symbols (such as the flag, the national anthem, and even eligibility for some types of military service) and in all of the state-controlled means of socialization such as radio, television and text books. By contrast, democratic policies in the state-making process are those that emphasize a broad and inclusive citizenship where all citizens are accorded equal individual rights.

In the territories of the former Soviet Union and across East and Central Europe, conflicts over nationality, borders and stateness have been woven into modern history and the fact that the region has historically been riven with unresolved nationalist demands is a crucial part now of its resurgence. However, these long-standing conflicts were made worse by the fact that, as Communist states dissolved, politicians, the bureaucracy and the *nomenklatura* sought to divert state resources towards themselves and their allies. Thus the breakdown of the Stalinist state and the power vacuum that ensued are as much an explanation of the nationality problem now as the persistence of ethnic identities and conflict in the region over time.

Separatist aspirations always present the state with the spectre of breakup. They are particularly dangerous at a time when regimes are in collapse. Even in Spain, one of the most successful of contemporary democratizations, violent Basque separatism constituted the most intractable of issues. In some cases, the peaceful breakup of a country into distinct territories and the formation of new nation states, as in the Czech–Slovak split, means that democratization is still possible. In others, although ethnic tensions are considerable, negotiations have prevented conflict. Kaplan (1998: 268) traces how Estonia moved peacefully to independence in 1991 and Tartastan to the status of sovereign state 'united with Russia' in 1994 as a result of negotiations with Russian authorities. She attributes the peaceful negotiations to diplomacy between strong presidents who themselves had little commitment to the politicization of ethnicity. It should be noted, however, that whilst negotiations prevented the outbreak of violent ethnic conflict, they did little or nothing to nest ethnic identities within democratic politics.

In the worst of cases, ethnic conflict has led to social breakdown, violence and disintegration of apparently fixed national boundaries. Violent unrest and civil war has erupted in particular in the ex-Yugoslavia and in parts of the Russian Federation, most notably in Chechnya. In the ex-Yugoslavia a resurgence of ethnic difference and conflict after 1989 was exacerbated and fuelled by the ambition of particular groups that sought to colonize the state at the expense of others. One of the most important factors holding Yugoslavia together before 1989 was the federal state. Able to deliver relative independence from the Soviet bloc, and prosperity, at least to the urban centres, it commanded the loyalty of many individuals in the constituent parts of the country, including Serbia, Croatia and Bosnia, territories where violent conflict erupted following the collapse of Communism. The disintegration of the federal state was therefore an important catalyst for the upsurge of ethnicity in the territories of Yugoslavia. Building the post-Stalinist state in the wake of Communism became an excuse for 'cleansing' the state of 'undesirable' groups.

Apart from the terrible human cost, the impact of the wars and the violence on the process of democratization is considerable. Violent ethnic conflict violates the basic principles of democracy. Civil war also implies complete state breakdown, as force becomes the prerogative of particular social groups. And, finally, its lasting impact can be the embedding of ascriptive identities for generations and the triumph of uncivil nationalisms which conflict with the democratic ethos. Dentich (1994) argues that nationalism in the ex-Yugoslavia not only led to the breakup of that country but created opportunities for the imposition of strong populist presidencies, exceptional powers and the triumph of violent nationalist mythologies as the foundation of state-building in Serbia, Slovenia and Croatia, rather than embedding democratic cultures of tolerance and power-sharing. Similarly Seligman (1992: 163) suggests that 'the continued existence of strong ethnic and group solidarities...[in East and Central Europe] have continually thwarted the very emergence of those legal, economic and moral individual identities upon which civil society is envisioned'.

Nationality problems result in social exclusion, as well as ethnic conflict. In Latin America, where societal antagonisms are rooted chiefly in economic, cultural and class-based differences, rather than ethnic ones, social exclusion has an ethnic dimension. This has become very clear in the case of Mexico; the Chiapas rebellion which is, at one and the same time, a struggle for Indian political rights and for economic justice for the rural poor (Harvey 1999). Similarly, indigenous peasant movements are strong in Colombia, Ecuador, Brazil, and Guatemala, although their demands are social and cultural rather than separatist (Barton 1997). Amerindians, the 'orginal' inhabitants of America, struggle for recognition of their rights within the national state (Radcliffe and Westwood 1996).

Diminished Sovereignty

A clearly defined state with firm and undisputed boundaries is an essential precondition for democracy (Rustow 1970). Weber identified the lineages of the modern state through the establishment of a rational bureaucratic entity for management and control. Tilly (1990) and Mann (1993) offer narratives of the 'modern state' as the establishment of sovereignty through the centralization of military and political power. But this history is not, in fact, a universal story. Vast swathes of the globe have histories of fractured or failed sovereignty. It is imperative, therefore, to analyze how diminished or contested sovereignty impacts on the democratization process.

For the territories of sub-Saharan Africa, sovereignty is a relatively recent attribute. African states were created, by and large, in the wave of decolonization that followed the Second World War. But the problem of African states is much more than the fact that they are relatively new. The state in Africa is also extremely fragile; indeed, in some cases it would be more accurately described as a surreal artifact. For Cruise O'Brien (1991), statehood in Africa is merely a 'show'. According to Jackson and Roseberg (1982a), the weakness of the African state is due to the fact that it is juridicially (*de jure*) sovereign without enjoying sovereignty in an empirical (*de facto*) sense. In other words, it is an internationally recognized entity but is unable to fulfil even the most basic functions associated with the state, – raising revenue, maintaining a monopoly on violence, administering public goods and upholding the law. Sorensen (1999: 396) explains:

> to achieve permanent juridical sovereignty in Europe, rulers first had to demonstrate substantial capacities for domestic rule, including the

creation of order, the extraction of resources, and the creation of legitimacy and infrastructural power. No such demands were visited upon the rulers who achieved independence in the context of decolonisation. The 1960 United Nations declaration on colonial independence explicitly rejected any requirement for state substance as a precondition for independence.

As a result, decolonization has created states that have neither demonstrated substantial capacities for self-rule nor command the acceptance of a majority of their citizens, but whose existence is protected by international law. Such states do not enclose a political, and still less a cultural, community. They have few vertical linkages to society. Their fragility makes them ineffective and vulnerable to challenge from within. In some cases, this has led to the 'failure' or the collapse of the state (Zartman 1995). In these cases, state-building becomes a first-order task alongside, or even prior to, democratization.

Although not all African states have experienced breakdown in this way, most are fragile. Allen (1995) identifies a number of distinct historical paths in Africa which produce contrasting patterns of (nondemocratic) state formation. In particular, post-Independence was characterized by the emergence of either 'centralized-bureaucratic states' or 'spoils politics'. Senegal, Cameroon, Cote d'Ivoire, Congo, Kenya, Tanzania, Zambia and Malawi are examples of centralized bureaucratic politics. After Independence, these countries developed strong tendencies towards patronage and clientelism, centralization of power in the executive and a developed party structure or bureaucracy for the disembursment of resources. The state was therefore stable, strong, and authoritarian, as well as relatively inclusive, since clientelist states co-opt groups they owe loyalties to *and* those that have important resources with which to bargain. Unresolved competition between groups or military intervention led, on the other hand, to 'spoils politics' in which executive control eliminated competition, institutions were poorly developed or absent and economic looting was common, leading to crisis. Nigeria, Somalia, Sierra Leone, Liberia, Uganda, Ghana and Upper Volta are examples of 'spoils politics'.

What are the implications of this kind of fragility for democratization? For Allen (1995: 312–13), the centralized bureaucratic state is capable of some form of democratization, especially where there is strong popular opposition. But where the state is organized around spoils politics, the economic crisis of the 1980s and 1990s tended to rule out democratization and led to the implosion of the state. In Liberia, Sierra

---

Box 4.4   State Collapse in Sierra Leone

Politics have been unstable in Sierra Leone since the beginning of the 1990s. The international system demanded signs of democratization in Sierra Leone which was dominated regionally by its neighbour, Nigeria, a state which was capable and willing to intervene in neighbouring states. A pro-democracy uprising against the authoritarian regime of President Momoh began in 1991. Initially, Momoh survived although he had to seek support from outside in order to do so. Nigeria sent troops to defend Freetown. Civilian rule and elections were introduced, in 1996, as a result of external pressure and the evident bankruptcy of the military regime. This led to the election of Ahmad Kabbah as president. Kabbah faced armed rebellion from two different fronts. First, armed gangs under the rebel leader, Foday Sankoh, secured control of important national economic resources and parts of the country. At the same time, the civilian government faced challenges from within the Armed Forces. In May 1997, a successful coup was staged by Commandant Johnny Paul Koroma. The coup was defeated, but once again only by outside intervention. Nigerian troops fought on behalf of the elected government though the summer of 1997. Since the capital Freetown had been captured by the military rebels, Nigerian troops focused their attacks upon the city, killing hundreds of civilians in the process. By June 1997, some 4,000 Nigerian soldiers were deployed in Sierra Leone as part of a West African regional peace-keeping force. UN peace-keeping missions followed, but failed to bring order to the country. British troops were then deployed in Sierra Leone in 2000 in support of the peace process. Having secured the arrest of Sankoh, they withdrew a year later, leaving behind an uncertain peace and a precarious state in the grip of collapse amidst rising banditry and rebellion. All of this points to the fact that there is, in effect, no state to democratize.

Leone, Somalia and Rwanda the state has effectively collapsed. Box 4.4 looks at how this has happened in Sierra Leone in more detail.

Poor State Capacity

Successful democratization requires that states have the capacity to carry out complex functions since all democratic states assume responsibilities and commitments to their citizens and must be flexible enough to respond to pressures from them. As Nelson (1989: 16) explains:

> the process of democratic transition itself … generates pressures. New democracies usually must contend with high levels of political

participation and expectations as well as with discontinuities in policy making authority and institutions.

Democratization, then, brings the state apparatus into focus. States with only a minimal level of technical capabilities will not be able to withstand popular pressure or carry through reform. Whitehead and Gray-Molina (1999: 5) argue that effective and sustained policies of redistribution or anti-poverty measures, which it can reasonably be assumed will follow from democratization, can only work where 'policy making capacity [has] been institutionalized'.

There are four basic goals which states should meet. They should:

- enforce the rule of law throughout the state's entire territory and population;
- promote economic growth;
- elicit the voluntary compliance from the population over which the state claims control; and
- shape the allocation of societal resources (Huber 1995: 167).

Meeting these goal requires technical capacity and relative state autonomy (Evans, Rueschmeyer and Skocpol 1985).

An important question is the extent to which democratizing states have the capacity to fulfill the promises of democracy. In order to do so, they need infrastructural power (Mann 1993) – an effective state apparatus and durable, legitimate institutional structures which provide the tools to intervene in society without using coercion. States with ineffective apparatuses, poorly managed states or states which only respond to the needs of a few almost inevitably experience corruption, faulty application of the law, the privatization of power and low-intensity citizenship (Huber 1995). For Huber (1995: 166), state strength is related to its 'extractive capacity' and means that incumbents can set and achieve goals. Of course, state capacity does not necessarily lead to democratization. But it is certainly difficult for democratization to proceed without it.

Furthermore, state capacity has become more crucial than ever because of the range of technical and political challenges states now face. States that are currently coping with the challenge of democratization are also dealing with, *inter alia*, the consequences of increasing economic interdependence, globalization, a relative loss of fiscal control and the growing authority of markets (Castells 1996; Held *et al.* 1999). As a result, successful states are under pressure to re-think how to deliver services and public goods, and what state capacity means is being re-defined. For Rosenau (1992: 14), *capable* states now steer rather than command and rely on a web of relations with society-based actors who act on behalf of the state.

So, newly democratizing states are caught between pressure to take on more functions, to be flexible and to deliver goods for their citizens on the one hand, and, on the other, to become leaner, in order to cope with the consequences of globalization. Fulfilling these two tasks – delivering more for citizens and competing in the global economy – is extremely difficult for *any* state. For states with an underdeveloped capacity to act, with poor connections into civil society or where civil society is not capable or willing to take on governance tasks, the task becomes herculean. In the light of this, it is surprising, perhaps, that any state has been able to rise, even partially, to the task. The Chilean state in this sense stands out. Chile has been able to integrate into the global economy while at the same time developing its autonomy vis-à-vis other regional states and domestic elites. As a result, moderate policies of economic reform which have extended benefits to the poor and the very poor have been possible. This was achieved partly because the transition to democracy created opportunities for the state to use non governmental organizations (NGOs) to deliver social services while at the same time enhancing its own authority (Taylor 1999). State-building in Chile has been sufficiently successful, in fact, to allow the government to break the terms of transition and, in 2000, to legally charge the ex-head of state, General Pinochet, for crimes committed during the dictatorship.

Nevertheless, for most states, the story is not so positive. Developing states have, for the most part, found it difficult to adjust to the simultaneous challenges of increasing their capacity, delivering more and better services, and responding to the pressures of globalization. Undoubtedly one reason why democratization has been more successful in Southern Europe is that these states enjoy greater technical, extractive and policy-making capacities, compared to other newly democratizing regions. Furthermore, democratization began in Southern Europe in the 1970s when the states retained more control over their domestic economy than is currently the case. In sub-Saharan Africa, by contrast, by the 1990s the state was too fragile and too poor to deliver the reforms that democratization promises. The absence of efficient state agencies, the under-developed capacities of the state to raise revenue, the inability of the state to shape national strategies for economic development all undermine democratization.

In sum, then, the relationship between state capacity and democracy is complex. State capabilities during democratization are shaped by a number of factors, including:

- the technical capacity of the state. Clearly some states enjoy more economic and cultural resources than others. Some states are able to count on trained, well-educated and skilful people to run it; in other countries, the state has very poor human resources at its disposal;
- how states are affected by globalization and how well (or poorly) they are able to respond to the challenges posed by economic reform and governance; and
- how far democratization itself operates as a force for effective reform of the state.

These three factors are interlinked. In cases where there is some level of technical capacity and the state adapts to the changing global order, then state capacity may be enhanced. Democratization may be deepened as well, although this does not necessarily follow. But this virtuous circle of achievements is tantalizingly difficult to achieve, in particular for developing countries.

Authoritarian Legacies

Democratization requires not only the election of a government committed to implementing democracy; it also involves a transformation in the way the state takes and implements decisions. But democratization is never a complete break with the past and the drive to reform the state is frequently blocked by interests embedded within it. The way the state behaves after transition, then, is dependent at least as much on the weight of the past as it is on the imperative for change. The past continues to shape the culture, legality, composition, direction and ideology of the state. Given that the past is non-democratic, democratizing states are bound to contain ambiguities, paradoxes and authoritarian enclaves. This observation runs counter to the early assumptions of democratization studies, which emphasized an almost limitless potentiality for change, irrespective of the past, and tended to 'understate the problems inherent in the transition from authoritarianism [and] the legacies of authoritarianism' (Caspar 1995:3).

Latin America offers a good example of how the weight of the past constrains the democratization of the state. For O'Donnell (2000), democracy is elusive because of the hangover of past state practices and authoritarian traditions. This explains why, despite democratization, undemocratic executives and low levels of popular participation remain the norm. The tradition of the 'strong man' in Latin America dates back to the emergence of Latin American republics as independent nation states. Its first modern expression was the populist presidency in the 1940s and 1950s. Executive domination over society intensified during the period of military domination of politics in the 1960s and 1970s, when authoritarian governments sought to increase the autonomy of the state. It is difficult now to change governing cultures and representation practices built on populist, clientelist and macho representations of leaders. Consequently, the traditions of delegation and *machismo* continue uninterrupted. Across the region, this tradition hinders the consolidation of democracy and stunts the development of the state by concentrating power in the hands of one person. It also upholds cultures of deference, restricted contestation and patrimonial state–society relations. Nevertheless, it is hard to imagine radical change because these cultures are deeply embedded within elites and societies alike.

In Russia, the tradition of the strong presidency also constrains the democratic impulse. Shevtsova (2000) traces the origins of the current superpresidentialist system that followed the forced dissolution of the Supreme Soviet in 1993 back to the habits and traditions of monolithic government, from Tsarism to Stalinism. In the 1990s, Yeltsin actually intensified personalist rule in Russia. Even after he stepped down, government continued to depend upon a 'presidential pyramid' in which the president is supported exclusively by personal appointees and is able to govern by presidential decree, bypassing parliament in the process.

In short, patterns of privileged access and practices of secrecy built up over time are encoded within state institutions. These shape the attitudes, beliefs and moralities of those who run the state. These patterns become part of the historical legacies inherited by newly elected democratic governments and form part of the institutional culture of state–society relationships. Such patterns are not consciously part of the state tradition, but they are fundamental for understanding why states behave the way they do. Furthermore, because they are carried unconsciously in the mindsets of both the governors and the governed, they are extremely resistant to reform. So for example, in Latin America, patterns of access to the state are such that they exclude indigenous groups (Radcliffe and Westwood 1996) – and ignore the poor, especially poor women (Craske 1999). At the same time, states are open to business groups and landowners (see, for example, Bartell and Payne 1995; Huber and Stafford 1995; Crisp 1998). In Africa, democratization presents, if anything, even less of a break with past state traditions than in Latin America. The cultural codes which have governed the state since Independence mostly go unchallenged. Even South Africa is only a partial exception to this pattern. For Mbembe (1991), this means that the politics of coercion in Africa are upheld through a form of consent which is actually the social practice of coercion routinized in everyday behaviour. State traditions are replicated in society by citizens who participate and reproduce their own subjection.

Finally, the legacies left from the immediate non-democratic period have to be taken into account. Authoritarian governments rely on distinctive patterns of state–society interaction which, in different ways, all demand unquestioning submission to the state. Where dictatorships are long-lasting, these patterns of behaviour shape everyone in society, including even those who are ideologically or morally opposed to the system. In cases where the system has been in power for more than a generation, it becomes difficult for people to imagine other ways of being. Authoritarian rule constitutes a 'time of eternity' (Garcia Marquez 1976: 206); it is hard to imagine that it will ever end and it is unclear what can follow. Even when there is a generalized desire for new and democratic forms of government, it is unlikely that anyone is really clear what this means. At the same time, change means upheaval and uncertainty. Bauman (1994: 18–19) uses the following anecdote to explain how Communism structured Polish society, shaping the mindsets and expectations even of those who were opposed to it:

> In May 1992 Adam Mitchnik, the unimpeachable voice of conscience of the anti-communist revolution, appeared on French television alongside the man he did more than anyone else to overthrow, General Wojciech Jaruzelski. …Mitchnik and Jaruzelski talked to each other amicably, understood each other without difficulty and seemed to agree on most points. The audience was shocked; some were furious with Mitchnik, their yesterday hero. What the shocked and the furious failed to comprehend was that Mitchnik and Jaruszelski were integral (though mutually opposite) partners in the same historical discourse; only together, in their conflict, could they gestate that discourse which led eventually to the dismantling of the communist legacy.

The price of dictatorships, in terms of social beliefs, behaviour, expectations and attitudes to the state, continues to be paid for a long time after the regime actually falls.

The Political Fallout from Economic Reform

One of the greatest differences between democratization in Southern Europe in the 1970s, and Africa, Latin America and the post-Communist bloc in the 1980s and 1990s is that these latter countries are trying to build new democracies just at a time when the state is being forced to cut back and to re-shape its role as a provider of public goods, as the arbiter of national economic policy-making and as the source of welfare provision. Asian countries, in this respect, fall somewhere between the Southern Europe position and the developing or post-Communist world, in that the capacity of the state to engage within the global market and to deliver services remains strong. So, for the developing and post-Communist world, the burden of the transition to market competition shapes state responses to democratization.

Changes in global capitalism, the crisis of protectionism, problems of international indebtedness or the need to remake the national economy according to the demands of the global market, all combined to push developing and post-Communist states towards policies of economic reform at the same time as they embarked upon democratization. As a result, both democratization and state capacity have been affected by this reform process. In a number of cases, the economic reforms have added to the crisis of the state and deepened already-existing problems of poor state capacity (O'Donnell 1993). In order to understand why this should be so, it is important to examine the kinds of policies generally undertaken in order to increase global competitiveness and integration (see Box 4.5). Policies to increase global integration generally require in the first instance short-term stabilization measures to control inflation and create some trade surplus through reducing imports and increasing exports. Short-term adjustment may then be followed by a longer-term set of policies aimed to move the economy towards a more marketized and internationalized system of production.

How do these reforms impact upon state capacity and democracy? First, they can weaken the legitimacy of office-holders, especially in cases where economic reform is overseen by international agencies, because policy initiative lies with external agencies and international lenders. Secondly, they can diminish the quality of public goods, undermine the public sector and lead to a loss of faith in the state and a resurgence in privatized solutions to social and economic ills. Thirdly, the introduction of policies such as privatization, tax reform, industrial and commercial liberalization and currency reform may lead to a decline in state revenue and public services. The effects of the reform process may also be to strengthen the organization of (some) social and economic groups vis-à-vis others and the state. So the authority of business in particular is usually strengthened at the expense of labour organizations. In some cases, economic reform has also been associated with the rise of

Box 4.5 Aims and Objectives of Economic Liberalization

The primary aims of economic liberalization are to:

- generate a profitable export sector independent of state protection
- lower the fiscal burden of the state
- generate a culture of private enterprise
- resolve external debt problems by generating foreign exchange
- attract private and multinational investment
- encourage saving and cut 'unnecessary' and 'imprudent' consumer spending
- restructure the role of the state in the economy from one promoting and leading development to one which enables development to take place through the market
- adjust national policies to a global environment that rewards the adoption of free trade
- allow the market to determine the allocation of most resources.

In order to achieve these aims, a raft of policy reforms are introduced. These include:

- liberalization of import–export regime
- single exchange rate
- currency devaluation
- rise in interest rates
- privatization of state assets
- rationalization of the public sector (reduction in the number of those employed in the public sector; transformation of the contracts; contracting-out of public services, etc.)
- liberalization of labour law (increasing the power of business over employees so as to lower costs to business, encourage private and foreign investment and increase output)
- removal of public subsidies on certain goods and services (e.g. food, fuel and transport)
- lower state spending on social services
- removal of restrictions to foreign investment and active encouragement of it.

informal markets, further eroding the state's legitimacy. Finally, economic reform can weaken democratization because governments may try to bypass opposition to it by pre-empting discussion and resorting to presidential decree.

It is difficult in practice, therefore, to simultaneously deepen democratization and carry through economic liberalization, given that reform encourages authoritarian styles of government and diminishes the quality of public space. Where the reforms are driven from outside, the erosion of democracy may be particularly acute. The fact that aid-dependent states are forced into negotiations with international agencies over national economic policy is itself a brake on democratization, as Stiglitz (2000), Chief Economist at the World Bank in the 1990s, argues:

> although international agencies support democratic institutions...in practice [they] undermine the democratic process by imposing policies. Officially of course, the IMF doesn't 'impose' anything. It negotiates the conditions for receiving aid. But all the power in the negotiations is on one side.

In some cases, such as Poland, economic reform has contributed to stabilizing post-transition politics, by reducing inflation and creating conditions of greater certainty. In others, economic reform has enhanced state capacity. In Argentina, Bolivia and Chile, economic liberalization in the 1990s contributed to strengthening the state. Nevertheless, in all these cases, economic reform also coincided with the rise of technocratic decision-making and a depoliticization of society (Hershberg 1997; Silva 1999).

Conclusion

This chapter has looked at what democratization means for the state. It has analyzed why remaking the state in a democratic mould is so difficult. Formal institutional change and institutional engineering are certainly important, but they are not a substitute for a full democratization. It has been argued that change to the visible institutions of the state – the executive, the electoral system, etc. – is not sufficient for a full democratization of the state. These kinds of changes mark the opening of democratization, but there are no grounds to assume that spillover to deeper state reform will automatically follow on. Furthermore, in some cases, the institutional arrangements developed during the transition actually hinder deeper democratization.

Democratization does not constitute a complete rupture with the past. Democratizing states cannot be understood outside of their histories, contexts and capacities. This means that the introductions of elections and the writing of new consititutions do not, in themselves, challenge non-democratic state cultures and practices. No do they necessarily transform power relations within society. For developing countries especially, democratization is further beset by problems of poor state capacity, the inability of the state to respond to the demands of the global political economy and the challenge of governance. The chapter has emphasized, then, the centrality of state cultures, practices and embedded legacies as a means to understanding why democratization projects so often fail to live up to their initial promise, even where there is strong domestic and international support. States are, in sum, notoriously resistant to change.

5

Democratization and Civil Society

Democracy occurs when subordinated social groups achieve sufficient access to the state so as to change the patterns of representation contained within it (Rueschmeyer, Stephens and Stephens 1992). A democratic state claims to represent the whole of the community and to act on its behalf. The state can no longer, straightforwardly, serve simply as an instrument to protect the dominant class. Democracy requires that subordinated groups have sufficient resources to play an important role within civil society and therefore also in relation to the state. Any explanation of democratization, consequently, must pay attention to the concept of civil society and to the struggles to extend rights and citizenship throughout society.

This chapter looks at the role of civil society and of social struggles in contemporary wave democratizations. The chapter first discusses what is meant by the term 'civil society' and why it is so central for democracy. It then establishes a framework through which to interpret and classify forms of social activism and identify their role in democratization. It goes on to examine the ways different societal groups and organizations have mobilized to promote democracy and evaluates their success. The chapter also considers whether civil society groups frame their struggles in exclusively national terms or whether they are able to access global resources and what the impact of this might be. Finally, it evaluates the degree to which civil society struggles are eclipsed after the transition. This, it is argued, constitutes a considerable impediment to democratic consolidation.

Civil Society and Democracy

Minimalist or Schumpeterian theories of democracy allocate little importance to civil society. However, with the revival of social protest and political turbulence in the 1960s, there was a renewed interest in the democratic potential of social organizations independent of the state. The anti-system movements or anti-capitalist protest groups which emerged across Europe and within the US in the late 1960s were seen as a sign of the continuing salience of conflict and protest in politics. More recently, the study of social activism – student-led demonstrations, 'political' strikes by workers, gender struggles, community-based activities, etc. – have been placed within the perspective of 'civil society'. 'Civil society' has become a term which is now increasingly used to encompass social activity and societal organizations which, directly, or indirectly, support, promote or struggle for democracy and democratization. Invoking 'civil society' as the bedrock of democracy has become popular within both policy-making and intellectual circles. At the same time, the notion of 'global civil society' has emerged to describe transnational social relationships and the thickening of ties between non-state actors across national frontiers and the search for global justice (Shaw 1994; Colas 1997).

What is meant by 'civil society', however, is not always clear. Civil society is said to refer to the space between the state and the individual (Walzer 1992). It is the arena of associations, of individual and community agency. It is, as John Hall (1995: 2) points out, 'at one and the same time a social value and a set of social institutions'. There is agreement, in a broad sense, that it comprises socio-political institutions, voluntary associations and a public sphere within which people can debate, act and engage with each other in order to deal with the state (Perez Diaz 1993: 55). Civil society is crucial for democracy because it is the space between the public and private spheres where civic action takes place. Organizations and individuals from within civil society can hold the state accountable, share their experiences, promote their interests and learn values of civility and trust. Putnam's (1993) work on 'social capital' as the thread binding societies together has done much to popularize the idea that the denser the web of social interactions between people, the stronger the democracy.

Part of the confusion about the concept stems from the fact that it is understood in quite different ways. Diamond (1994: 5–6) offers a predominantly liberal perspective, in which civil society is understood to be

> the realm of organized social life that is voluntary, self-generating, (largely) self-supporting, autonomous from the state and bound by a legal order or set of shared rules. It is distinct from the society in general in that it involves citizens acting in a public sphere to express their interests, passions and ideas, exchange information, achieve

mutual goals, make demands on the state and hold state officials accountable. Civil society is an intermediary entity, standing between the private sphere and the state ... Actors in civil society need the protection of an institutionalized legal order to guarantee their autonomy and freedom of action. Thus civil society not only restricts state power but legitimates state authority when that authority is based on the rule of law.

The democratic functions of civil society, according to this liberal perspective, are described in Box 5.1.

However, the liberal understanding of civil society does not pay sufficient attention to the question of power. Thus a more radical position criticizes the liberal assumption that civil society is automatically inclusive and identifies how unequal economic, social and cultural resources shape the contours of civil society itself. Participation in civil society requires resources, knowledge, self-worth and recognition; under capitalism, therefore, not everyone can participate equally. Consequently, for Jelin (1996: 104), civil society should be used ana-

---

Box 5.1   The Democratic Functions of Civil Society from a Liberal Perspective

The role of civil society in democracy is to:

- limit state power and subject governments to public scrutiny
- provide an arena for citizens to participate in voluntary associations, increasing their democratic awareness and skills
- offer a space for the development of democratic values such as tolerance, moderation and a willingness to compromise
- create channels other than political parties for the articulation, aggregation and representations of interests
- generate opportunities for participation in local levels of governance
- cut across sectional interests and mitigate political conflict
- recruit new political leaders
- provide non-partisan election monitoring which deters and checks fraud and monitors judicial and legal reforms in new democracies
- disseminate information and, if necessary, contradict official information
- provide the resources to carry out economic reform
- lower the burden and demands placed upon the state.

(Diamond 1994)

---

lytically to refer to a 'conflictive practice related to power – that is, to a struggle about who is entitled to say what in the process of defining common problems and deciding how they will be faced'. This means it is important to identify who is active in civil society, or how citizenship is constructed, in order to analyze its democratic potential.

The liberal perspective sees civil society essentially as an aid to the state, especially in terms of reducing the load the state carries, and as a check on state excesses. It envisages the democratic state as a minimal state. The radical perspective, in contrast, takes the view that the role of civil society is to transform the state. Community activism is a way to challenge unequal power relations and engage with the state, so as to require it to use its capacities for the benefit of all citizens. Civil society thus becomes an instrument to correct the imbalances of the capitalist state, and struggle between civil society and the state is a means to achieve democracy. The radical perspective assumes that collective action, social organization and protest are healthy signs of democratic life (Ekiert and Kubick 1998: 578). Social struggles facilitate democratic consolidation because they can lead to the reform of the state, the extension of citizenship and the entrenchment of rights. Box 5.2 summarizes the democratic functions of civil society from the radical perspective.

This chapter adopts an approach that combines elements of both the liberal and the radical perspectives. The most important democratic function that civil society can perform is its engagement with the state

---

Box 5.2   The Democratic Functions of Civil Society from a Radical Perspective

Cohen and Arato (1992) suggest that civil society has two main democratic functions. First, associations and movements from within civil society cooperate, develop identities, offer the opportunity for participation and create networks of solidarity. Secondly, civil society organizations and associations try to influence or reform the state. At times they also take on issues of corporate power and have pressed states to redress the power imbalance generated by capitalism. They also, increasingly, organize globally to promote social justice transnationally. Civil society thus has a dual function, offering a vision of a more participatory system and engaging in the public sphere to promote change. For Iris Marion Young (1999: 152), 'the critical and oppositional functions of the public spheres of civil society perform irreplaceable functions for democracy'.

as a force for change. The capacity of civil society organizations to press for reform and to engage with the state is perhaps a key for understanding whether democratic consolidation takes place. But Diamond's view that civil society organizations play central role in holding the government accountable, in providing an arena for political discussion and in disseminating information, is also important.

It should be noted that civil societies, are, in practice, all very different in their composition. As a result, there is some confusion, in an empirical sense, about who exactly is in civil society and who is not. Whereas in Latin America, civil society is used overwhelmingly to designate popular social movements and the organizations of the excluded and the poor (Pearce 1997), in East and Central Europe the civil society project is strongly identified with the intellectual movement. Lomax (1997) attributes the weakness of post-1989 democracy in Hungary to the fact that intellectuals were actually demanding power for themselves; civil society was used to designate the 'progressive' middle class concerned with maintaining its own superiority, not popular organizations such as labour or community groups. In Africa, civil society has been used to describe local groups pressing for change and NGOs, even though many NGOs rely on foreign aid for survival. In Asia, civil society refers to labour and social movements, environmental groups and human rights organizations. Furthermore, the boundary between civil society organizations and those of political society is not always clear. In particular, whether political parties more properly belong in the realm of civil or political society is a vexed question. In Africa, Latin America and Asia, parties are generally seen as part of political society because the aim of most of them is to enter and control the state. In Europe, including post-Communist Europe, the picture is perhaps more ambiguous, as parties grew out of the civil society project itself. But as the civil society project disintegrated, ties between parties and society diminished and parties became elite organizations. As a result, 'civil society' in this book conceptually refers primarily to pro-democracy subordinated groups and social movements, rather than political parties.

Conceptualizing the Role of Civil Society in Democratization

Tilly (1984; 1995) argues that national social movements and democratic struggles emerged alongside the consolidated nation state. Tarrow (1998) has drawn on Tilly's work to develop the 'political opportunity structure', which explains social movements activity through their engagement with the state. He argues that

> people engage in contentious politics when patterns of political opportunities and constraints change and then, by strategically employing a repertoire of collective action, create new opportunities, which are used by others in widening cycles of contention. When their struggles revolve around broad cleavages in society, when they bring people together around inherited cultural symbols, and when they can build on or construct dense social networks and connective structures, then these episodes of contention result in sustained interactions with opponents – specifically in social movements. (Tarrow 1998: 19)

He stresses the importance of the following in order to understand the impact of social movements:

- *political opportunities or constraints*
  State structures and political cleavages create relatively stable opportunities for engagement; changes in the opportunity structure may mean that resource-poor actors can engage in contentious politics and possibly create sustained social pressure.
- *the repertoire of contention*
  The forms of collective action which people adopt varies. The 'conventions of contention' may form part of a society's culture. Leaders may decide on new forms of action. History and collective memory or forms of protest which are copied from abroad may form part of the 'repertoire of contention'.
- *consensus mobilization and identities*
  A particular way of understanding the world frames collective action or social movement activity which dignifies and justifies it. These identities can excite passion, emotion and commitment; they are the reason why people mobilize, even when they may themselves be in danger.
- *mobilizing structures*
  Social networks determine who participates in social networks. The more embedded in social networks – through work, family structures, institutions, neighbourhoods – the more receptive people are to collective action. Tarrow calls these 'connective structures'.
- *the dynamic of movement*
  To sustain protest, sustained political opportunities are needed. Ultimately 'movements fail or succeed as a result of forces outside their control'.

- *cycles of contention*

  As opportunities widen, more social movements may become involved in the struggles and may shape how they are framed. Networks become more dense and interactive. The cycle of contention widens. This may lead to 'outcomes in the sphere of institutional politics; at its most extreme, it may lead to revolutionary change' (Tarrow 1998: 19–25).

The political opportunity structure is a useful way to conceptualize why and how civil society organizations become important in democratization. The breakdown of authoritarian regimes, the loss of legitimacy of dictatorships, the collapse of the state, all create opportunities for social mobilization. The state is too weak to contain social protest or to coerce people into submission. Once protests begin, the balance of power between civil society organizations and the state changes. Reform of the state becomes a possibility. However, the cycle of contention may be broken if the authoritarian state can reorganize and generate new tools for repression or find new sources of legitimation. Sometimes, however, the cycle of protest develops so strongly that either it brings the authoritarian regime down or causes it to enter into crisis. There is then an opportunity for a change to the state and to the balance of power between civil society and the state or democratization. Box 5.3 examines how such an opportunity opened in the Soviet Union as a result of the changes taking place within the state.

Opportunities for protest are no longer confined to moments of state transformation or crisis. They can emerge as a result of significant change within the global order and social movements can now appeal to powerful actors located outside the state. This means that the outcome of contemporary social protests is no longer determined solely by the structure of national political opportunities and constraints. Internationalization affects protest from below in different ways and to different degrees. The repertoire of contention adopted by social movements can, for example, incorporate forms of protest which have been learned from the television or the newspaper, and the cycle of contention can widen to include the activity of social groups based abroad. Pressure can be brought on the state from inside and outside the country. Box 5.4 provides an example of how a Brazilian social movement came to frame its struggles in such as way as to attract international support which then sustained and enlarged the range of actors pressurizing the Brazilian state for change.

**Box 5.3   Political Opportunities and Democratization: The
Collapse of the Soviet Union**

In the late 1980s, contentious politics – protests, social mobilization, etc.
– erupted after years of repression in the former Soviet Union. The reforms
that were undertaken by Mikhael Gorbachev transformed state structures
and therefore presented a political opportunity for change. Openings in the
state were created, and new groups, such as 'Citizens Dignity' or
'Memorial', pro-human rights groups trying to investigate human rights
abuses under Stalinism, were able to use the new channels into the state.
Over time, they began to count on the sympathy of some party officials,
increasing their access into the state. Meanwhile labour organizations
mobilized, strikes occurred and independent unions formed. The elections
of 1990, rather than providing support for the government, led to waves
of demonstrations against it. According to Tarrow (1998: 76), the most
important factors explaining the emergence of contentious politics of
1989–92 in the ex-Soviet Union were:

- the opening of access to participation for new actors;
- the evidence of political realignment within the polity;
- the appearance of influential allies;
- emerging splits within the elite; and
- a decline in the state's capacity or will to repress.

Despite the protest movements, social movements have failed to have a
sustained impact on politics. Social networks are weak and collective identities are principally national, not sectoral or class-based. As a result, the
dynamic of protest ran out of steam once the Soviet Union had been
broken up into independent nation states. This brought to a close the option
of democratization from below.

Civil Society Organizations and Contemporary Democratization

Whereas it was possible only to identify subordinated classes as agents
of democratization in the nineteenth century, a range of very different
civil society actors have emerged in struggles for democracy since the
1970s. We consider in this section the very different roles played by a
number of these groups. In particular, women's movements, labour
movements, community organizations and indigenous associations can
be identified as engaging with the state in pro-democracy struggles.
Only some, however, were able to influence the transition to democracy
and fewer have been able to play a major role in shaping the politics of
new democracies. This was due to changes in the political opportunity

---

Box 5.4   The Formation of a Transnational Protest Network: The Rubber-Tappers in Brazil

International environmental activists began a campaign to sensitize the World Bank to the environmental impact of its loans and development policies in the early 1980s. Attention soon focused on the World Bank loan to Brazil's Polonoreste Programme in the North East of Brazil and the Amazonian area. While environmental activists were concerned about the damage to the ecostructure and deforestation, the anthropologists who joined the campaign were more worried about how the development programme affected the indigenous people of the region who were being forced off their land by ranching and other development initiatives. An opportunity to exert leverage over the Brazilian state opened, as Brazil began a tentative political transition and, at the same, was forced into negotiations to restructure its international debt. This was exploited by international NGOs who brought pressure to bear to incorporate environmental issues into the negotiations between the World Bank and the Brazilian government.

This presented some local organizations and NGOs with an opportunity for protest of their own. Rubber-tappers who worked in the Amazon and whose livelihoods were threatened by the encroachment of ranching, were able to forge a relationship with activists in Washington to argue against the way the development plans were proceeding. The rubber-tappers began to frame their struggles for land rights as a struggle against the environmental degradation of the tropical forest. The international outrage that followed the murder of the leader of the rubber-tappers, Chico Mendes, by the landowners brought home how far the issue had transnationalized. The rubber-tappers were now a part of a global social network and were able to call on groups outside Brazil for support. They could appeal beyond Brazil to international environment groups and other international organizations who provided resources which they lacked to gain global attention, once the issue was framed as one of environmental protection.

Source: Keck (1995).

---

structure and to a disruption in the cycle of contention. With the onset of democratization, the legitimacy of the state increased, while the unity of civil society was shattered. Furthermore, with the start of the transition, the autonomy of civil society actors from the state diminished.

Women's Movements

Pro-democracy women's movements emerged in Southern Europe, Latin America, some East and Central European countries and in parts of Africa. They have been rather less evident in Asia. Based on a sense of common identity and ethical purpose, women's movements evolved as important pro-democracy actors at the national and the international level. Women's movements lay claim to a shared commitment to protecting life, and therefore by extension, to democracy. This has enabled the formation of national and transnational networks, the articulation of a coherent gendered critique of different kinds of authoritarian practices and the presentation of gendered or feminized visions of democracy. Nevertheless the unity these movements sometimes achieve under conditions of authoritarianism is fragile in that the identity which holds them together can easily be unravelled by class or other kinds of crosscutting social identities. As Rai points out, 'there is no *essential woman or womanness* that can be isolated when we scrutinize their lives under any type of regime' (Rai 1996: 226; italics in the original).

As a result, women's movements are usually stronger and more cohesive when they are struggling for democracy under authoritarianism than as organizations trying to push a feminized version of democracy onto the political agenda in the post-authoritarian period. The role of the women's movements in authoritarian and post-authoritarian Latin America offers a good example both of their achievements in ending dictatorships and of the post-transition problems they encounter. Authoritarian governments in Latin America in the 1970s and 1980s articulated a gendered discourse which was designed to keep women within the family and to keep the family out of politics. Nevertheless, repression and poverty combined to force women into the public sphere. Mobilized in defence of their families, they became 'militant mothers' (Alvarez 1990; Craske 1999). As such, they were a major strand of opposition to dictatorship. Members of the women's networks that developed came from very diverse background in terms of class, lifestyles and ideology. They were able to unite, nonetheless, both to defend the right to life against military terror and to propose a feminization of politics, meaning the incorporation of values such as sharing, compassion and support into the political world.

The groups with the biggest profile were the human rights groups. Of these, the Mothers of the Plaza de Mayo in Argentina became the most internationally known, although similar organizations also sprang up in Chile, El Salvador and Guatemala. The Mothers of the Plaza de Mayo used the cloak of motherhood and the disguise of being 'just housewives' or 'mothers' to search for their disappeared children. They were able to establish a very narrow space for dissent and opposition to the military regime which ruled Argentina from 1976 to 1983. They went on to become internationally known through the support they received from human rights groups in advanced democracies. In this case, the gendered identity of motherhood undoubtedly travelled well across national, cultural and developmental frontiers. Connecting with human rights transnational networks increased the domestic profile of the Mothers quite dramatically (Brysk 1993). They were able to use the transformation of the international agenda in the 1980s, as pro-democracy movements got off the ground in the US, and were successful eventually in penetrating US and Western European policy-making circles. As Martin and Sikkink (1993) have shown, by framing their protest within the context of mothering and at the same time playing to the growing international and US concern with human rights in the 1980s, they became the most internationally visible of the organizations active against the dictatorship. International support legitimized the women and to some degree protected them from the arbitrary violence which the Argentine military was accustomed to using against the opposition.

Partly due to their efforts, human rights consituted a focal point of the Argentine transition in 1983. An investigation into human rights abuses committed under the dictatorship began in 1984 and trials of members of the Armed Forces were held through the mid-1980s. However, the commitment to human rights waned as time passed. The insistence on human rights and their search for justice was eventually judged counter-productive for democratic consolidation as the new democratic government struggled with massive international debt, economic collapse and hyperinflation. Inside Argentina, support for the Mothers also waned and their moral legitimacy declined precipitously. At the same time, the transition opened up fissures between the women themselves. In Argentina, as elsewhere, the onset of formal democratization transformed the relationship between the state and social groups and between individuals who had previously been able to cooperate successfully together. So, while a part of the Mothers have continued to fight for justice for the disappeared, others have made their peace with the new system, even though it did not deliver justice.

At the same time, it has become clear that what the pursuit of 'women friendly' policies means, once democratization has begun, varies according to how differently situated women perceive their interests (Waylen 2000). In particular, divisions open up between middle-class professional women, many of whom consciously define themselves as feminist, and the popular women's organizations, concerned with surviving in a hostile economic climate. Also, women make very different choices in terms of the tactical issue of how to gender the new democracies.

Some seek incorporation within the new state structures; others seek to maintain their autonomy (Taylor 1998). Divisions in previously united movements are the inevitable result. It is difficult to escape the conclusion, in fact, that fragmentation is inevitable after the transition.

Labour Movements

Made up of individuals who share material interests, labour movements are strongest, nevertheless, when they also constitute social, interpersonal and community networks (Tilly 1978). Under authoritarianism, labour organizations have the potential to become the touchstone to community or even national protest when they articulate community grievances rather than the narrow pursuit of sectoral interest.

Labour movements in Southern Europe and Latin America were important pro-democracy organizations because their historical evolution and the structure of employment opportunities meant that unions regarded themselves as representatives of the labouring population broadly speaking, rather than simply their members. They therefore found it relatively easy to become community rather than factory-based actors (Collier and Mahoney 1997). In Spain, labour opposition was the most important sign of the far-reaching rejection of the Franco regime in the 1960s and 1970s (see Box 5.5). In Chile, the copper workers' union, the strongest union in the country, was the initial force behind the Days of Protest in 1983, the first mass opposition to the Pinochet regime. In Argentina, the powerful national labour federation eventually came out against the dictatorship after 1979. By 1982, it was fully involved in the mass opposition front, the *Multipartidaria*, along with human rights organizations and community groups. This prompted the military junta to embark on its disastrous war to recover the Faulklands/Malvinas islands, leading to defeat and a rapid disintegration of the regime. In Brazil the emergence of independent unions, especially in the cities, was a focal point for social protest against the military dictatorship in the 1970s. The Brazilian labour movement, in fact, consciously moved beyond narrow labour-related demands to articulate the concerns of the working and lower-class generally. More than elsewhere in Latin America, Brazilian labour became a 'social movement', linked to other lower class social movements such as shanty-town or community groups, demanding a political, not an economic, solution to its problems.

In Southern Europe and Latin America, it is impossible to unravel the processes of disintegration of the authoritarian regimes without

---

Box 5.5   The Spanish Labour Movement and the Demise of Francoism

Labour was a significant source of opposition to the Francoist dictatorship (1939–76). Labour opposition emerged for the first time after 1959. Rapid industrialization in Spain at that time allowed for the creation of independent trades unions, the Workers Commissions (*Comisiones Obreras*) which were gradually able to operate at the factory level, especially in Madrid and the industrialized northern regions. By 1966, delegates from *Comisiones* were winning union elections in preference to the candidates from the state-controlled official union movement. However, after 1966 the dictatorship adopted a policy of overt repression of the independent labour movement, bringing to a close the first cycle of labour protest. During this first period of labour militancy, the independent unions were unable to find support from other actors within society or from political parties, which remained repressed. At the same time, international opposition to Francoism was muted and the repression of the labour movement attracted only cursory protest.

The second phase of labour militancy occurred in a changed socio-political and international context. On the one hand, labour protests in the late 1960s and early 1970s linked up with regional opposition from nationalists in the Basque Country and Catalunya. And, on the other, labour organizations were supported by community protest from working-class areas such as the industrial belt around Barcelona, At the same time, increasing international hostility towards Francoism gathered pace after the Burgos trial in 1970, in which sixteen ETA (the Basque Nationalist organization) members were tried in military courts and nine sentenced to death (later commuted to life imprisonment after international intervention). International interest in events in Spain meant that the regime could no longer opt simply to repress and this helped to create spaces for dissent.

The dynamics of labour protest was twofold. In the first place, there was the logic of collective action against employers, in order to improve wages and conditions. Secondly, strike activity was rooted in political protest against the dictatorship. These two dynamics were of course in practice intertwined. Labour protest against Francoism was therefore the result of a combination of factors, including the process of industrialization and the disciplinary and production regime under which workers were employed, as well as a rejection of the authoritarian regime. Its impact was, however, chiefly political in that it undermined, nationally and internationally, the dictatorship.

---

reference to labour. But labour organizations have not been key actors everywhere in contemporary transitions. Communist regimes did not usually leave enough space for independent labour unions to develop.

At the same time, their official ideology was pro-worker and the state consciously colonized workers' organizations. Only Poland is an exception to this trend. The Workers' Defence Committee, an independent labour organization, was formed in Poland in the 1970s, with the aim of defending victims of repression by the state in the aftermath of a wave of anti-government strike activity. This inspired the creation of Solidarity, the independent trade union which eventually achieved legal recognition and went on to successfully challenge the state. Solidarity undoubtedly drew its strength from the large, culturally distinct and geographically concentrated working-class movement in Poland. But it also benefited from the protection of the Catholic Church which, uniquely in East and Central Europe, had survived as an independent institution, autonomous from the state. The support of the Catholic Church endowed Solidarity with legitimacy beyond the labour movement and afforded it protection. Despite the imposition of martial law in 1981, which made independent organizations such as Solidarity illegal, it survived intact to win legal recognition in 1988 and later enter the Round Table negotiation, leading to the first (partially) free elections.

Kopstein (1996) argues that workers' protest was also important in bringing about the demise of Communism in East Germany. Based on the assumption that workers protest in diffuse as well as direct ways, he suggests that 'small-scale, largely non-political acts of everyday resistance ...chipped away at the long-term capacity of communist regimes to meet the demands of society at large' (Kopstein 1996: 393). Shop-floor resistance to the East German dictatorship included opposition to the introduction of piece-work in factories because of labour exploitation, feet-dragging over the production targets that were decreed centrally and demands for egalitarian pay structures rather than productivity-oriented pay structures. These practices date back to 1948 and, though not consciously aimed at democratizing the state, were important forms of resistance which denied the Communist state legitimacy and undermined it socially.

What about the role of labour organizations elsewhere? In general, African unions represent only a small percentage of the population, concentrated in the few urban or trade centres. Unions have also suffered co-optation because of their relative weakness and have been unable to forge more than a precarious independent existence. As a result, labour struggles have generally concentrated on 'non-political' issues of pay and conditions (Chazan *et al*. 1999: 89). In South Africa, however, labour did form part of the political struggle against apartheid. The African National Congress (ANC) created the non-racial South African

Congress of Trades Unions (SACTU) in 1955. The key to its moderate success – it represented 19 affiliate unions and 55,000 members in 1961 – was that it linked pay and conditions to broader questions of rights and African nationalism. Nevertheless, its political impact was limited. Consequently, labour did not become an important organization of protest until the 1970s. Nevertheless, the South African labour movement, even at this time, was less organically connected to the popular movements than in Spain or Latin America. South African labour law had succeeded in dividing and weakening the unions, making a common position vis-à-vis the state difficult to achieve. At the same time, some union leaders calculated that their impact would be greater – and their physical security assured – if they eschewed political unionism. Instead, they concentrated on building union strength and union democracy (Marais 1998: 45). As a result, the capacity of the unions to engage in strike activity increased in the 1980s, especially following the legalization of black trade unions after 1980. But political unity was difficult to achieve because the unions themselves were divided on whether to engage with the popular opposition that was now emerging in the black townships. Some unions did so and helped organize community actions such as school boycotts, consumer boycotts and resistance within communities. Labour organizations thus contributed in two distinct ways to the demise of the apartheid state: by disrupting economic activity through strike action and through their role in popular movement against the state in the 1980s.

How important have labour organizations been following transition? Here, the key variables are:

- the national patterns of institutionalization of labour;
- the strength of the labour movement itself and of societal organizations in general vis-à-vis the state; and
- the kind of developmental project newly democratizing governments pursue.

Where labour is seen as a key actor for economic development, it will be able to play a role in shaping transition and post-transition politics. Thus the Spanish trade union movement was crucial for stabilizing democracy in the immediate post-transition period. However in Chile, where economic growth has been based since the mid-1980s on export-led growth in agricultural or non-industrial commodities, labour has been relatively unimportant after 1989, despite a long history of organization and politicization.

Community Organizations

Authoritarian regimes attempt to seal the state off from the masses. They are unreceptive to pressure from below. This sometimes has the effect of shifting the locus of political activity to the community rather than depoliticizing society, as the state intends. Popular or community activism may increase just as the authoritarian regime breaks down and democratization gets under way because 'the nature of the state [is] potentially more fluid at ...moments of transformation than at other times' (Waylen 1996). This means that it is important to consider the impact of community-based organizations in democratization, even though they may not explicitly be 'political' organizations at all.

In Spain, urban social movements in large cities such as Bilbao, Madrid and Barcelona presented the Franco regime with a crisis of governance in the early 1970s (Hipsher 1996). They remained important throughout the first phase of the transition, between 1975 and 1977. They eventually demobilized as the leftist parties, which had initially supported community protests, were incorporated into the new democratic structures and urged caution upon community organizers (Castells 1983). For the left, the new democratic system was too important to risk, independent of whether it was economically redistributive, and they feared that the radical community protests would alienate the right, which was only partially convinced of the value of democracy. Their view was that the transition was fragile and could easily be overturned (Bermeo 1992). As a result, they pulled out of the popular social movements. In the process, the community groups lost their channels into the state, as well as their most vocal leaders, and the community movements subsequently collapsed.

Strong and well-organized community movements also appeared in Chile and Brazil during the military dictatorships. In both cases, they drew support from the crisis of the dictatorships in the early 1980s. They were also empowered by the rich tradition of organization among the shanty towns and communities of the poor which dates back to the creation of the *favelas* or the *poblaciones* in the 1960s. Because these groups distrusted the political class and the political parties, which they saw as part of a political elite that had deprived them of representation, they saw themselves as articulating a new model of democracy. Certainly they represented a critique of the kind of democracy which had traditionally existed in Latin America, in which popular organizations had achieved neither recognition or representation. So, not only did they challenge the authoritarian state but they also tried consciously to present a new way of doing democratic politics. They emphasized the importance of participation and internal democracy and insisted that politics should be concerned with the daily experiences of the poor – for survival, for employment, for housing, for security, for basic services (Escobar and Alvarez 1992). In Chile, these groups have largely been marginalized by the rapid re-emergence of the civilian political class. However, in Brazil, the shanty-town organizations remain active. Through the Workers Party, they continue to try and change the face of post-transition 'official' politics (Keck 1992).

The experiences of Southern Europe and Latin America are not mirrored in Africa. In much of sub-Saharan Africa democratization is a far more timid affair, for the simple reason that the central state has reduced meanings for people, and its reach – though not its ambition – is normally less. As a result, community groups are accepted as instruments for survival, provided that they do not try and enter the political process. Self-help and local economic networks are the normal site of social activities, but these activities exist in a different universe from that of the state. Popular organizations rarely engage directly with the state and concentrate instead on supporting their members. The political impact of civil society organizations, therefore, in sub-Saharan Africa has been rather less than in Europe and Latin America, mainly because it is so difficult to enter the public sphere.

The South African story is different. The ambition of the apartheid state was to control and organize the entire social community. As a result, the range of initially small-scale organizations that sprang up under apartheid, many of them centred on neighbourhoods or shanty-towns, were seen as subversive. Groups excluded from the formal circles of politics, and indeed from citizenship, organized in townships, communities and schools because other, more formal, channels of participation and organization were closed to them. Some of these groups were explicitly self-help oriented: soup kitchens, for example, were set up so that children could be fed in times of high unemployment and hardship. But these groups also engaged directly with the authoritarian state. The township protests in South Africa in the 1980s, for example, organized by young black people, had the aim of demonstrating the non-viability of the apartheid regime and demanding change. Strong networks within the townships meant that the community was able to act together and even to protect members from the police. The townships were also able to draw support from other domestic actors who shared their commitment to ending apartheid. Additionally the violence and the repression in black townships in South Africa drew international condemnation.

Thus the township protests were an important catalyst to the transition in South Africa, directly and indirectly. They created a crisis of internal governance inside the country, and they connected with other groups inside and outside the country in coordinated condemnation of the South African apartheid regime.

In East and Central Europe, community or individual opposition to Communism took a completely different form. Communist governments aimed at a total control over society. Community and individual protest therefore represented a critique of state power and a desire for less, never more, of the state in daily life. Opposition to the state took the form of an individualistic retreat into the private sphere. Under the Communist regimes, dissidents tended to romanticize the individual's non-cooperation with the state as a form of civil society. Kuron (1990: 72) thought that the state's 'monopoly is so total that if citizens gather and discuss freely a matter as simple as roof repairs on a block of apartments, it becomes a challenge to central authority'. This led to an assumption that autonomous institutions could emerge from within society at large, becoming a kind of 'parallel polis'(Havel, Klaus and Pithart 1996). As it turned out, however, social organizations were actually very weak on the ground and networks were thin. After the fall of Communism, the transitions to democracy were very quickly seized upon by elites who became the 'voices' for democracy, amid very little opposition from popular organizations.

Indigenous Movements

Since authoritarianism represents the centralization of power, ethnic nationalist groups, if they are not in control of the state, find themselves in the opposition. For these groups, the end of authoritarianism represents an opportunity to make secessionist demands. Such movements have emerged in Spain, East and Central Europe, the Balkans and within the territories of the former Soviet Union. They stress ascriptive identity and comprise people who wish to opt out of a pre-existing 'nation state'. It is difficult to see these groups as part of civil society. They do not engage with the state for the purpose of reform or a democratization of power; nor do they contribute to the democratization project through the diffusion of liberal values of tolerance or civility. It is not clear that they are democratic movements at all, in fact, although they may have played a part in bringing to a close a period of authoritarianism. In Africa, Latin America and Asia, such movements are much rarer. Although some indigenous or ethnic groups may wish to retain and use cultural symbols (language, dress, production practices, etc.) that are different from the dominant culture, they do not generally exclude themselves from the polity. They may, however, be excluded and ignored by the state. Any meaningful project of democratization, therefore, must include extending rights and citizenship to these excluded groups.

State-building in Africa has meant the creation of a state at the service of one ethnic group to the exclusion of others. Ethnic identities are ways of playing out social and political roles, and of determining inclusion and exclusion. Ethnicity functions to buttress populist and clientelist relationships and as a way of establishing social networks. The strength of ethnic identities, as well as their fluidity, are responses to the increasing fragility of the state. Playing – and creating – ethnic tensions can serve the interests of local leaders in a search for a share of state power. As a result, the 1990s in particular witnessed a resurgence of ethnic tensions in Africa as a response to crises of the state. It is, however, difficult to situate ethnic struggles within pro-democracy struggles. Instead, they constitute survival and exchange networks. Nevertheless, in some cases, the rights of groups in Africa have been taken up by international groups and, in this way, been framed as a part of democratization. This happened in Nigeria. The military dictatorship found itself under international pressure in the 1990s to enter into negotiations with the Ogoni people who were protesting against the exploitation of their land by oil companies, as a sign of commitment to human rights and democracy. Respect for the Ogoni, in fact, became a test, at least as far as the international community was concerned, of how far democratization was actually occurring.

In Latin America, state building came to mean ignoring the existence of the indigenous population or their 'otherization' (Radcliffe and Westwood 1996: 42). Liberalism and modernization were interpreted through a crudely racial lens, in which indigenous culture was seen as backward (Yashar 1997). Modernizing states therefore sought to eliminate indigenous cultures through repression. This was the case even in countries such as Guatemala, where the indigenous people were a numerical majority.

Invisible, conceptualized as a problem or simply excluded from the polity altogether, indigenous groups in Latin America have traditionally been able to call upon precious little social or political capital with which to demand rights. Until very recently, strategies to deal with indigenous populations have been packages of integration and assimilation – through language, education, etc. This began to change in the 1970s. Indigenous groups began to engage with the state, stressing their ethnic identity. This was evident in Guatemala especially. The Guatemalan indigenous population is particularly numerous and the repression of the indigenous communities under the military dictatorship was particularly violent (Trudeau 1993). In general, across the region, democratization has been taken to represent an opportunity for *indigenista* organizations (see Box 5.6). Explicitly political organizations have emerged in Southern Mexico, Brazil, Bolivia, Ecuador and Guatemala and, to rather a less extent, in Chile and Paraguay. They receive support and validation from a range of pro-democracy international activists. Their demands vary and include the establishment of

---

Box 5.6 Indigenous Movements and Democratization in Latin America

Democratization in the 1980s presented opportunities for indigenous groups. Yashar (1998) argues that indigenous movements have been unleashed in a number of countries due to the increase in opportunities and institutional transformation. Local institutions have been restructured and previous forms of rural incorporation have been reversed as a consequence of technocratic government practices or of the reduction in state authority in the rural areas. These changes have disadvantaged indigenous communities. As a result, 'indigenous peasants have both gained and used greater autonomy to contest the terms and practice of citizenship. In this changing institutional and social context, indigenous movements have emerged to (re)gain access to the state and secure local autonomy' (Yashar 1998: 34).

Indigenous movements in Latin America which are pressing for reform include:

- The *Ejercito Zapatista de Liberacion Nacional* (EZNL) in Chiapas, Southern Mexico, which emerged on 1 January 1994. The *Zapatistas* have forced the Mexican government to enter into negotiations over autonomy and cultural politics.
- In Guatemala, Mayan organizations organized the Second Continental Meeting of Indigenous and Popular Resistance in 1991 in order to increase their political profile. Indigenous movements also formed an electoral alliance, *Nukuj Ajpop*, to compete in municipal and legislative elections.
- In Bolivia, indigenous movements have put forward claims for territorial autonomy. An indigenous grouping, the *Kataristas*, were represented in government for the first time in 1993.
- In Ecuador, indigenous movements have campaigned for agrarian reform, bilingual and bicultural education and territorial autonomy. In 1996, they began to contest elections for the first time.

legal rights, territorial rights and the right to decide how the natural resources found on the land they inhabit are used. Since land is essential to the survival of these communities, the struggle to retain land for community not commercial agriculture is particularly important. They are not therefore seeking to establish independent nation states but to obtain packages of rights – to land, to cultural autonomy, to collective representation – within the existing state system. Pushing collective rights onto an agenda of democratization which is overwhelmingly liberal in its understanding of democracy in this way is not easy. Despite a dawning awareness in Latin America that collective indigenous rights are important, and growing mobilization to demand them, democratization processes in practice have largely ignored these issues. But, as a result of the increasing activism of indigenous groups in Latin America, regime change has sometimes allowed a formal recognition of their existence for the first time – in Brazil and in Nicaragua, for example. Nevertheless taking indigenous rights seriously is hampered by the political economy of democratization which links democracy to the market. This creates tension over the use of land as indigenous communities struggle to prevent commercial farming eliminating traditional practices (Barton 1997).

Civil Society after the Transition

Schmitter and O'Donnell (1986) argue that the beginning of democratization is accompanied by a resurrection of civil society. However they also suggest that this moment of revival gives way to eclipse. A number of reasons have been put forward to explain this apparent decline in civil society activism. These include (a) the idea that the expansion of political society necessarily eats away at civil society; (b) 'movement fatigue', that is, members of social movements choose to disband and live 'normal' lives; (c) the notion that the democratizing state consciously colonizes civil society as a strategy of governance or of cooptation; and (d) the loss of external support and/or external pressure to moderate their demands or the kind of tactics (the repertoire of protest) they assume.

What is certain is that the opening of the process of democratization signifies a change in the political opportunity structure for civil society organizations. They are engaging with a changed state apparatus – one with greater legitimacy, internally and externally and, consequently, one with greater resources. As Hipsher (1996) argues, it is reasonable to assume that democratization represents a contraction of opportunities supportive of protest. Furthermore, the introduction of democracy changes the way in which social struggles can be framed. Groups that had been able to forge a common identity under authoritarianism as pro-democracy movements may find that this is shattered with the beginning of political reform, and class, sectoral or gender tensions and hierarchies begin to reassert themselves. They may be fundamentally divided over what, precisely, democracy means. The opening of democratization can therefore spell the end of a cycle of contention. For Schmitter and O'Donnell (1986) this represents the normalization of politics, as the state reasserts its control over society.

However, the extent to which civil society movements *do*, or even *should*, weaken in consolidating democracies is more debatable than has been suggested. For a number of both liberal and radical theorists, the strength of civil society is almost a test of the strength of democracy itself. From this perspective, the evaporation of civil society organizations after the transition is not part of the normal pattern of democratic politics at all; rather it implies that democracy is thin, and that the chances for building a substantive democracy, based on rights and citizenship, are weak.

It is unlikely, in fact, that civil society always disappears in quite the way that was initially thought. Post-transition states try to regulate civil society activity and they may be partially successful in this enterprise. Consequently, the kind of groups that are active and the demands that are being made on the state change once democratization gets under way. This is a response to the very different circumstances of democratization, the new role of the state and the divisions that inevitably open up in civil society itself, as some anti-authoritarian groups find that they are satisfied with the progress of democratization, while others are disappointed. It is also a response to the changed opportunities for engaging with or against the state that democratization implies. Furthermore, some organizations consciously opt for a non-confrontational policy towards the new democratic state in order to 'give democracy a chance'. This does not necessarily represent weakness but could be construed as 'responsible behaviour'. Concerned not to destabilize the transition, for example, the Spanish labour movement accepted a wages policy which tied wages increase below the rate of inflation with the conscious goal of underwriting the construction of democracy. Their aim was to provide a period free of labour unrest for the early years of the transition. This could be read as strength and responsibility, instead of weakness and decline. Of course, if democratization is merely a manoeuvring by cynical elites to gain international acceptance and no substantive concession to internal opposition groups are made, then there is no reason to suppose that a decline in activism occurs at all.

It is also possible to question the extent to which there is an absolute decline with democratization. Hochstetler (1997), for example, argues that social movement activity is inherently cyclical and that to present a simple picture of decline is misleading. She suggests that experiences and repertoires of protest carry on from one cycle to another. As a result, in the case of Brazil, she argues that 'any account of social movements organizing in Brazil after 1985 must be able to address not only movement decline but also some striking innovations in grassroots and middle class organizing as well such as the growth of non-governmental organizations (NGOs) and new movements like the landless movement (MST) and the various anti-violence movements' (Hochstetler 1997: 1). This suggests that while the immediate transition period can sometimes generate a lowering of protest from civil society groups, as democratization gets under way, it increases again.

Conclusion

In this chapter, we have reviewed the importance of civil society in the creation of new democracies. Many of the civil society organizations discussed here were crucial in generating opposition to authoritarianism. Others were important in connecting opposition to the international community. The crisis of authoritarianism generated an opportunity for civil society activism. At the same time, this activism contributed to deepening this crisis of the state further and played an important role in catalyzing transitions. The decomposition of authoritarian regimes constitutes, in fact, a rare moment of autonomy for civil society. More than anything else, this explains why civil society activism is more visible under authoritarianism than after democratization has begun.

After the initial transition, levels of activism tend to diminish and the unity of civil society movements is disrupted. Some tend to fade away completely. Others find that the state takes on their roles, at least formally. Still more find that it is now difficult to make themselves heard in the new regime. And some find themselves confused by the fear that activism could destabilize the fragile new democracy. For some groups, it is not that they alltogether disappear or are deactivated but that the kind of activity they undertake changes. This may make them less immediately visible, or more cooperative in the eyes of the state. So, for example, labour in Spain and Poland continues to play a role in politics but this role is less conflictual. Finally, for some organizations, the new democracy has actually signified wider possibilities for activism than were possible before. This is the case for the indigenous movements in Latin America.

Nevertheless, it is hard to escape the conclusion that the new democracies do not adequately channel or represent the diverse range of civil society groups that have grown up. This is partly because of the difficulties of establishing democratic mechanisms for the representation of civil society organizations in democracy. How can we know that these groups are representative of the community at large? Are their leaders democratically accountable? But it is also a consequence of the elite-led transitions and the fact that the 'political class' rapidly re-established its dominance in the new systems. As a result, most new democracies are failing to represent adequately the demands for inclusion and participation which emerged at the end of dictatorships. Of course the picture varies widely. It is less the case in Europe than it is in Latin America; less so in Latin America and Asia than in Africa. A final question is, does it matter if civil society is weak if there are other channels, through political parties and elections, for representation? This chapter suggests that it does. A strong civil society matters because it helps determine the *quality* of democracy. Civil society organizations are not an alternative to other forms of political representation; they are a means for checking and controlling the state and a tool to push the state towards deeper reforms. A weak civil society implies a thin democracy, where patterns of participation are low and where the state has few obligations to listen to society, conceptualized broadly and inclusively.

6

Democratization and Globalization

Until the 1990s, the established view was that democratization was domestically driven. International factors were regarded as, at best, supplementary (Whitehead 1986) and the external element to democratization was the 'forgotten dimension' (Pridham 1991). But as democratization began to take off in East and Central Europe and, more tentatively, in Africa and Asia, the international dimension of democratization moved to centre stage. Moreover, a number of empirical studies (Mujal-Leon 1989; Grabendorff 1992; Whitehead 1991, 1996; Grugel 1996) provided evidence of the importance of the international dimension in particular cases. Pridham (1991) identified interactions at the boundary between domestic politics and the international order as crucial for shaping the politics of democratization. Finally, Huntington (1991) argued that globalization was the primary cause of the third wave, turning the original theories of democratization on their head.

But how, precisely, do international factors, or globalization, produce democratization? And what kind of democratic project do they favour? This chapter argues that the creation of a global political economy and the emergence of global governance mechanisms generate pressures for democratization. However, they do so in ways that are frequently confusing and ambiguous. Furthermore, there is no uniform agreement about the kind of democracy that international agencies wish to promote. The result is that whilst there is no shortage of international programmes or activity in support of democracy, their impact on politics on the ground is often exaggerated.

Globalization and Democracy

Democratization is part of a distinct set of changes within the global order. In particular, it is related to the creation of a genuinely global political economy; to the emergence of institutions of global governance; and to the creations of a global communications network.

The Global Political Economy

Strange (1992: 2) sees democratization as a consequence of the formation of a global political economy:

> Most of the recent changes in world politics, however unrelated they may seem on the surface, can be traced back in large part to certain common roots in the global political economy. We see common driving forces of structural change behind the liberation of Central Europe, the disintegration of the former Soviet Union ... and the U-turns of many developing country governments from military or authoritarian governments to democracy and from protectionism and import substituting industrialisation towards open borders and export promotion.

The creation of a global political economy has its origins, overwhelmingly, in the globalization of production, trade and finance. Academics – and more importantly governments – agree that there is now a greater extensity of trade than at any other time in human history and that we are witnessing the emergence of genuinely global markets in finance and production (Held *et al.* 1999). The process of globalization is both cause and consequence of a seismic shift in national economic policies and the global movement towards economic liberalization and global integration. It is no longer possible to posit development behind sealed or insulated national frontiers. This is the case for developed societies; if anything, it is more true even for developing economies which are short of capital, technology, know-how and confidence. Thus globalization is an uneven process that affects states differentially (Holm and Sorenson 1995). Its impact is greatest in vulnerable and weak countries where states are less able to mitigate its effects (Hurrell and Woods 1995).

The creation of a global political economy is linked with democratization in diverse ways. First, it establishes the authority of Western capitalist centres more tightly over the developing world. It reduces the political and economic options available to developing states. Developing and post-Communist countries have repeated and regular contacts with agencies or governments from the capitalist core. This is a result, for example, of aid regimes that rely on political conditionality, the development of programmes of humanitarian intervention, in for example, the ex-Yugoslavia or Somalia, and the emergence of regionalized trade blocs, which have begun to dissolve the previously firm borders distinguishing the North from the South and the West from the East. Southern or post-Communist countries now find that they are 'locked in ' to a particular model of development which depend on formal democracy and an open economy. They are tied into a set of political relationships with developed states which include a commitment to the liberal democratic model of development. Furthermore, integration suggests that the fortunes of the developed world have become bound up with those of their developing partners in a way never before experienced. Global integration means that economic crisis in the developing world can spread rapidly to the core economies. As a result, for Western Europe, security and development are now tied to events in East and Central Europe and the post-Communist Balkan states. Meanwhile in the Americas, NAFTA implies that economic fragility in Mexico can easily contaminate the US and Canadian economies. It makes sense now, more than ever, for the core countries to try and shape political processes elsewhere. Democratization, then, is part of a wider process of deepening hegemonic control over the developing and semi-peripheral world.

Secondly, the global political economy is built upon strategies of global liberalization. From a liberal perspective, liberalization encourages global democratization. Trade liberalization was expected to create free markets which, in turn, would facilitate the creation of citizenship, a middle class and a civil society. Markets would act to limit state excesses by creating 'agencies of restraint' and therefore work to encourage democracy (Collier 1991). These would lead to successful transitions to democracy (Callaghy 1993). For a cluster of countries, democratization coincided with economic liberalization. In some, economic liberalization unleashed political change. This included the empowerment of national and transnational groups with a preference for institutional reform and perhaps even democracy, for a range of instrumental or ideological reasons. Liberalization also sometimes undercut the authoritarian state's capacity to 'buy' support by reducing its income and its penetration of society, creating a crisis within the state itself. This happened especially in states dependent on 'spoils politics' because it transformed financial and production practices, creating new circuits of capital which bypassed the state (Allen 1995). In short, liberalization occasionally acted as a catalyst to democratization.

However, the assumption that export-led growth automatically promotes democratization ran into problems by the mid-1990s. Evidence suggested that whilst economic liberalization was supportive of democratization in some cases, in others it weakened the state so much that democratization became impossible. This was certainly the case in parts of sub-Saharan Africa (Baylies 1995). At the same time, for most people in developing countries, economic liberalization has proved impoverishing and socially polarizing. It is leading not to the progressive empowerment of civil society but to the creation of hierarchies of global and local power. It excludes the poor, weakens the developing state through internationalization and deepens the North–South divide (Cox 1997). Integration into global markets deepens inequalities within and between countries and makes the developing world vulnerable to political pressures to 'catch up' or copy models of development from the West. Under these conditions, democratization is difficult to achieve because it is difficult to make an argument, or find funds, for redistribution.

Global Governance

The global economy is the essential background to the emerging forms of global governance. Because globalization diminishes the autonomy of all states, it is leading to the emergence of a 'post-Westphalian order' characterized by the rise of international agencies and institutions of global governance which replace or operate alongside the inter-state system (McGrew 1997). These include the International Monetary Fund (IMF), the World Bank and the World Trade Organization (WTO) which regulate the international economy, and the United Nations (UN) which attempts to impose global order and establish global norms. The moves to establish an international court with a remit to investigate global human rights is also part of the emergence of transnational governance regimes. The power these institutions wield is a reflection of the fact that they represent, however loosely and indirectly, the interests of the West. Their financial, political and economic resources are drawn from Western states. They are not, therefore, independent, although they are not directly managed by Western states. For Cox (1997), they are part of the covert structures that regulate global capitalism, which he terms the *nebuleuse*, along with meetings of the G7, the Organization of Economic Cooperation and Development (OECD) and more informal meetings between heads of the Central Banks of leading economies. These emerging institutions of global governance reflect the structural inequalities between the rich and the poor, between those that control significant and valuable resources and those that do not (O'Brien *et al.* 2000).

Global governance institutions have embarked upon a range of policies to promote democracy. Interventions in the ex-Yugoslavia, as well as campaigns in sub-Saharan Africa, have been carried out in the name of democracy. Programmes of economic development now explicitly have democracy as part of their goal and the promotion of global human rights is seen as international backing for democracy. But because of their composition these institutions tend to favour a particular version of democracy which is consonant with Western power and capitalism. In general, they have prioritized the holding of elections and alternation in power, over slower but more effective programmes of reform of the state or a redistribution of economic and social resources. As such, their programmes tend to be directed towards the creation of low-intensity democracies. There is, furthermore, some doubt concerning how far it is legitimate or democratic for institutions, which themselves have no mechanisms of democratic accountability and which represent predominantly the developed and capitalist world, to impose democracy from outside. It could even be argued that intervention of this sort is a violation of the principle of state sovereignty.

It is not surprising, then, that attempts to impose a limited democracy through the institutions of global governance have led to the emergence of strategies of resistance within developing countries. For example, the Chiapas rebellion in Mexico, led by the *Ejercito Zapatista de Liberacion Nacional* (EZLN), is a response to the perceived imposition of policies of economic liberalization and limited democratic reform from outside. Instead, the EZLN calls for the introduction of development programmes that are respectful of local traditions of production and social organization. Other strategies of resistance are undertaken by organizations which lay claim to representing global civil society. The 1990s witnessed the emergence of mass movements that oppose globalization through the imposition of global capitalism and limited democracy. Instead, mass protests at global governance meetings have called for an end to imposition from the West and the empowerment of civil societies across the world. At the same time, transnational networks, formed around issues of justice, human rights and ecology, and composed mainly of globally active NGOs, present an alternative vision of globalization from below. These groups promote a version of global democracy which they see as the creation of genuinely global citizenship rights.

The Diffusion of Democratic Values

Globalization is not just a matter of economic exchanges or of the emergence of a new architecture of governance. It affects the daily lives and life experiences of most people across the globe. This is the result of the technological advances, the emergence of global communications networks and time–space compression which means that we continually experience events thousands of miles away in real time. The technological advances in the West and the communications revolution have contributed to a loss of faith in the ability of the developing and non-Western worlds to resist the onslaught of free market capitalism or Westernization.

Demands for political change, social justice, environmental protection, etc. can now be heard many thousands of miles from their place of origin. For Giddens (1990) this means that cultures are now global, not just national or local. An interconnected world means that political crises and conflicts, whatever their local and particular origins, are couched in the same language. Democratization becomes the common linguistic currency to describe social struggles and political change. 'Democracy' offers a way of ordering complex and particular events in a language that is universally understandable; it is, according to Held (1996: 297–8), the only 'grand or meta narrative that can legitimately frame and delimit the competing "narratives" of the contemporary age'. As a result, a wide variety of social and political conflicts are described as 'democratization', whether, in fact, they are or not. Furthermore, the creation of elements of a global culture acts as a force behind the creation of a global civil society, demands for internationally enforced human rights norms and the formation of transnational advocacy networks. It acts, therefore, as a stimulant to global campaigns for democracy from below.

Promoting Democracy

Global governance institutions, states, NGOs and transnational networks have all developed different strategies to promote democracy. Most of the contemporary policies have been in place since 1990. However, democratic promotion actually has a history dating back to the Cold War. The US, some European states and some political parties developed embryonic policies for democratic promotion as early as the 1960s and 1970s. In this section, we examine the different ways in which actors go about trying to push democratization and the different models of democracy they promote. In order to do this, we first establish a typology of pro-democracy interventions. The typology is summarized in Box 6.1.

Whitehead (1996) proposed that international factors in democratization be analyzed as processes of contagion, control or consent.

Box 6.1   A Typology of Democratic Promotion

Type	*Actors*	*Example*
Contagion	Domestic elites	Spain/Portugal 1974–6; South America 1978–89; East-Central Europe 1989; Southern Africa 1990–4
Control	US; Western Europe	Dominican Republic 1965; Grenada 1983; El Salvador 1982–9;
Consent	Western states/elites/ institutions; domestic elites	Spain/Portugal 1974–6; Latin America 1990s; South Africa 1994–; Czech Republic/ Hungary/Poland 1989–
Conditionality	Global governance institutions; Western states	Sub-Saharan Africa 1982–
Citizenship	Transnational NGOs global civil society	Environmental/indigenous rights campaigns in Brazil and Nigeria; international support for EZLN in Mexico

Contagion suggests that democratization spreads in waves from neighbouring countries. This explains democratization in regional clusters, where domestic elites appear to control the process, such as in East and Central Europe. It is the result of the diffusion of democratic values across borders. Democratization through *control* refers to cases where democracy is imposed as a form of subordinating countries to Western dictates. Democracy is seen as a way of 'vaccinating' countries against the threat of revolution or defiance of global norms. Democratization through *consent* is more complex than either of the above models. It suggests the incorporation of democratic norms, initially from outside, by groups and actors inside the state-in-transition. Democratization by consent implies a gradual learning process within societies in transition.

Schmitter (1996) adds the concept of democracy through *conditionality*. He explains:

[conditionality's] hallmark is the deliberate use of coercion – by attaching specific conditions to the distribution of benefits to recipient countries – on the part of multilateral institutions. The *locus classicus* for this kind of behaviour in the past was (and still is) the IMF ... More recently, it has been the European Community ... that has insisted upon a certain standard of political behaviour as a condition for membership. (Schmitter 1996: 30)

Conditionality is an increasingly important tool for democracy programmes. Finally, we should note the increasing use of democratization policies via *citizenship*. Here transnationally active networks promote democratization from below. They transmit solidarity, support, the weight of numbers and technical assistance to campaigns for human rights, indigenous rights, sustainable development and people-centred democracies.

The most important actors, in terms of the resources they deploy and the influence they wield, are Western states; institutions of global governance; political parties; and transnational NGOs. We look now at the scope of their activities in support of democratization.

States

Stabilizing the developing world and vaccinating it against the threat of Communism during the Cold War was the motivation for the first generation of pro-democracy policies adopted by Western states. Western states pushed democracy as a way of creating a more secure world for themselves. But supporting democratization in the 1960s and 1970s was a difficult enterprise. Liberal democracy disintegrated, failed to take off or was weakly embedded in most of Africa, Asia and Latin America. Where democracy survived, it tended to borrow the form from US and European models but the substance was markedly different. The British Caribbean, for example, followed the Westminster model of government on Independence, but political cultures of personalism, weak institutionalization, the relatively small electorates, the limitations of civil society, the impact of racial and ethnic tensions and massive socio-economic divisions combined to undermine the institutions and limit the creation of a culture of citizenship (Payne 1991). In Africa, there were attempts to establish one-party or no-party democracies, based on the view that liberal democracy and the tradition of party representation was alien to African cultural traditions. In Latin America, populist or even revolutionary democracies were the norm, with very few countries demonstrating any stable commitment to the institutions of liberal democracy between 1950 and 1980.

In the US, funds for the promotion of democracy abroad were established as early as 1961, with the Foreign Assistance Act. This established a mechanism through which the US assisted anti-Communist parties and individuals in Asia, the Middle East and Latin America, in the name of democracy. By the 1970s, economic aid had become the principal foreign policy tool for the US with which to reward friends and punish enemies. This was presented as a way of promoting democracy abroad. At the end of that decade, President Carter attached respect for human rights as a condition to US aid, in an attempt to break with the style of previous pro-democracy policies. US democratic promotion in this period had a geopolitical rationale. It was concerned above all with upholding US ideological and material interests. In Latin America, for example, pro-democracy policies served to contain nationalist pressures and maintain an asymmetrical relationship based on US dominance (Arnson and Mendelson 1992; Nef 1994). It is worth noting here that pro-democracy policies did not apply to Eastern Europe, however global the US government's rhetoric might have been. For all its promised support for Europe's 'liberation' from Soviet domination, in practice no assistance was delivered to the few democratic movements which materialized before the 1980s.

European policies in support of democratization date from a similar period. For Western European countries, pro-democracy policies emerged out of decolonization. They were similarly motivated by security and material concerns. Britain and France committed to programmes of gradual decolonization in Africa, for example, which were essentially exercises in 'teaching' African elites how to govern. Eventually, European withdrawal led to the holding of elections and the establishment of a general suffrage. The forms of democracy left behind did little to democratize the state or to incorporate the indigenous traditions of local organizations and forms of representation (Chazan *et al.*1999). The first period of detente in the 1970s created an opportunity for Europe to take up democratic promotion more broadly and marks the beginning of a serious engagement with democratization in the developing world.

The nature and importance of democratic promotion policies in the US and in Europe changed gradually. The 1980s opened a new phase of support for democracy, buoyed up by the end of the decade by the transformation of East and Central Europe and the collapse of the Soviet Union. The main changes introduced in the 1980s were:

- policies were formalized and institutionalized in sets of governmental, non-governmental and regional bureaucracies;

- pro-democracy policies were awarded a higher priority than in the past;
- the amount of funding for pro-democracy policies increased;
- the policies were extended to embrace new geographical areas to include countries such as China, Hong Kong, South Africa and South Korea for the first time, as well as the ex-Soviet Union and Warsaw Pact countries; and
- pro-democracy intervention shifted from experiments in control to policies of consent and conditionality.

As a result, by the 1990s pro-democracy strategies were about creating hegemonic control in the developing and post-Communist world through consensual agreement or cooptation with key domestic elites.

As a response to the new strategy, the United States Agency for International Development (USAID) created a programme called the Democracy Initiative, which grafted a democracy focus onto development assistance (Hirshmann 1995). But the most significant institutional change was the creation in 1983 of the National Endowment for Democracy (NED), an autonomous non-governmental organization. Most NED funding is channelled through four separate organizations which each have policy autonomy (the Centre for International Private Enterprise, the Free Trade Union Institute, the National Democratic Institute for International Affairs and the National Republican Institute for International Affairs). The NED promotes the classic US vision of democracy: a two-party system and a minimal state, resting on a free market and a free trade union movement. Programmes vary from seminars to promote awareness of how the market functions, to civil education programmes, from funding elections to conferences of constitutional reform or civil–military relations. After 1990, the NED expanded out of Latin America where its first programmes were directed, and moved increasingly into East and Central Europe. Other changes in the US pro-democracy programme have included strengthening regional organizations such as the Organization for American States (OAS) through the incorporation of a pro-democracy unit (Ramirez 1993). New pro-democracy foundations have also been created, such as the Carter Foundation. Additionally, long-established charitable foundations such as the Ford Foundation also began to incorporate pro-democracy work within their remit.

Within Europe, the opening of a new phase of democratic promotion in the 1980s coincided with the strengthening of European institutions and the European Commission acquired an increased protagonism in EU external affairs. A significant part of the EU's external role in the

1990s, especially in relation to developing countries, was the promotion of peace through conflict negotiation and development through democracy. Within these programmes a particular weight is attached to the development of civil society and respect for human rights. This built upon the established role the European institutions had played in promoting democracy within Europe itself in the 1970s, notably in Spain and Greece (Tsingos 1996; Powell 1996).

The geographical range that US and European democratic promotion policies now encompass is spectacular. They have both moved beyond their old colonial and geopolitical areas of engagement. Policies are aimed at Asia, the Middle East, East and Central Europe and the territories of the former Soviet Union, as well as Latin America and Africa. In the 1990s, pro-democracy policies were directed particularly at the ex-Soviet territories and East and Central Europe where they were frequently developed in tandem with pro-market policies. In most of East and Central Europe, US government funding for pro-democracy policies has been backed up by a range of commitments from US charitable foundations, such as the Rockerfeller Brothers Fund and the Ford Foundation, with the result that funding is channelled into the region on a number of different levels. The US government has funded initiatives which include judicial and institutional reform as well as civil education programmes and party reform initiatives, while foundations have concentrated on either civil society programmes or market-based and enterprise initiatives, with the usual assumption (at least inside the US) that pro-market policies are also automatically policies aimed at promoting an open and democratic society.

The rationale for these policies is not only a geopolitical one, that East and Central Europe need to be 'won' for the West. They are also generally about winning new markets for US-produced goods and financial services. It would be wrong, however, to assume that only material interests lie behind US pro-democracy policies. Romania, for example, has been an important target for US programmes, although there are few material incentives for the programmes (see Box 6.2). Meanwhile, in Latin America, US perceptions of its security interests are a better explanation of pro-democracy programmes than market expansion. So policies of institution-building and judicial reform are aimed principally at the drug-exporting countries of Colombia and other Andean countries, for example (Carothers 1994).

Somewhat in contrast to the US, European pro-democracy assistance tends to be conditional on the introduction of basic freedoms (Pridham 1999). This is evident in the policies it has pursued in East and Central

Box 6.2   US Pro-Democracy Policies in Romania

The US inherited a special relationship with post-1989 Romania partly as a result of having cultivated Ceausescu in the 1970s in his bid to establish independence from Moscow. Of the Eastern European countries, Romania was the tardiest in introducing political and economic reform after 1989, and policies were aimed at exerting sufficient pressure to force the country towards democracy and marketization. Between 1990 and 1996, the US government spent approximately $US 13.5 million in pro-democracy work in Romania. Most of this was channelled through USAID or through the NED. Between 1990 and 1992, funding went mainly into programmes of electoral support. Overall, the priorities of the aid programme are the creation of a free media, holding elections, developing political parties, building the trade union movement and establishing and funding civil advocacy NGOs. Most of these policies have been implemented in a 'carrot and stick' approach typical of the US dealing with developing countries. According to Carothers (1996), the US has offered diplomatic attention and praise, technical and financial assistance, and trade benefits in return for political and economic reforms and has withheld or reduced such benefits when Romania has been perceived as backsliding.

The policies assumed that Romania could be expected to move towards a democracy quickly; in fact, a number of US officials, especially those located within the US Embassy in Bucharest, criticized the US government for having over-optimistic expectations about the possibility of rapid change. But hard-line negative conditionality continued to shape policies through the 1990s. The results have been slight or even disappointing. Romanian political parties, despite substantial external funding especially for the Peasant Party and the National Liberation Party, remain weak and poorly connected to society. External funding has made this, if anything, worse, as parties have become attuned to trying to provide what their foreign backers want. Funding pro-market pro-democracy parties has also had, paradoxically, the effect of increasing the appeal of the ex-Communists.

Source: Carothers (1996).

Europe. The EU has played a role in encouraging a political dialogue with East and Central Europe – especially important given the desire for integration into the EU on the part of the East-Central states – and has facilitated social, civil and party links between Western and Eastern Europe. Making the East ready to 'join' Europe has been the *leitmotiv* of EU policies, rather than the more idealistic and loose commitment to full democracy. Efforts have been made to involve civil society organizations in the pro-democracy policies aimed at East and Central Europe, through, for example, the PHARE (see Box 6.3). The overall success of

---

Box 6.3   The PHARE Programme

East and Central post-Communist states have set their sights on member-ship of the EU as a way to expanding their markets and increasing their access to capital. However, the EU insists on democracy as a criteria for membership. One of the ways in which the EU encouraged democracy was the PHARE Democracy Programme, established in 1989, which the EU used to coordinate European aid in order to sustain the political and eco-nomic reform process. The aim of PHARE was :

> to support the activities and efforts of non-governmental bodies pro-moting a stable open society and good governance and focuses support on the difficult or unpopular aspects of political reform and democratic practice, where local advocacy bodies are weak and professional expert-ise is particularly lacking.

PHARE funding has been directed at a variety of small-scale projects aimed at deepening the democratic process. These have included support for trade unions, employers associations, professional associations, con-sumer organizations, local governments and environmental NGOs. Training has been provided for future parliamentary leaders and cam-paigns undertaken to promote public awareness about what democracy means. By directing its funding to non-governmental actors, PHARE has demonstrated the EU's conviction that democratization requires citizen-ship awareness as well as, for example, the establishment of multi-party elections.

Source: Pridham (1999).

---

policies in East and Central Europe has been mixed. In those countries where the transitions to democracy and capitalism count on local support and legitimacy (such as the Czech Republic and Hungary), external funding, assistance and know-how in underwriting democratic institutions has been a source of support for a process of democratiza-tion based on consent. But in countries such as Romania, where the political culture tends rather towards passivity and dependence, where political elites are only partially convinced of the values of democracy and where the traditions of democracy are weak, then external assistance has had poor results.

Pro-democracy policies are also aimed at Hong Kong and China. However, this coincides with a general decline in Western authority in East Asia overall and a resurgence of Asia-Pacific identities (Sum 1995,

1999). This raises the possibilities that pro-democracy policies are simply a replacement for the loss of economic power in the area and an attempt to establish ideological control as a replacement. If this is so, the project has garnered so far relatively few successes. Curtis (1997) suggests that the decline in US 'soft power' in the area might actually weaken the attractions of liberal democracy in Asia as a consequence.

Governance Institutions

Governance institutions have occasionally attempted to impose democracy, or at least peace, the first stage to democracy, without the consent of local elites. But in general, they have preferred policies of persuasion or conditionality. Aid regimes have been reshaped since 1990 to reflect a democracy bias and aid has become a weapon in the struggle to promote democracy globally (Burnell 1997). The introduction of political criteria for aid implies that economic development is only possible through political reform, or the introduction of 'good governance'. The Fourth Lomé Convention in 1989 set a precedent in Europe in this sense because it established the option of aid suspension in cases of human rights violations.

The process by which international agencies have come to encourage democratization can be monitored through the changes that have occurred in the World Bank. Once concerned exclusively with the process of *economic* development, which it viewed as separate from *political* development, in the 1980s it came to see democracy as functionally linked to economic progress. In 1981, the World Bank argued that the African economic crisis was due not to a mistaken policy focus by African governments but, more fundamentally, to the persistence of authoritarian states with a predatory and rent-seeking logic. This constituted the beginning of the focus on the role of political institutions for economic development. By 1989, the World Bank had defined 'good governance', as the drive for democratic government came to be termed, as part of the reform package recommended to aid-dependent states in Africa, thereby linking political change to the introduction of market-led economic reforms. Thus in the case of a number of African countries, 'democratization' is, in fact, simply a reflection of the leverage of international agencies.

The World Bank launched a Comprehensive Development Framework in 1999 that laid down an integrated approach to aid, which 'gives equal weight to the institutional, structural and social underpinnings of a robust market economy' (World Bank 1999a). For the Bank, democratization requires the creation of parties, a civil society and reform of the state. These require additional and specific sorts of support. According to one World Bank advisor to Africa:

> Private enterprise needs an enabling environment and only government can provide this. So the problems of governance must be faced: they cannot simply be willed away by privatisation, economic liberalisation and reliance on market processes. (Young 1995)

The World Bank and other donors have sufficient authority in aid-dependent countries to force at least cosmetic changes in the political order. But how far is conditionality conducive to long-term democratization? Crawford (1997) argues that it not effective at all. Moreover, aid conditionality is only partially implemented anyway. A concern with human rights and pro-democracy policies is subordinated to 'other dominant foreign policy concerns, especially economic self-interest' in countries that are central to Western interests such as China, Nigeria and Turkey (Crawford 1997: 71). Democracy through conditionality, then, is visited mainly, or at least most thoroughly, on the poorest countries. Aid sanctions have been applied primarily in sub-Saharan Africa where they have generally undermined social networks and social cohesion, rather than having been a mechanism for the creation of democracies (Hellinger 1992). In sum, governance institutions have taken a strong line rhetorically, but their policies have fallen short of full support for democracy, even democracy understood chiefly as the introduction of elections and some institutional mechanisms of accountability. The weight of governance policies has consistently been mediated by security and market concerns, except in the very poorest of countries.

Political Parties

A number of Western political non-state organizations have also become involved in democratic promotion. In contrast to the motivations of states and global institutions, these organizations do not work from a security logic. Political parties play an interesting role, straddling concerns with development, political culture and participation alongside a commitment to the 'Western' way of life. Their influence has, at times, been extensive, not just in the discrete sense of having a direct impact on events but more diffusely in terms of producing a set of images of how democracy works and of providing expertise and know-how from which actors located inside democratizing countries can choose to learn.

They are, therefore, organizations that contribute to democratization through the diffusion of values. Their role is supportive in cases where democratization is primarily an internally driven process, although they have at times become enmeshed in policing policies of conditionality imposed by Western states.

Political parties operate in two main ways in terms of their pro-democracy work. First they direct their attentions towards transforming the mentalities of elites in countries in transition, suggesting a generally unreflexive view of privileging elites and issues of leadership in democratization. Secondly, they fund, organize and support campaigns of mass education, awareness and training, suggesting a commitment to participation and, to some extent, a socially embedded democratization. The precise weight given to the particular policies depends partly on the ideological orientation of the funding parties. So, European social democratic parties and Christian democratic parties have tended to engage in both sorts of activities, while liberal and conservative parties have, on the whole, concentrated on maintaining and deepening elite ties. The US organization, the National Republican Institute for International Affairs, usually funds like-minded parties and institutes, while the National Democratic Institute for International Affairs has been more concerned with promoting civil society organizations and with issues of governance, including problems of consolidation and civil–military relations.

European and US political parties have been most actively engaged in the transitions to democracy in Latin America and in East and Central Europe, where cultural and geographical proximity mean that party ideologies find an echo in the democratizing societies. One way of influencing events is through granting or withholding membership for local parties in the party internationals – the transnational organizations of political parties. According to Andreas Khol, Executive Secretary of the European Democratic Union in 1987, the primary international function of political parties is to provide their members with democratic legitimacy through membership of the Internationals (Grabendorff 1996). According to Pridham (1999: 69), transnational party links between Western Europe and East and Central Europe have operated at different levels. First, they have been able to sanction or reward local parties through membership (or rejection) of the Internationals. Secondly, they have been a force for coordinating European policies towards East and Central Europe, through, for example, activity in the European Parliament. And thirdly, they have engaged directly with issues of 'training, moral and material support as well as political monitoring...party identity, early programmatic development, the acquisition of political experience and building up organizational mechanisms' (Pridham 1999: 69–70). Pridham places particular weight on the process of political socialization of East European politicians by Western politicians.

In Latin America, the parties' roles were somewhat different. They began serious operations in Latin America in the 1970s, in protest at the wave of authoritarian governments in the region and in support of democratic forces, although their work was somewhat constrained by the Cold War. In view of the unresolved problems of human rights in the region the parties, especially the Socialists and the Christian Democrats, have directed some of their activities in support of mechanisms to establish the rule of law and strengthen respect for human rights. These have included cooperation in designing programmes of judicial reform and, at times, packages of support for the extradition and trial of torturers. These have been tempered, however, by the pragmatic view that prosecutions can sometimes destabilize the transition. The influence of parties over the transitions in Latin America has waned as regimes moved towards consolidation, or at least semi-democratic stability, in contrast with the still-important role the parties seem to exert in East and Central Europe (Grugel 1996).

Parties were early advocates of policies of democratic promotion, but are now less visible. This is in part a reflection of the fact that parties have tended to regard their role as one of supporting domestically driven processes; they have not, therefore, been enthusiastic backers of democratic imposition. Furthermore, Western parties have had little of relevance to say to countries in Asia or Africa, where political cultures and traditions of participation are different from the Western model. And finally, the party-led model of democracy has been subject to a range of criticisms within Western Europe itself, ranging from allegations that it is elitist and exclusionary, to a view that it is outmoded and unresponsive to society's diffuse needs for local and community representation. For some, party-led European democracies are themselves in crisis (Mair 1997). As a result, having opened up the field of pro-democracy activities abroad in the 1970s, by the end of the 1990s they had been eclipsed by the vigorous campaigns undertaken by transnational NGOs.

Transnational NGOs

Transnational NGOs have become key institutions within the global political economy in two distinct ways. Some transnational NGOs are part of the formal and informal networks of resistance to globalization from above. These organizations search for and promote alternative visions of democratization to those of states and the governance institutions. Others, however, have become partners with the global institutions and act as service deliverers for them. They are therefore intimately tied up in the strategies of democratization through conditionality. But in fact, the division is less marked than would initially seem possible, and a number of transnationally active NGOs not only participate in networks stressing alternative models of democratization from below but also work with the institutions of global governance.

New forms of governance or the development of 'national and transnational governance networks' (Rosenau 1992) require the participation of non-state sectors including NGOs. As states have moved towards privatizing policy areas, they have delegated to NGOs a significant role in shaping and delivering aid policies. Hence, especially within the European aid regime, NGOs such as OXFAM and Christian Aid now are part of the decision-making process that decides how aid – of which an increasingly important part goes towards democratic promotion – is carried through (Van Rooy and Robinson 1998). Similarly, within the US, the autonomous NED plays both a flagship and a pioneering role for US democratic promotion, outlined above.

Meanwhile, the democracy through citizenship network has tended to concentrate its pro-democracy work in the following areas:

- global advocacy campaigns;
- pressure for the creation of international regimes which respect democracy;
- small-scale participative development and pro-democracy schemes; and
- transnational social movement activity.

The democracy through citizenship network is part of the range of 'transnational ethical networks' that have emerged in the post-Cold War order (Grugel 1999). The most active, in terms of pro-democracy work, has been the human rights network (Sikkink 1993, 1996; Keck and Sikkink 1998). Transnationalized activity saved lives and changed state policies in the 1980s and 1990s (Brysk 1993; Martin and Sikkink 1993). Meanwhile tactics learned in the Argentine case, which led to the formation of the first transnational human rights network, have since been applied in Rwanda, Bosnia and East Timor. But NGOs have also undertaken other kinds of campaigns, such as lobbying and protesting, to change policy within the UN or the WTO. For example, the UN has been lobbied by NGO networks to increase its pro-democracy work and to orient its focus more towards citizenship. NGOs have also been active in pushing for reform of the WTO. The WTO meetings in Seattle in 1999 and Prague in 2000 attracted thousands of activists from NGOs to protest at the impact of WTO rulings in the developing world. Similarly, NGO networks have lobbied regional organizations such as the Summit of the Americas meetings held between American heads of state to issue statements in support of democracy and to bring trade and investment policies in line with their pro-democracy policies.

Although the larger US and European NGOs now form part of the governance networks, many also try and participate in small-scale projects aimed at encouraging democratization from below. They are therefore simultaneously engaged in trying to implement governance 'with a human face' and bottom-up development and democratization strategies. Of course, there are difficulties in straddling both agendas and NGOs struggle to fulfil the expectations of both funders and partners (Grugel 2000). Box 6.4 describes some small-scale programmes typical of the sort that NGOs present as contributions to 'bottom-up' democratization. A different strategy, but with the same aim, is through transna-

---

Box 6.4 British NGOs and Bottom-Up Democratization in Latin America

A number of small-scale British NGOs support democratization in Latin America through project work, transnational networking and advocacy campaigns. Project work is the most traditional form of NGO activity and was adapted in the 1990s to incorporate a democracy focus. Project work involves supervising, staffing and running a development project or supporting a local NGO or social movement to do so with funds or training. As a pro-democracy strategy, it assumes that civil society, democracy and development should be built from the bottom up. Furthermore, since many of the projects are aimed at supplying the means to alleviate economic hardship, it also links democracy with economic entitlements. A good example of this kind of project is an initiative which involves two small UK NGOs, CODA and WOMANKIND, and a Nicaraguan collective of women builders, the Maria Jose Talavera Collective in Codenga. The collective was formed in 1987 with a membership of eight. It erects small houses, makes concrete blocks to be used in the construction industry, and offers electrical services. The collective was a response to high levels of female unemployment caused by the exclusion of women from formal sector employment and a sexist work culture which prevents male employers taking on female labourers. External assistance has meant that the collective has not only been able to survive but has expanded, taking on more members.

tionalized networking. Chalmers *et al.* (1997) argues that some local popular movements are now part of transnational 'associative networks'. Cook (1997) noted the expansion of cross-border labour alliances in response to the signing of NAFTA. Because these groups are generally grassroots movements and depend upon 'people-to-people networking' they constitute a new form of citizen diplomacy devoted to the democratization of politics in Mexico. Beard (2001) traces similar alliances in the Caribbean.

Evaluating Policies in Support of Democracy

Having identified the range of pro-democracy actors, and the different strategies that are undertaken in support of democracy, we are now in a position to evaluate their effectiveness. There are good reasons to be sceptical of their impact. Pro-democracy programmes have been carried out in Latin America, Africa, post-Communist countries and in parts of Asia. The amount of money spent, and the number of programmes and missions carried out, seem to bear no direct relationship with the success or failure of democratization experiments. This is essentially because democracy, if it is to be stable, enduring and substantive, needs to count on significant support across a range of internal elites and civil society actors and to be embedded within an enabling and relatively efficient state. External support, however generous, cannot provide this domestic setting, if it is lacking.

Carothers (1991, 1994) suggests a further reason why democratic promotion policies have only a limited impact. On the basis of extensive research on the NED, he argues that their approach is methodologically flawed and fails to think through *how* democracy is supposed to result from external programmes. Underlying the NED, he suggests, is a belief that spending a modest amount of money can bring about dramatic political changes in a short space of time. In addition, he suggests that the NED is forced constantly to justify its existence to Washington policy-makers, with the result that it tends to talk up its activities, 'concentrate its efforts on countries that are "hot" in US policy terms rather than those that are fertile ground for democracy and emphasize high-profile events with strong VIP participation rather than true development achievements' (Carothers 1991: 235). This kind of behaviour is not exclusive to the NED; it is typical of pro-democracy programmes generally, partly because of the absence of any effective way of testing effectiveness and institutions' need to blow their own trumpet in order to assure themselves of further funding. Furthermore, many external organizations do not sufficiently understand and connect with social and economic issues to work efficiently. The NED operates from the assumption that democratization is a matter of relatively straightforward institutional reform, rather than a complex process of transformation requiring socio-economic change, cultural shifts and a redistribution of power. This skews the programmes that it funds, a problem shared by the pro-democracy policies undertaken by most Western states.

If policies that aim to positively support democracy are limited in their success, what of policies of conditionality? In countries suffering extreme dependence on the West, external actors have seized the chance to determine, almost by force, the norms that condition the democratization experiment. Indeed, they are often responsible for the introduction of a discourse of democratization in the first place. Governance institutions, backed up by Western states, have played a particularly significant role in democratization in sub-Saharan Africa. Far from guaranteeing success, the dominance of Western donors has meant simply the imposition of models of democracy that are imitative of the form, but which enjoy none of the underpinnings, of democracy in the West, namely an efficient and relatively open state, strategies of economic distribution and development or class structure that limits the power of economic elites and strengthens civil society. It is hard to escape the conclusion that policies of conditionality are really exercises in power politics, in which the West 'teaches' developing countries, frequently against their will, how they should organize their domestic political sphere. It should not be surprising, therefore, that the results are poor.

For Whitehead (1996), only democratization by consent can generate genuine democratization. Where democratization has strong domestic foundations, pro-democracy policies from outside can serve to assist and deepen democracy. But it is unrealistic to expect either conscious pro-democracy policies or even the 'triumph of democracy' at the discursive level to transform what, in many cases, are centuries-old, deeply embedded authoritarian practices. Pro-democratic programmes cannot produce rapid and major transformations in the short term:

> Problems ... such as political violence , the weak rule of law, and the absence of real democratic norms are problems that go to the core of [some] societies. They represent deep-seated economic and social structures, long-standing political habits, and fundamental cultural patterns. The notion that some modest amount of training seminars,

exchange programs and technical assistance can solve these problems has no logical foundation. (Carothers 1991: 218)

Strategies of democratization through citizenship networks are, in a sense, policies of consent. They bring together non-state actors and NGOs from inside or outside developing countries in voluntary collaboration. Can this strategy result in more stable or substantive processes of democratization? In the long run, the answer may be yes. Social action over time may change the shape and the function of the global political economy, as transnational activism aims to do. But this is unlikely to be achieved in a short time-frame. Furthermore, the efficacy of transnational networks and the future of the global political economy are dependent on so many factors that it is impossible to say with any certainty what the results of transnational activism will be. Participating in transformative transnational networks is a leap of faith that the world could, and should, be different. It is important as a strategy of resistance to globalization from above, but there are no guarantees as to what it will deliver.

The second strand of the NGO repertoire, as it were, is the more mundane set of policies of democratic promotion through encouraging civil society organizations and bottom-up development in democratizing countries (Robinson 1995). But, even here, although the NGOs are supportive of democratizations that 'make sense' to local people, we should be cautious about results. It is unlikely that small incremental improvements at the local level will, on their own, achieve a democratization of the state. They could even generate new sets of problems. Social demands might outstrip state capacity to deliver, for example, leading to disillusionment with democracy's capacity to 'get things done'. Ndegwa (1996) suggests, furthermore, that as local NGOs become more enmeshed in transnational networking and more dependent upon foreign funding, they become less responsive to the development needs of their own societies. They run the risk of being stripped of their links with local societies. NGO pro-democratic assistance programmes also need to be assessed with caution. Their successes are small-scale and incremental. They have a role in supporting initiatives, in demonstrating international solidarity and in indicating the deep desire of a number of social actors in the developed world for a better and more just global order – and their willingness to work to construct it. But their importance lies ultimately in making the point that building democracy requires social, institutional and international changes; they are not themselves a solution to these problems.

Why then, if democratic promotion is such a flawed enterprise, has the West taken it so seriously? Carothers argues that the fashion for pro-democracy programmes is the result of Western, especially US, naiveté:

Americans tend to view democracy as a natural political state; non-democratic systems are an aberration from the norm. This view of democracy leads to the view that political development (defined by the Americans as progress toward US-style democracy) is a relatively easy process ... The implicit assumption is that democracy should naturally succeed and that success is just a question of making the right adjustments. (Carothers 1991: 220)

Even European actors, which have rarely demonstrated quite the degree of naiveté Carothers talks of, were over-optimistic in the 1990s about how far democracies can be created from outside. Just as important, though, are the geopolitical, economic and security considerations that lie behind the penchant for pro-democracy policies. Once democratization became part of the global agenda of change, it was caught up and shaped by the uneven processes of global development. The West and the agencies of global capitalism are as much engaged now as in the past in developing political and economic strategies that assure their domination and limit independence elsewhere. However, strategies of containment and control have been replaced by those of hegemony and consent.

Conclusion

The role played by globalization, the global order and reflexive global actors in democratization went from being ignored in the 1970s to being grossly exaggerated in the 1990s. This chapter has argued that it does not make sense to expect change that is engineered from outside to be lasting or profound. It is likely that external intervention on behalf of democracy will fail where there is negligible commitment to it by domestic groups. Moreover, external assistance will play only a supporting role in cases where democratization springs from domestically generated social pressures.

More influential, then, in shaping the project of global democratization, are the pressures generated by the global political economy, leading to the emergence of new patterns of dependence, marginality and exclusion. Along with the creation of a global communications network, these guarantee the diffusion of a stylized image of democracy, alongside the

penetration of capitalism, the creation of new marke
tionships and the establishment of new modes of co
than anything else, the emergence of a global poli
responsible for the prevalence of democracy as a disc
because it is able to penetrate dependent societies and
talities and aspirations. So far, the attempt by transnati
networks to decouple democracy from capitalism, corpor ..uns and consumption, and relocate it within discourses of autonomy and citizenship, have had rather less sustained impact in shaping the meaning of
democracy.

But the pressures generated by the global political economy are, at
best, ambiguously pro-democratic. On the one hand, they account for the
diffusion of the ideal and the belief that democracy represents the only
legitimate version of the 'good society'. But on the other, globalization
reproduces and intensifies patterns of inequality and reduces the autonomy of peripheral and developing states, making substantive democracies difficult to build. At the same time, defining what constitutes
democracy is in the hands of Western governments, institutions and
agencies who recommend technical recipes for democracy-building,
divorced from the social reality where they are to be applied. The result
is that, ultimately, the dominant project for democratization is simultaneously a project of Westernization.

Democratization in Southern Europe

In 1974, the long dictatorship in Portugal came to an end and the rule of the Colonels in Greece gave way to the re-establishment of a liberal regime. In 1975, General Franco died and the Spanish people, tentatively, and self-consciously, embarked on a project of democratization. Together these experiments are frequently referred to as the democratization of Southern Europe. Huntington (1991) is certainly correct that the Southern European transitions, especially that of Spain, were of global significance. But there was no sense, at the time at least, that by bringing an end to dictatorships and embarking on projects of political change, Southern Europeans were making anything other than national histories.

The Southern Europe transitions have since became paradigmatic both for theory-building and for shaping normative views of how later democratizations 'should' develop. It is not hard to see why. The democratizations in Southern Europe are undoubtedly the most successful of contemporary experiments. By the end of the 1980s, democracy was secure, though not without its problems. It is sometimes easy to forget now that this success was by no means assured and was, for many years, a matter of some considerable doubt. The intention of this chapter is to analyze events in Portugal, Greece and Spain and to explain the particular models of democracy that have emerged. Democratization has been most successful in Spain, due, it is argued, to a combination of a relatively successful and capable state and a very dynamic civil society, especially before and during the transition. Moreover, democratization in all three countries was aided by a very supportive external environment.

Portugal: Democratization or a Revolution Contained?

Portuguese democracy emerged not only from the collapse of authoritarianism but, just as importantly, from a failed revolution. It therefore differs substantially from the gradualist and reformist road, which has come to be seen as the modal path of transition in the region, that characterized Greek and Spanish democratizations. In contrast to the Spanish experience especially, democratization in Portugal proceeded in a series of bumpy and ambiguous spurts, and key elites have shown a less than wholehearted acceptance of liberalism.

In 1926 the Portuguese military came to power, putting an end to a corrupt, restricted parliamentary regime (Gallagher 1983). By 1929, Antonio Salazar, initially as Minister of Finance, had established himself as the key figure in the new regime. The new regime evolved towards a system of dictatorship that relied for its survival on civilian domination, peasant support and an active security force. Salazar oversaw the introduction of a corporativist Catholic constitution in 1933 and the creation of the *Estado Novo*, frequently described as the Portuguese variant of fascism. According to Maxwell (1995: 16–17), the Salazar regime

> had at its core a condominium of conservative and quasi-fascist intel-
> lectuals, a brutal political police and a handful of large monopolistic
> family concerns. In the country at large, the regime sought support
> from the church, the small rural peasantry of the north, the large
> landowners of the south and petty functionaries who dominated the
> bureaucracy.

The regime tried to freeze development in the country in a mould which allowed for the reproduction of the social and cultural dominance of Catholicism and the economic hegemony of the oligarchy. And indeed, for many years, it was able to prevent social and economic change. Interestingly, the dictatorship was not solely dependent upon Salazar himself, as became evident towards the end. The ageing dictator fell into a coma in 1968 from which he never recovered. He died in 1970, the powers of government having been in the hands of Marcelo Caetano since his illness. Caetano remained in office until 1974 when he was overthrown by a revolutionary movement led by General Spinola, supported by the Armed Forces Movement (MLA). The 'Revolution of the Flowers', so-called because the officers who took to the streets in support of the revolution filled their rifles with carnations in a symbolic gesture of reconciliation with society, marks the start of Portuguese democratization.

The revolution was a rejection not only of dictatorship but also of empire. Until 1974, Portugal had retained an empire stretching over Guinea, Mozambique and Angola. The country's small elite was bitterly divided over how to deal with its slow collapse. General Spinola became a national figure following his open criticism of Caetano's decision to resist decolonization in Africa. Commander-in-Chief of the Armed Forces in Guinea, Spinola not only saw that defeat would be inevitable but argued that compromise with the guerrilla leadership could result in a continued role for Portugal in the area. Thus the immediate detonator for the opening of the transition was neither regime collapse nor irresistible popular democratic demands. Democratization followed from state crisis. The Portuguese state was too poor to maintain the empire and many within the state refused to accept that withdrawal was the only realistic option. Portugal, a late arrival at industrial capitalism, was, moreover, also suffering from the social and economic consequences of uneven development.

The difficulties of maintaining the empire led to widespread dissatisfaction within the Army. Eventually a movement of disaffected junior and middle-ranking officers was formed. The MLA, as it came to be known, was initially moderate, and aimed to channel grievances relating to pay, conditions and status. But it quite quickly radicalized. Influenced by anti-imperialism, a sympathy for national liberation movements which characterized centre-left politics in Europe in the early 1970s, and a belief that the Armed Forces could be a vanguard of national development, the MLA moved to the left during the African wars. A number of MLA officers thus sought not only to disengage from empire but wanted to establish a Portuguese-speaking Socialist bloc, provided that 'our brothers in Guinea, Mozambique and Angola accept, desire and demand it' (Maxwell 1995: 98).

The character of the revolution, then, was determined by the fact that opposition to the authoritarianism regime came mainly from within the state, from the Armed Forces, rather than civil society. The weakness of civil society and the belief within the Army that it had a mission to modernize the country, together, were to have a significant impact on the politics of transition. However, the fact that the Army could not speak with one voice – there was no underlying agreement about how Portugal should modernize – led to a deep confusion in the new government following its seizure of power. General Spinola was the head of the movement in 1974 by virtue of his anti-colonial stand and his reputation. But he had no real political affiliation and he was far more conservatively minded than the members of the MLA, the organization on which the revolution rested. The MLA was able to shape the orientation of the new regime, with the result that it adopted a pro-socialist stance. But a vague sympathy for socialism and a genuine desire to decolonize did not make for a workable programme for government,as it quickly became clear. The government found that it was quite difficult to actually do anything, especially because of the weakness and inefficiency of the state – which had, in fact, accounted for the ease with which the officers took power. Furthermore, cooperation with the old, displaced elite was simply not possible, making the task of governing even more difficult.

Nevertheless, Spinola initially held the government together through personal prestige. Moreover, the revolution was strengthened by the popular euphoria with which it had been met. While some of the support was rather unorganized and inchoate, the Communist Party, which had a strong base and organizational presence and quickly emerged as the most powerful force after the MLA, offered support to the revolution. The Socialist Party, by contrast, although it certainly supported the revolution, was weak and had been manufactured into existence barely a year earlier, with help from the West German Social Democratic Party which was, for reasons discussed below, particularly active in Southern Europe in the early 1970s.

The new government promised constituent elections within a year of taking office in April 1974. Electioneering began, and parties began to emerge. Spinola threw his weight behind the new parties of the centre-right, the Popular Democratic Party (PPD) and the Centre Democratic Party (CDS) which he hoped would have sufficient force after the elections to restrain the MLA in the constituent assembly. Nevertheless, Spinola also brought the Communists, the most organized political force in the country, into government as a way of pre-empting opposition and with the aim of curbing the labour movement. Together with the MLA, the Communists represented a force for deepening the revolution rather than moderating it, as Spinola sought to do. As a result, the government was riven with ideological in-fighting. Spinola was forced to resign in September 1974 after a show of strength from the left. He was replaced by fellow moderate, General Costa Gomes, but the left continued to gain the upper hand. When Spinola attempted a come-back in 1975, he was forced into exile in Spain and a new round of resignations from the centre-right followed. After this the government shifted considerably leftwards. Banks were nationalized and the expropriation of the large landed estates was promised.

These measures were popular and the MLA appeared strong. But in fact the movement was disintegrating internally because of a lack of agreement between members. As a result, the government was rapidly becoming leaderless. By the end of 1975, it was on the point of collapse. For Maxwell (1986), the rapid disintegration of the revolutionary government was the result of fundamental ideological division within the

MLA, which was exacerbated by the process of decolonization, the worsening economic situation which gave outsiders leverage over politics, and the displacement of the Communists by the Socialists as the most popular party. The trend from Communism to Socialism had been clear from the time of the constituent elections of April 1975. Mario Soares's Socialists became the largest party in the new Constituent Assembly, with 37.9 per cent of the vote in comparison with the Communists' 12.5 per cent. Meanwhile, external actors, convinced that this was a vote for democracy over revolution, seized their chance to turn Portugal into a Cold War *cause célèbre*. Western European powers and the US, all of which had been taken by surprise by events in Portugal in 1974, were alarmed at the radicalism of the MLA and the presence of the Communists in government. They poured assistance into the Socialist Party in the hope of derailing the revolution. After the constituent elections, they argued that the moderate Socialist victory should prevent the government moving any further to the left.

But the Communists and a section of the MLA continued to insist that the revolution was still viable. Unwilling to accept that a liberal democracy might result from the constituent process, they pushed radical policies through. But by now, some of the MLA were opting for the rising Socialist Party. Thus 1975 was marked by intense crisis, as the fate of Portugal was caught between internal disorientation and Cold War politics. The US Secretary of State, Henry Kissinger, who had played an important role in defeating the left in Chile only two years earlier, was determined to prevent the Communists from establishing a revolutionary framework for government in a country that was not only located in the heartland of Europe but was also geopolitically central to Western defence. Although it was not clear what could be done from the outside, an atmosphere of external threat hung over Portugal.

As these tensions were being played out, and amid popular demonstrations, strikes and violence, the Constituent Assembly, dominated by the Socialists, wrote the new constitution. The Constitution of 1976 came down in favour of liberal democracy and the ad-hoc revolutionary bodies created by the revolution disappeared. Nevertheless, there were important left-overs from the revolution period, many of which were at odds with the trend towards liberal democracy. First, the Constitution was not submitted to a popular referendum, indicating a strong a belief in the authority of the state and a lack of faith or even respect for popular sovereignty. And second, the Constitution proclaimed many of the radical measures of 1975, such as the bank nationalizations, to be legal and binding. As a result, Gallagher (1989: 14) describes the Constitution as a 'stalemate'. Moreover, the bitterness of the revolutionary period had a very negative effect for post-1976 politics. The transition had not been able to produce a shared view of what democracy should be. Liberal democracy was certainly not embedded within society in this period and faith in the new order was not great. Nor did the Constitution provide the opportunity for reconciliation between the opposing bands. Indeed, divisions within the political elite, especially on the left, deepened between 1974 and 1976, as the Socialists and Communists found themselves on opposing sides of the political debate.

The first democratic general elections were held in 1976 and were won by the Socialists. In government for two years, the Socialists did little to challenge either the cultural deference which characterized Portuguese social life or to remedy the worst effects of uneven development for the Portuguese working class or peasantry, the party's own electorate. Always a minority government, Socialist Soares was removed as Prime Minister in 1978, amidst parliamentary opposition and a collapsing economy. Three different short-lived governments followed. Elections in 1979 and 1980 led to the victory of a centre-right alliance. This was then the victim of the instability and fluidity of the new party system. Parties were enclosed within a world of elite politics, separated from the mass of the electorate by a system of social privilege. The new system had done nothing to address the underlying problems of elitism or to strengthen the social bases of democracy. In other words, Portugal suffered from its lack of democratic tradition and the new democracy was unable to create opportunities for broader participation or deeper citizenship. At the same time, even though the attempted revolution had failed, it had garnered sufficient support to split the political class. This meant that stable elite-led democracy was also difficult to achieve. Democracy was stunted. It was, according to Maxwell (1986: 135), only a 'truce', papering over real political divisions rather than signifying either consensus or social democratic reformism.

Democratization in Spain

General Franco, who had come to power in 1939 following a three-year civil war, died after a long illness in November 1975. But demands for change had been building up in Spain long before then. The Francoist state, built to enshrine the victory of the Nationalists following the defeat of the Republic, was in deep crisis from the 1960s. Following years of severe hardship and repression, the state had engineered successful economic development that brought prosperity to some parts of the country and created a growing and more vocal middle class, especially in cities such as Madrid and Barcelona. But political liberalization had been slow, tentative and unconvincing. By the early 1970s, growing social pressure, from regional nationalists, students, trade unionists, ordinary people and even the Catholic Church, made the task of government almost impossible. Meanwhile, the rest of Europe – which the Francoist technocratic elite wished desperately to join for reasons of economic growth and markets – looked on uneasily as violence and repression increased in the last years of the dictatorship. A generalized crisis, then, was palpable inside the dictatorship before Franco died (Grugel and Rees 1997).

The crisis of governance in the 1960s and early 1970s was responsible for important bureaucratic and political change inside Francoism itself, some of which was eventually to bring sectors of the right into cooperation with the opposition following Franco's death. For these people, cooperating in the establishment of a democratic state after 1975 was, initially at least, less the sign of an ideological commitment to democracy and more a reflection of their need for order. That they accepted, however reluctantly, the inevitability of democracy was nonetheless an important indication that the right, at long last, had been 'civilized', that it would accept the democratic compromise (Areilza 1983: 119). This transformation of the Spanish right was enormously important. It meant that it was possible for the first time for the Spanish people as a whole to view the civil war as a national tragedy, a repeat of which was to be avoided at all costs, rather than a glorious campaign, the image Francoists had clung onto for so long.

Consequently, underpinning and sustaining the Spanish transition was a slow and painful process of national reconciliation. Tentatively at first, but gradually with greater confidence as the transition progressed, people began to speak out about how a future of tolerance and an end to fear mattered far more than 'winning' or being proven 'right'. This process can be documented through the press, and the cultural production of the time. It is echoed in the statements of the political class and the elites. Thus, democracy became the conscious theme of the transition, 'the new civil religion' (Desfor Edles 1998: 51). It was this conviction that ultimately allowed for the construction of democracy in Spain, especially since the conflicts which had led to the civil war – the challenge of regionalism, the ambiguous role of the Army in politics and intense social and class conflict – had by no means disappeared.

Cultural transformation was not divorced from social and political change. It was, furthermore, strengthened by how the transition itself unfolded. After the death of Franco, a short-lived and ineffectual government led by Arias Navarro gave way to the leadership of Adolfo Suarez, a moderate ex-Francoist and, for many, the architect of the new Spain in conjunction with the King himself . Suarez was the victor in the first democratic elections of June 1977 with a hastily formed party, the Union of the Democratic Centre (UCD), leading to the first democratically elected parliament since the 1930s. He rapidly made clear his intention of working with the opposition in the creation of a new democratic framework for politics, marginalizing the groups within the state who sought continuity. At the same time, since the process of constitutional change would be determined by a government which had emerged from the institutions of the dictatorship – the state bureaucracy, through the medium of the King – the path to democracy was also marked out as a gradualist and inclusionary one (meaning the inclusion of the right and the Francoist establishment) rather than one that signified a complete break with the past (Share 1986).

For Maravall (1982), after 1977 democratization became largely 'the task of the political class'. Elites focused on the task of writing the new constitution. This was the work of representatives from seven political parties, including the left (Socialist and Communist), the right (Popular Alliance) and the Catalan Nationalists ,as well as the governing party, the UCD. The discussions leading up to the Constitution were kept secret, partly due to a fear of antagonizing the Army and the ultra-right. The period 1977–8 was also one of significant demobilization, partly because of the threat of reprisals from the extreme right. Popular pressure never quite disappeared, however, and it re-emerged strongly after 1979 in defence of the nascent democratic order.

The new constitution was approved by the Cortes (the parliament) in October 1977. It laid the groundwork for regional autonomy and made reference to the different 'nationalities' contained within the state, and, as such, was a major concession from a previously highly centralized state. The Constitution was ratified by popular referendum, with 89.7 per cent of the Spanish people voting in favour, a resounding vote for a democratic future. Ominously, however, in the Basque Country, over 50 per cent of the population abstained and only 30.86 per cent voted in favour. Separatist regionalism, one of the causes of the civil war in the 1930s, clearly was not about to evaporate with the onset of democratization. The question was, rather, whether the nationalists would adapt to the new democracy. Furthermore, there were still doubts as to how far the Army and the ultra-right, all of whom opposed any concessions to regional nationalism, could be trusted to act within the law.

The transition (1977–82) was a period of concentration on the framework for formal democracy and the new institutions that would guide and govern the state. Less attention was paid to social and economic reform. Indeed, the transitional government of Suarez created a kind of corporatist pact with the labour unions in an attempt to put social and economic demands from below on hold. The Moncloa Pacts, as they were known, were the result of tripartite negotiations in the autumn of 1977 between the government, the opposition and the unions. The unions agreed to accept wage rises below the rate of inflation so as not to undermine the fragile political system, in return for a promised comprehensive reform package after the political transition was complete. They seized on the chance to show how 'responsible' they were. In effect, the contribution of the labour movement to slowing down the pace of social demands in the face of considerable violence and opposition from diehard authoritarians was immensely important. But the Pacts also had a negative effect on Spanish democracy, by sealing off elite negotiations and politics from social pressure and making sectoral demands from below look 'undemocratic'.

So the transition remained fragile, even after the new Constitution was approved. After 1979, violence increased as the 'ultras', the right-wingers who opposed democratization and who remained committed to Francoism as a grand Catholic nationalist crusade, and the Basque separatists stepped up their activities. The Suarez government ran out of steam, amidst its failure to control either the ultra-right or the nationalists and its inability to cope with a deteriorating economy. Suarez won the elections of 1979 but was able to form only a minority government. Spain then entered a period of crisis not completely dissimilar from that of Portugal. The Spanish Socialist Party, now the main party of opposition, sought to distance itself from the government for electoral advantage, only to weaken the minority government still more. The Moncloa Pacts were abandoned in December 1978. Meanwhile the government tried to implement the regional autonomy programme with little political support from other parties and with opposition from the Basque nationalists. The process was made more difficult by the rising tide of violence, as the Basque terrorist group ETA sought to force the government into further concessions. Alarmingly, rightists groups also embarked on campaigns of terror and violence. As a result, 123 people were killed in 1979 through acts of terrorism.

The government's evident inability to control events and the collapse of consensus paved the way for the military's attempted return. In February 1981, a coup attempt took place. The parliament was taken hostage by a unit of the civil guard and army units mobilized in Brunete, just outside Madrid, and seized Valencia. It was the coup attempt more than anything that pulled Spanish democracy back from the brink of collapse. The decisive intervention of the King, who insisted that he would prefer exile to the collapse of democracy, the sudden unity of the political class around the new institutions, and, overwhelmingly, the eruption of mass public demonstrations in favour of democracy brought it to an end. But the problems the coup attempt highlighted were solved rather more gradually.

Between 1981 and 1982, when the next general elections were due, politics in parliament was cautious and cooperative. When the Socialists were elected into office in October 1982, one of their main tasks was the reform of the Armed Forces (Heywood 1995: 62–6). These reforms have on the whole been successful but plots to overthrow democracy surfaced as late as 1985. It is not so much that the Army is 'democratic' now – surveys usually indicate high levels of nostalgia for the 'good old days' of Franco. But the threat is institutionally contained. The military is socially, and now even numerically, weak.

The story of the Spanish transition is therefore one of slow and gradual change, with high points of tension and conflict. Democracy was not an inevitable outcome in 1975, 1977 or even 1979, despite a social structure, a geopolitical environment and cultural context all of which were favourable to democracy. But at some point in the early 1980s, a reversal to authoritarianism became difficult to imagine. The transformation of the right was particularly important for stabilizing the Spanish system. At the time of the transition, the right was electorally weak and culturally insignificant. That it accepted the new Constitution, including reform of education, Church–state relations and devolution, was less a sign of its conversion to democracy than an indication of the juggernaut of irresistible change. But over time the right also accepted that the constitutional settlement could not be undone and gradually came to accept full participation in democracy. Nevertheless, it only fully made its peace with democracy in the 1990s. Despite this success, however, other problems – of inclusion, of the state and of separatist regionalism – remain as yet unsolved.

Democracy Returns to Athens: The Greek Transition

The transition to democracy in Greece which began in 1974 brought to an end a much shorter dictatorship than either Portugal or Spain had suffered. The 'Colonels', led by George Papadopoulos, came to power in 1967. The Colonels had by no means replaced a fully functioning democracy, however. Greek politics had been unstable both before the Second World War and, more unusually for a European country, after it. Before 1945, class conflict, significant underdevelopment, military defeat and a fear of revolution all combined to make the Greek bourgeoisie suspicious of too much liberalism. The political system excluded the rural and urban working class while satisfying elite demands for economic privilege in an under-productive economy. The monarchy was restored – having been abolished in 1923 – and threw its weight behind the anti-Communist state which emerged in Greece before the Second World War (Diamandouros 1986: 142).

Following the Axis occupation and the Second World War, there was a civil war (1946–9), which pitted the left against a right-wing determined to keep exclusive control of the state. In this, it was aided by Western powers who needed to shore up Greece against a perceived Communist expansion in the Balkans. For Diamandouros (1986: 142), after 1949, 'anti-Communism was transformed from a mere instrument of state legitimization to the governing principle of an aggressive strategy of social demobilization and of social control designed to safeguard the closed nature of the Greek political system, to reinforce it and above all to ensure its perpetuation'.

The civil war led to the brutal suppression of the left. Some years after, a liberal Constitution was passed but was never fully implemented. Thus the return to conservative civil rule in the 1950s fell far short even of formal democracy since the political rights of a large number of Greek people remained curtailed. At the same time, the military played an important role in politics, ostensibly because of 'national security' problems. In this politically restricted and controlled arena, the right was under little pressure to modernize or to democratize. But it was also unable, ultimately, to prevent a resurgence of a range of leftist movements. This was aided by the economic growth experienced in Greece in the 1950s. Greek politics in the 1950s thus suffered a triple crisis: the liberal institutions had little internal legitimacy because of popular exclusion; the Army was in theory and in practice the guarantor of the parliamentary regime; and the weak and emerging left was, as a result of the above, cast in opposition to the regime. The liberal state was almost completely hollow (Mouzelis 1978). The right lost the general elections of 1963. This defeat was confirmed a year later. But the new centrist government that replaced it was weak. In the political vacuum, and with the backing of the right, the Colonels came to power in 1967 with a mission to restore order. The coup could only win at best an ambiguous response from Greece's international allies in NATO, committed as they were to maintaining at least the formal institutions of democracy. At the same time, the military intervention was able to unify the centre-left opposition, in a way that had been impossible before. Thus, paradoxically, the coup, which was carried out to prevent a resurgence of the left, brought about its revival and temporary unification. Further problems ensued when the military regime attempted to distance itself from the conservative elite and rule more autonomously. The monarchy left Greece, in protest at the military's republican tendencies.

In the absence of firm social support, the military turned, disastrously, to the cult of the nation in the hope of sparking a nationalist revival and uniting the country behind the regime. The military hardliners that took control of government after 1973 embarked on a bid for external grandeur by becoming involved in adventurism abroad. Cyprus, which contains both Greek and Turk populations and which Greece had long tried to assert some control over, became the focus of their attention. An adventure in Cyprus seemed to offer the government the chance to play the nationalist card. Presenting itself as a government committed to the protection of Greeks living abroad and to Christian values, the Greek government supported a coup attempt in July 1974 against the democratically elected government of Cyprus, led by Archbishop Makarios. The Cypriot crisis led rapidly to the collapse of the regime.

For Linz and Stepan (1996: 130), although the immediate factor behind the ending of the dictatorship was military adventurism, the crisis of the Greek authoritarian regime was institutional: its power base inside the state, indeed even within the Armed Forces, was always weak. Opposition to the regime should not be discounted either as a factor pushing the regime towards disintegration, for it never quite went away. And, although Linz and Stepan are undoubtedly correct to emphasize the failure to institutionalize the dictatorship, it is important to see why this proved impossible. Ultimately, in the Europe of the 1960s and 1970s, authoritarianism could find no place. The environmental dimension was therefore central to undermining the regime. The Colonels could never achieve international legitimation: history had simply moved on.

Nevertheless, as in the Portuguese transition, the final demise of authoritarianism was precipitated by the regime's inability to handle an external crisis. It was caught between its own nationalist rhetoric and its weak military capability. For the Greek army, the Cyprus problem played a similar role to the African decolonization in Portugual. The Colonels first tried to remove the elected government of Cyprus, and then intervened, with the pretext of protecting the Greek population, following the Turkish invasion of Cyprus. Only days after the invasion, they were deposed. Civil society and civilian elites actively supported the coup and the military were so soundly defeated that they were unable to impose conditions on their exit.

The conservative focus of the civilian restoration was quickly made clear, as the conservative politician Constantine Karamanlis, who had dominated politics before 1967, was brought back from exile. To an extent, the events of 1974 represented an attempt at a rightist restoration of 'politics as normal', a return to the conservative-dominated anti-left liberalism of the years before 1967. But Karamanlis's strategy for post-1974 politics also contained some new elements which presaged a move towards national reconciliation.

The transition to formal democracy – the establishment of the new institutional framework – was remarkably rapid, far quicker than in either Portugal or Spain. This was because the political elite proved far more autonomous during the transition in Greece than in either Portugal or Spain. In November 1974, the first democratic elections were held, which the conservatives, led by Karamanlis, won. Popular and student opposition to the military, initially so powerful in July when the military fell, weakened as the threat of war over Cyprus came to dominate the agenda. Karamanlis's policy of judicious, but limited, concessions to the left proved successful and the separation of the conservatives from the military had, apparently, pushed them belatedly towards adopting a more inclusionary form of liberalism than in the past. He accepted that parliamentary government had to be built around the inclusion of leftist parties. The Communist Party was legalized. Karamanlis delayed trials of the military, but accepted that they ultimately take place. He emerged, in sum, as a powerful figure, offering to oversee, at least to some degree, a real reform of the political class. Testimony to this was the decision to hold a referendum on the future of the monarchy, tainted with perhaps the most anti-democratic past of all the European royal families. In December 1974, nearly 70 per cent of the people voted for a republic.

In October 1981 the Socialists won the general elections, signifying that alternation in government and the peaceful handing over of power to the left was possible. The biggest problem for democracy, however, is the separation of the political class from society at large. The new system broadened political society by opening it up to the left. But it remains unresponsive to pressure from below. PASOK, the Greek Socialist Party, is in reality a populist rather than a social democratic party and reproduces traditional forms of personalism and cooptation as organizational principles (Lyrintzis 1989). Ties between parties and civil society are weak. The Socialists present themselves as the party of the people, not by including the people amongst its ranks, but rather by the advocation of paternalistic welfare policies. The lavish personal spending and corruption that accompanied the Socialist government of Papandreu in the 1980s were clear proof of the insulation of the political elite from society. Also, the operation of the state is such that it ensures the retention of privilege and protects the commercial, industrial and state-dependent bourgeoisie. Consequently, the state remains a formidable obstacle to deepening democracy.

Theorizing the Transitions

Democratization in Southern Europe has been theorized in a number of ways. Giner (1986) advocates a political economy focus on transition in Southern Europe. This allows him to identify a common pattern and a common explanation applicable to all three cases. He argues that they are the outcome of a shared pattern of development: history moves in stages from oligarchic control to bourgeois domination, fascist dictatorship to constitutional order. Similarly Sole Tura (1988) argues that Southern Europe constitutes a distinct area of Europe with its own political traditions and developmental rhythm. These arguments depend on more than the fact that all three transitions, Portugal, Greece and Spain, began within a few years of each other. They emphasize the regional pattern of capitalist development and the key role played by all three states in encouraging and shaping the development process. In other words, Sole Tura adopts a structuralist explanation which ultimately puts the state at the centre of his analysis. A statist focus provides one way of explaining why the transitions began at roughly the same time.

In contrast, a majority of scholars have emphasized agency (that is, the agency of elites) and contingent choice in the period following regime collapse (Share 1986; Preston 1986). Others have analyzed the democratizing activities of social organizations (Fowraker 1989; Fishman 1990; Tarrow 1995; Blakeley 2000). Desfor Edles (1998) has produced a culturalist analysis of the Spanish transition which prioritizes mass and elite cultural transformation, leading to a genuinely new way of understanding national history. Other more partial studies of aspects of democratization in Greece have emphasized the importance of cultural transformations over time in explaining how democracy takes root. These studies all stress that transitions were not inevitable but were, instead, the result of conscious and unconscious actions by individuals and organizations.

All these interpretations have something important to offer to our understanding of the process of regime change in Southern Europe. Rather than privileging one level of analysis (national or global) or one actor (elite or popular movements), we will now try to identify the different factors that have contributed to democracy in Spain, Portugal and Greece, concentrating on the role of the state, civil society and the global order.

The State

The State as Actor in Democratization

The weakness of industrialization in Southern Europe meant that state intervention was necessary for the expansion of industrial capitalism. Civil society, especially in the form of an independent-minded bourgeoisie, was poorly developed across the region, until the 1960s at least. As a result, the state was relatively strong, with significant infrastructural capacity. Late development gave rise to the idea that Southern Europe is a 'semi-periphery' of the capitalist world, subordinated to global capitalist centres through trade and investment, and with politics shaped, at least in part, by the exigencies of maintaining a capitalist order. The state was strong vis-à-vis its own civil society but weak in relation to external actors, especially capitalist powers or transnational companies (Giner 1986). It was assumed, then, that the absence of democracy was functional for capitalism in the region.

The semi-peripheral state in Southern Europe was not autonomous or independent of all social groups. In all three cases, the state historically enjoyed close relations with the upper classes. In Greece, for example, a set of oligarchic families (the *tzakia*) more or less controlled the state until the military coup of 1967. In fact, the difficulties of legitimizing the 1967 intervention was partly due to the fact that it disrupted the traditional patterns of upper-class access to the state, leaving the Colonels without a firm base of support in society. In Portugal, the interests of the large landowners and the small commercial and industrial bourgeoisie had been protected by the Salazar regime. And in Spain, Franco's close relationship with capital (with the exception of Catalan capitalism) is well documented.

Thus in all three cases, the state itself is important in politics and state actors were significant in the politics of democratization. This was most certainly the case in Spain. The party of the transition, the UCD, and the main political leadership, emerged from within the state bureaucracy. Many members of the Francoist elite or the bureaucracy went on to form right-wing parties in the new democracy. It was true in a different way in Portugal. The 1974 uprising came from within the state itself, from the Armed Forces. The state was an important political base after the collapse of the Caetano regime. It was, in fact, far stronger than any organization from within civil society. This explains why the MLA was able to establish such influence over policy so rapidly. In Greece, the Colonels failed to build on the past or to create a genuinely new framework for state activity. Nevertheless they did not remove the economic or social privileges the upper class enjoyed. Their efforts to build greater state autonomy at the expense of civil society failed. As a result, the state itself was rather less important in the transition, one reason why the transitional period, in the sense of the period between collapse and democratic elections, was short: the civil elite was able to reassert itself extremely quickly and was, fundamentally, unchanged.

The weight of the state was to prove a stabilizing factor in Spanish politics during the initial period of transition. In Portugal this was true to much less a degree. Capturing the state did not really give the MLA any long-term structural advantage. Nor did the Socialists who came to power use the state as an instrument of democratization. Ultimately it proved both weaker and much more an instrument of the upper classes than the 'semi-peripheral' model would suggest. Gladdish (1993:119) points out that the post-transition party structure, while important as instruments for controlling and disputing the state, remains essentially true to the image of 'inter-elite competition'. Bermeo (1978) argues that the Portuguese state was tied throughout the transition to the commercial and industrial bourgeoisie. In the Greek case, the strength of the state was mediated by its loss of control during the transitional phase. Nevertheless, following the first elections, the state once again returned to the centre stage of Greek politics. However, how far the state plays a role in supporting democratization is rather more doubtful: it essentially remains an instrument available to elites to further their own power.

State Institutions and Democratic Change

Transforming the state is at the core of democracy. Certainly Spain, Portugal and Greece have experienced significant state transformation since the onset of democratization. All three have introduced liberal democratic constitutions, regularly hold free and fair elections and have multi-party systems. In all three countries, the parliamentary system introduced during the transition has weathered economic and political crises and remains in place. There is a minimal level of consolidation, at least, throughout the region.

A more important question, however, is the extent to which more profound institutional change has been achieved. In this, the picture is rather more patchy and there are important differences between the three countries. In Spain and Greece, the relationship between socio-economic and political elites and the state – elites continue to view the state as to some extent an instrument for private gain – has proved difficult to change. The Greek Socialists lost power at the end of the 1980s amidst scandals of corruption and maladministration, which indicated just how far the politicians saw themselves as above society at large. Similarly in Spain, the Spanish Socialists lost office in the early 1990s amidst charges of corruption and embezzlement of public money (Heywood 1998). Becoming a politician is still seen as a way to make money – one of its traditional functions in Southern Europe.

Nevertheless, there are also real successes in terms of how state institutions work. In particular, there has been a consistent pattern of rooting the democratic state through welfare reform (Esping-Anderson 1994). Maravall (1995) shows how income disparity decreased significantly in Spain and Portugal as a result of democratization. However, this tendency towards democracy through welfare was far more marked in the early years following transition than it is today. In fact, all three countries experienced a new political economy in the late 1980s that was designed to weaken the direct role of the state in the economy, following the typical path of other European countries in shrinking the state. This has had the effect of weakening the state as a source of income redistribution.

The State as Obstacle to Democratic Consolidation

Of the three countries, only Spain could be said to have a 'stateness problem' (Linz and Stepan 1996) to any significant degree. The unity of the Portuguese state is beyond question and Macedonian nationalism is, as yet, a minor problem in Greece. But in Spain, separatism has proved an intractable problem. While it has not seriously threatened the survival of the Spanish state itself, it has undoubtedly undermined the quality of democracy. The emergence of a federal state as a result of the new constitution did not significantly undermine the legitimacy of the armed Basque Nationalist group, ETA, in the Basque Country. As the nationalist struggles have continued, both ETA and the Spanish security forces have engaged in anti-democratic activities. In 1977, anti-terrorist legislation led to the suspension of a number of detainees' rights, including the right to have a lawyer present during questioning. Furthermore, the police in the Basque provinces, amongst whom anti-Basque feeling is high, have consistently abused their powers of detention. Also, in its efforts to defeat ETA, the Ministry of the Interior undertook a 'dirty war' in the 1980s, killing a number of innocent people in the process. The party in government at the time, the Socialist Party, went to great lengths to keep this secret from the public and the courts, thereby attempting to subvert the judicial process. In sum, the presence of separatist nationalism has pushed the Spanish state towards adopting methods as violent and undemocratic as those of their opponents. Even so, separatist nationalism remains far less contentious an issue than in East and Central Europe.

Democratization and Civil Society

Economic development in the 1950s and 1960s contributed to the strengthening of civil society in the region. Until then, the social and cultural resilience of the upper classes meant that they had enjoyed exclusive access to the state. In the cases of Spain and Portugal, the dominance of the Catholic Church and the links between the Church and the dictatorships also contributed to preventing the development of a strong autonomous civic culture. Democratization presented opportunities for the expansion of civil society organizations across the region. Nevertheless, the strength of the state tradition has tended to limit the effectiveness of civil society organizations. Democratization of political

society (the political parties and the political elite) has been successful
but the state remains suspicious of the powers of civil society.

Popular Mobilization and Democracy

Before the onset of democratization, the upper classes, both the landed
and commercial elites, were excessively privileged. In Portugal and
Spain, the upper classes had directly preferred authoritarian government
as a means to defend their wealth and status. Movement from below was
a force behind democratization, although the scale, nature and effectiveness of popular mobilization varied between the three cases and peaked
and troughed at different moments within the democratization process.

Widespread and sustained popular opposition to the dictatorships surfaced for the first time at the end of the 1960s. This was especially true
in Spain, where opposition had been building up since the early 1960s
and where rural and urban popular movements counted on a history of
organization that pre-dated the Franco regime. Labour protests, student
unrest and, in Spain, opposition from Catalan and Basque nationalists
erupted in a significant way for the first time. This process was less
marked in Portugal than elsewhere in the region due to the fact that,
beyond the Communist Party, there was little tradition of organization
of the part on non-elite groups. Much of Portugal was effectively still
cut off from political life as late as the early 1970s. In Greece, the
Colonels faced intense student protest in the early 1970s. As in Spain,
these protests were fuelled by the fact that the regime was clearly entering its twilight years as well as by the fact that the international trend
appeared to be towards popular activism: students in Spain and Greece
took heart from the wave of student and mass protest that erupted across
Western Europe and the US at this time.

Civil society activism, however, had only a limited impact on the dictatorships, especially in Greece and Portugal. It would be difficult to
attribute the collapse of the Greek dictatorship to popular protest. Nor
were popular organizations able to shape in any significant way the
terms of the transition. Similarly, despite the outpourings of popular
sympathy for the coup in 1974, especially in Lisbon and Oporto, the
dynamic of the revolution was determined by elites from within the
state. Only in Spain was a 'cycle of contention' (Tarrow 1998) established which impacted upon the politics of the transition. Protests from
some community-based groups, regionalist groups, labour organizations, students and, rather more tentatively, women's groups, built up
through the late 1960s and early 1970s, pushing elites towards consen-

sus and closing the option of a continuation of the dictatorship after the demise of Franco himself. One reason for their success lay in the fact that popular organizations, especially in Madrid and Barcelona, could count on traditions of organization which were magnified and mythologized so as to encourage participation. Another was the maturity of the organizations themselves and their adoption of a clear political agenda. Almost all popular organizations by the early 1970s aimed to overthrow the dictatorship and to promote a democratization of politics – though they were not necessarily clear on what precisely that would mean. According to Blakeley (2000: 292):

> the key difference between civil society prior to the Francoist dictatorship and that which had developed by the twilight years of Francoism ... was the reorientation of associations and social movements towards the politico-institutional sphere. Contrary to the 1930s, those active in social movements and associations in the struggle against Francoism were concerned with the form and nature of the state and their relationship with political parties. ... Participation was therefore no longer solely understood in terms of self-organisation within civil society, but was increasingly directed at influencing government activity within the political sphere.

Despite this activism, however, civil society's role in shaping the framework of the new democracy has been rather more limited. After 1977, the political parties took the initiative and the spaces for a more participatory democracy slowly closed down. The labour movement sought institutional incorporation after the transition got under way; regionalist groups tended to fragment and community-based organizations were disorientated by state and party encroachment. As a result, even Spain now has few institutional legacies from this period of intense social activism.

Global Factors

Southern Europe was important to a number of different external actors during the transition period. At the same time, politicians in Spain, Greece and Portugal were all well aware of the constraints imposed by their countries' economic and geopolitical dependence on Western Europe and the US. In general the external dimension was positive for democratization in the region. Nevertheless, partly because these transitions so clearly worked to a domestic logic, and partly because democratization had not become a full-fledged international discourse by the 1970s, the weight of the 'global' over the 'national' was less in Southern Europe than in Latin America, Africa or East and Central Europe.

(Re)joining Europe

The underlying cause of the region's external dependence was the fact that it arrived late to key developments which have structured European politics. Greece, Spain and Portugal were slow to move towards industrial capitalism. Southern European bourgeoisies were also later than their Western European counterparts in learning, or more properly in needing to learn, to adapt to the uncertainty of democracy. For these reasons, Southern European countries came late to regional integration and the European Community (EC). As a result, 'Europe', constituted as a place of development and democracy, played an important role in structuring oppositional ideologies in Spain, Greece and Portugal. By the same token, resisting Europe was important for anti-democratic elites. Thus, for the diehard Francoists as well as for the radical elements of the MLA, refusing to join Europe was a way of resisting liberal democracy. So, accepting that Southern Europe was indeed a part of Europe, in a political and economic sense, was an important step of the democratization process.

Western European influence over events in Southern Europe was considerable because of what Europe represented symbolically. But for this very reason, it is difficult to trace and quantify exactly. Western Europe shaped outcomes in Southern Europe by weight of influence. Certainly, the fact that the EC rejected Spain, Portugal and Greece as members until they had put their house in order, so to speak, had weight inside the Southern European countries. But just as important, if not more so, was the cultural pull of a liberal group of countries so close by. This was enhanced by the fact that in the rest of Europe democracy went hand in hand with higher living standards for almost all of society than those of Southern Europe. Cultural penetration – through films, music, fiction and tourism – all combined to present Southern Europeans with an apparently stark choice: Europe and development or nationalism and decay. Calculating reactions in the rest of Europe to local or national events structured the choices that guided elites involved in the transitions. But equally, for the ordinary people, a sense that being close to Europe made them feel that democracy was their right. Indeed, merely the fact that these countries slowly came to conceptualize themselves as a part of 'Europe' rather than 'Latin' (Spain and Portugal), 'Balkan' (Greece) or just 'different and unique' is indicative of the major cultural change that both prepared the way for democratization and made it possible.

The EC admonished and encouraged Southern Europeans to move towards democracy in a number of tangible ways. Although membership of the EC was vital for their economic development, the Community rejected Portugal, Spain and Greece until democratic changes had been introduced. Moreover, it was made clear that democracy encompassed more than simply elections. In particular, the EC – and especially the European Parliament – emphasized respect for human rights. As a way of binding these countries into the Community without membership and, at the same time, as a sign of encouragement, the Mediterranean agreements were introduced in the 1970s to encourage trade dependency.

The Geopolitical Dimension

Western Europe and the US were all too aware of the immense strategic value that Southern Europe possessed for their security. Together, these countries controlled traffic through the Mediterranean and constituted the West's frontier with Africa and the third world. Such was the importance assigned to the area that the US had pushed a reluctant Western Europe into accepting Francoist Spain as part of the Western Cold War defences in the 1950s. Authoritarian Portugal and barely democratic Greece became part of the formal defence architecture and joined NATO.

The geopolitical dimension of Western support for nascent democracy in the region is most obvious in the Portuguese case. US concern at the events in Portugal in 1974 and 1975 is well documented (Maxwell 1995:104–6). But as Maxwell also points out, the efforts of the US to contain the revolution were constrained by US preoccupation with internal politics at the time as a result of Watergate, and equally by its weak sources of information on Portugal:

> As Cord Meyer, the CIA station chief in London at the time, put it 'When the revolution occurred in Portugal the US was out to lunch; we were completely surprised'. The US Ambassador in Lisbon was … in the Azores visiting the US base there when the coup occurred. Since Lisbon airport was closed he decided to go on to Boston to attend a class reunion at Harvard. (Maxwell 1995: 66)

The result was that action on Portugal was paralyzed due to a lack of will and confusion in Washington.

Nevertheless, the threat of displeasing the West and the fear of what the US *might* do were internalized in Portuguese politics. Dependency on external powers breeds a mentality of fear, leading people to police themselves. In this sense, for many, the idea of breaking with Portugal's tradition of alliance with Anglo-American defence, as the MLA wished to, and allying the country instead with the developing ex-colonial world, could only ever be a pipe-dream, and a dangerous one at that. Ultimately, it was felt, such rashness would provoke intervention.

The role of the US and a concern for keeping Southern Europe safe for the West should not be dismissed even in the Spanish case, where Western powers played a the least obvious role in the transition. It should be noted, for example, that King Juan Carlos made his first unequivocal declaration of support for democracy in a speech to the US Congress. And the US worked hard to persuade the governing Socialist party in the 1980s that membership of NATO would consolidate the transition. Indeed, it was US pressure and the argument that membership of NATO would shore up the transition that finally brought the Socialists around to accepting that membership was inevitable.

International Support for Democratization

Contemporary policies on the part of non-governmental agencies to aid democracy date from the time of the Southern European transitions. They were designed and implemented especially by European political parties who seized their chance to play an international role, to push what were seen as 'European' solutions to problems of social conflict and to ensure a peaceful climate for European development. Thus the political parties were in many ways the architects of the first pro-democracy policies of the third wave. According to Pridham (1993: 16), assistance to parties during transitions has a multi-dimension impact: not only does it strengthen the party that is in receipt of funds, training, know-how, etc., but it also strengthens the party system and helps create a broad-spectrum party system.

European social democratic parties played a considerable role in supporting democracy in Southern Europe from the outside. This was particularly so in Spain and Portugal where the (then West) German Social Democratic Party was especially active. Endowed not only with considerable financial resources but also a clear international mission, the West German Social Democrats set about creating or assisting Spanish and

Portuguese sister parties. Crucially, they also helped form them ideologically, pushing them towards policies of moderation and the abandonment of Marxism. They were remarkably successful in this. Not only did the West Germans help create a party capable of winning elections in Portugal, but that party was also in tune with the need for economic modernization. The Spanish Socialists, meanwhile, abandoned Marxism before taking office and embraced capitalist development enthusiastically once in government. Indeed, the Spanish Socialists were later to take on the mantle of spreading the 'good news' of moderate socialism to Latin America by the 1980s. In this way, Southern European socialists were able to shed their image of being radical anti-capitalist hotheads.

Conclusion

Of the recent democratizations, democracy in Southern Europe is strongest. It is also the region where democracy is most evidently built upon strong domestic foundations, notwithstanding the fact that the international climate was positive for embedding democracy. One reason that democracy stood a good chance of surviving in Southern Europe was that it had a history in the region, albeit a weak one. At the same time, democratization was also new, in that it was, for the first time, uncontested and reasonably inclusive. The democratic states which emerged after the transitions of the 1970s were seen as foundational rather than re-established after periods of suspension. Furthermore, democratization was tied for the first time to welfare and social improvement.

The Southern European transitions, then, have led to the establishment of both formal and substantive democracies. They benefited from a supportive international climate – expertise was lent from outside by particular actors; they had the option of joining an established regional organization of democracies, the European Community; and the economic conditions of the 1970s allowed for the adoption of state policies of growth with welfare. Nevertheless, in all three cases, the transitions were domestically-driven. Civil society actors were not insignificant and in all three cases pushed strongly for democracy. But the key actors, in guaranteeing peaceful transitions, were elites, especially from within the state. Only Greece was an exception to this and the unity of the conservative elite acted to some extent as an alternative.

All this is not to say that democratization is without problems in the region. In some cases, there are quite serious defects. The transition in

Portugal has done least to challenge old patterns of deference and therefore to make citizenship rights anything more than formal. In Greece and Spain, the expansion of democratic rights have been challenged by traditions of personalism and the impact of economic reforms. In Spain, the strength of popular organizations during the transition suggests one reason why democratization here was the most successful of the three, especially in terms of incorporation, participation and citizenship. But all three countries have witnessed the development of forms of social inclusion and, a gradual process of democratization of political society. The greatest obstacle to democratization in Southern Europe would appear to be the state itself, where institutional legacies from previous periods still remain in place.

8

Democratization in the Developing World: Latin America and Africa

In the 1980s the developing countries crashed into a profound recession. The debt crisis in the developing world had its origins in the problem of external debt repayments in the face of zooming global interest rate rises. But it soon turned into a long-term development crisis. Latin American and African economies collapsed, production plummeted, imports ended and credit dried up. In both regions, a majority of the governments at this time were not democratic. In Latin America, in the political turmoil that followed, many authoritarian regimes were replaced, tentatively and slowly, with civilian and elected governments. Nevertheless the crisis did not lead in any automatic way to democratization. It was only possible in those countries where there were credible political alternatives that could count on some minimal domestic consensus. In many countries, the civilian elites were, on the whole, ready and willing to take office again, although this was not so in Central America. Democratization was also resisted in Mexico. The new civilian elites sought domestic and international support through abandoning claims to exceptionalism. The introduction of liberal democracy was perceived as part of a package of changes – to development policies and to foreign policy, as well as political reform – that would allow Latin America to re-enter the Western mainstream.

Africa's economic performance in the 1980s was far worse than that of Latin America and its development crisis has been far more prolonged. But democratization has arrived late and remains weak. It is mainly sustained, in fact, because it is a part of the the power relationship between African states and the international order. Democratization is, in other words, an integral part of the agenda of the international financial agencies for the region and this accounts for its introduction. The vigorous, if problematic, process of democratization in South Africa in the 1990s stands as the only major domestically driven democratization in the region. Should we conclude, therefore, that there were no democratic alternatives for government in Africa in the 1980s and 1990s, despite the economic crisis and the de-legitimization of incumbent regimes? This is one of the issues that this chapter will explore.

Why is the trend to democratization stronger in Latin America than in Africa? Answering this question means probing not only the extent to which alternatives to dictatorship exist but, more fundamentally, the impact of underdevelopment on the state and civil society. It also means examining the relationships between underdeveloped countries and regions and actors from outside the state. In the case of Latin America, the influence of the US on political change in the 1980s and 1990s cannot be understated. Equally, Africa has been subject to a variety of external influences, chief among which are the international financial agencies, although the US and European countries have also played a role. Key questions, then, include:

- How is democratization affected by poor economic performance and increasing levels of poverty?
- What is the role of the state in democratization in underdeveloped countries and what kind of legitimacy can be established for new democratic institutions?
- What is the relationship between the international community and developing countries in terms of democratization and how does external dependence affect the democratization project?

Democratization in Latin America

Very different patterns of national history – different economic systems, social structures and positions within the international system – have shaped contrasting experiences of democratization in South America. In the first place, it is important to make the distinction between large countries of South America, such as Brazil, Argentina and Venezuela, and the smaller countries such as Paraguay and Bolivia. Brazil and Argentina are more industrialized and have a class structure very distinct from those of Peru, Bolivia and Paraguay. Chile and Uruguay, though relatively small, have patterns of political and economic development which are closer to the development patterns of the 'big' countries than to those of their smaller neighbours. In the larger countries, although wealth was still relatively concentrated, by the 1940s there were substantial and growing working classes in the cities and the countryside and the political systems expanded in order to incorporate participation from below. Until the 1960s and 1970s, these political systems in South America were, to greater or lesser degrees, inclusionary without being fully democratic (Cammack 1997). Dictatorships had emerged in almost all of South America by the 1970s (Venezuela and Colombia remained democratic in form, at least).

In contrast to South America, taken as a whole, Central American politics has been shaped very directly by proximity to the US. The US traditionally allied itself with the landed conservative elite in the region. Domestic elites retained exclusive access to the state, sometimes aided by their own Armed Forces and sometimes by US intervention. Elites presided over agro-exporting systems which rested on the intense exploitation of the poor and the peasantry. Political and economic struggles in the region were, as a consequence, rooted almost exclusively in disputes over the uses of land and labour. Elite responses to challenges from below were violent (Dunkerely 1988). Of the Central American states, only Costa Rica has been able to deal with challenges from below in a peaceful and democratic fashion. Furthermore, Central America has consistently been an object of intense interest in the US. In the 1980s, US security concerns led to an enhanced US presence in the region, in an attempt to roll back the revolutionary movements that emerged, starting in 1979 with the triumph of the Sandinista Revolution in Nicaragua.

For South America, relative isolation from the US meant less direct intervention. During the Cold War, this allowed for limited experiments with democracy. Chile, for example, maintained a precarious democratic order from 1931 until 1973, when a more radical government focused Washington's attention upon it and incurred the wrath of the domestic elite through policies of land reform and nationalization. The Argentine parliamentary regime developed early in the twentieth century but gave way in the 1940s to populism. Parliamentary systems in South America, where they survived, tended to be highly conflictual and unstable because they depended on exclusion, corruption, vote-buying, clientelism and a literacy qualification which served to exclude the rural poor. Populism – prevalent in Mexico, Argentina, Brazil and Peru – offered popular inclusion structured via a strong party-state. Clearly less democratic, populism was stable only as long as economic growth allowed for side-payments to the bourgeoisie and to organized labour. Populism has left an important legacy in South America: that of the strong state, capable of closing down independent activity from within civil society. In the 1960s, demands for greater democracy could be felt across South

America, challenging both the limited parliamentary model and the populist model. At this point, internal elites and the military reacted with repression and demands for 'order'. This occurred in Brazil in 1964, in Argentina in 1966 and 1976 and in Chile in 1973. For O'Donnell (1973), these dictatorships reflected not only elite distaste for reform but, more fundamentally, a project of industrial deepening which required the super-exploitation of labour, in contrast to the more inclusive period of populist development.

Other South America countries have a weaker history of parliamentary politics, partly because of divisions within the civilian elites. Bolivia witnessed a nationalist-populist revolution in 1952, and experienced military interventions throughout the 1960s and 1970s; Colombia experienced massive social, political unrest and intermittent civil war until 1958 and an elite pact afterwards which allowed for alternation in government; and Venezuela's troubled experiment with democracy dates only from 1958. In Ecuador, weak political parties, a small and poorly organized working class and a divided elite made politics unstable and allowed for military domination. With the exceptions of Venezuela and Colombia, the Andean countries also experienced military intervention in the 1960s and 1970s. In Paraguay, meanwhile, civil society was weak and the economy undeveloped and General Stroessner was able to establish a strong state in the 1950s with the collusion of elites and the military. In sum, there *is* a history of democracy in South America before the 1980s, but it is a complex one of restricted and elite rule, state cooptation of civil society and, frequently, also of electoral manipulation. Nevertheless, the legacy of democratic norms, however flawed, has proved an important reference for democratic reconstruction.

The dictatorships of the 1970s and 1990s generated mixed experiences in terms of growth and industrial development. While the Pinochet regime is credited with transforming Chilean political economy and creating the basis for economic growth after 1985, and the Brazilian military deepened industrial production at least until the end of the 1970s, most authoritarian regimes in Latin America presided over chaotic economies in which economic elites experienced unprecedented access to domestic and international loans and few restrictions on their activities. Extreme repression by the military and the security forces in their efforts to wipe out the 'cancers' of socialism and working-class activism meant that there was little space for open opposition, at least initially. The most notorious torture centres were perhaps in Argentina where 30,000 people disappeared and many thousands more were imprisoned and terrorized. But there were similar levels of state-organized violence in Chile, Brazil and Uruguay. Evidence also points to cooperation between the authoritarian regimes in creating a genuinely regional authoritarian project, and also, to support from the US in legitimizing the dictatorships internationally, until the middle of the 1980s, at least.

By the 1980s, the regional trend of authoritarianism was waning. A number of factors account for this:

- the economic chaos and the international debt after 1982 meant that the Armed Forces could no longer argue that the economy of their country was in safe hands;
- the revival of social opposition to authoritarianism – from the Catholic Church, human rights groups, neighbourhood communities and unions – supported in some cases by extra-regional organizations, created governance problems for the dictatorships; and
- a more sympathetic external environment for democratization projects as a result of changing US foreign policy meant that the international climate was unsettling and uncomfortable for non-democratic regimes.

Where re-democratization has proceeded most smoothly, the political class has reorganized and manufactured new bases for consensus, so as to assume control. In Chile, for example, where democratization was delayed until 1989, a new (or rather old) political class has re-emerged relatively painlessly, reconnecting Chile with its pre-1973 past. In Argentina, by contrast, elite responses were divided between the populist model of incorporation under Peronism and a liberal model of politics under the Radical Party. After the collapse of the first transition government of Raul Alfonsin (1983–9) the Peronists came to power under Carlos Menem. He then presided over a break in the traditional relationship between Peronism and the labour movement, making possible the introduction of economic liberalization. He also attempted, unsuccessfully, to put an end to the legacy of the human rights abuses by pardoning the military and attempting to impose forgetfulness. The task of reconciliation, however, remains uncompleted (Robben 2000).

Despite the problems which have beset Chile, Argentina, Brazil and Uruguay, these democracies could be said, for the most part, to be stable. But they are also incomplete and socially disembedded (Chalmers *et al.*1997) in that they survive with very low levels of active support from the majority of the population. Democracy in Peru, Paraguay,

Venezuela and Colombia is even more fragile. In general, Latin American democratization suffers from a substantial 'democratic deficit'. Access to the arenas of policy-making on the part of a range of social groups – the organized working class, part-time workers, shanty-town dwellers, the poor, especially poor women – is, throughout the region, very limited. Basic civil liberties are incomplete. At the same time, the establishment of new democracies, in almost all cases, has gone hand in hand with the deepening of poverty, economic marginalization and increasing international dependency. This state of affairs is not simply due to a reassertion of the tradition of restricted democracy following the collapse or the eradication of the left, though that is part of the explanation. Democracy is also constrained by the processes of economic liberalization and market-led global integration, which, by the beginning of the 1990s, were hegemonic in the region. The result is neo-liberal democracy (Grugel 1998) in which 'utopian' debates about democracy and development that fuelled politics in the 1960s and 1970s are now largely seen as irrelevant.

If democratization has led to 'neo-liberal democracy' in South America, what of the process in Central America? Remarkably enough, electoral politics were never suspended in Costa Rica, despite the upheavals of the 1980s. In the war-torn societies of El Salvador, Guatemala and Nicaragua elections were held in the 1980s because of US pressure. These were not 'founding elections' – that is, they did not symbolize the creation of a new political order (Karl 1986). Peace – as a step towards reconciliation – was first necessary, before elections could have any democratic significance. Peace accords, reached in Nicaragua in 1989, El Salvador in 1992 and Guatemala in 1996, have put an end to the civil wars and, theoretically, made some kind of democratization possible. But the process is fragile in the extreme. Peace has meant not only the end of armed conflict but also the end of the leftist project of revolution and 'the need to find new bases for a left-centred critique of elite power' (Pearce 2000). Partly because the left is so weak and in a state of ideological flux, democratization essentially means only electoralism. Civil society has few resources with which to control the state. The new democratic institutions are unrepresentative, and lack credibility, resources and authority (Cordova Macias 1996). Even in Honduras, which escaped war in the 1980s and therefore the traumas of state violence and failed revolution (Sieder 1996), democracy is very limited because elected representatives have little power and the notion of government accountability barely exists.

Democratization in Africa

At Independence, Western party systems were imposed on the newly created nation-states of Africa by the retreating colonial powers. These rarely bore any relation either to local traditions of power or to the social systems in which they were supposed to operate. The first democratic elections in the 1950s or 1960s were, in most African states, celebrations of liberation from colonialism rather than votes for one party or candidate over another. Shortly after, many African states moved towards one-party rule or authoritarian takeovers of government. The turn to authoritarianism by the 1970s was fuelled by:

- poor economic performance;
- the emergence of rent-seeking states;
- the manipulation of cultural diversity by political leaders, reducing trust and damaging the nation-state itself; and
- a social structure unsupportive of liberal democracy.

Democracy as an aspiration survived but its influence over state politics was minimal, even when elections were held, as in Tanzania where they served as a justification of single-party rule. Certainly *liberal* democracy was increasingly regarded as inappropriate in Africa on the part of many civilian elites. This conviction was shared by the Armed Forces, by now active in regional and national politics. Personalist, corporatist and factional interests were generally behind the military interventions.

The non-democratic regimes which emerged in the 1970s are difficult to classify. It not possible to identify a common pattern similar to the 'bureaucratic-authoritarian model' (O'Donnell 1973) in Latin America. Chazan *et al.* (1999: 141–55) identify seven different regime types in Africa since 1951: administrative-hegemonic, pluralist, party mobilizing, party centralist, personalist-coercive, populist and breakdown. All contain elements of authoritarianism except the pluralist model, which is confined to Botswana, Mauritius, Senegal and Namibia. Because the other regimes are both diverse and *sui generis,* it is difficult to establish a moment of collapse or regional transition. Certainly, Africa was late in getting onto the democratization bandwagon. Talk of Africa joining the third wave only really dates from the beginning of the 1990s. A trend was discerned when the long-time president of Zambia, Kenneth Kaunda, stepped down in 1991. Following this, early reports of African democratization circulated that were wildly – and baselessly – hopeful.

Experience has proved disappointing. Nevertheless, as Herbst (2000: 247) perceptively points out, politics in Africa has irrevocably changed since the 1970s. African societies have undergone such widespread economic and political changes that a return to pre-1980s politics is simply not possible:

> whatever else has happened it is clear that the old order – characterized by one-party states that had complete control over the media and public life and that faced little domestic or international opposition to their continued rule – is dead ... At the same time, it is hardly the case that democracy is inevitable.

African politics, in other words, are in a state of flux, in which elements of locally supported democratization projects are visible alongside externally driven experiments, chiefly in electoralist democracy, without these succeeding in establishing themselves as the only, or even the dominant, trend.

Similarly, it is not easy to establish with any clarity precisely what the legacies are from the past, especially since the 'past' (i.e. authoritarianism) is not really over. Nevertheless, if elections can be taken to signify the beginning of democratization, Africa has entered the first stages of the transition process. Elections were held almost throughout the continent in the 1990s. For Wiseman (1997), 'by 1995 pluralistic party systems were in place in more than three-quarters of African states, and in thirteen of them (Benin, Burundi, Cape Verde, Central African Republic, Congo Lesotho, Madagascar, Malawi, Mali, Namibia, Niger, Sao Tome and Principe and Zambia) change of government through the ballot box had actually taken place'.

However, elections, on their own, do not necessarily signify the beginning of democracy. In some cases, such as Nigeria and Sudan, the holding of elections has represented merely a cynical manipulation on the part of military governments seeking accommodation with the international community, following coups against elected civilian governments. These elections have been carried out in a climate of intimidation and have not been free or fair. In other cases, elections have been manipulated by civilian elites, intent on staying in power. In only a few cases have elections been called by incumbents where the consequence, however unintended, has been to liberalize the polity. This is the case, however, in Ghana where the Rawlings government called elections in 1996. The results were accepted by the opposition and the political climate improved, though the process stopped short of democracy. More usually, holding elections has had little or no impact on the political order. According to Herbst (2000: 250), in 21 of the 46 countries in sub-Saharan Africa that held elections in the 1990s, no political transition, either of government or regime, was discernible. Furthermore, there are even signs of a reversal of some tentative democratic experiments. In the Gambia the military came to power for the first time in 1994. In Zimbabwe, relatively stable if authoritarian through the 1980s, the process of holding elections in 2000 opened the country up to a intense wave of violence amidst a climate of intolerance for opposition. Finally, in some states, illness, poverty, AIDS and internal warfare threaten state survival to such an extent that disintegration is a constant threat. For a few countries, notably Liberia and Somalia, this has already happened, making the question of authoritarianism or democracy almost meaningless, since there is no undisputed national territory over which to govern (Zartman 1995).

In the light of all this, it is difficult to argue that democratization is an established trend in Africa. African politics have been driven since the 1980s by a dialectical relationship between economic crisis and external intervention, especially by the international financial agencies. There has, of course, been opposition to authoritarianism, but organized, cohesive oppositions, clearly committed to democracy, have been slow to emerge. So, with only ambiguous support from domestic elites, Africa is experiencing a process of externally driven 'transition without consolidation'(Sandbrook 1996). Harrison (1994) argues that this leads to 'unsustainable democracy' and greater instability. Certainly democratization is weak and new democratic states do not enjoy a solid domestic constituency of support. Any tentative processes of democratization are also threatened and undermined by the prolonged economic crisis, deepening poverty and crises of the state.

Only in South Africa is the experience of democratization somewhat different. The main obstacle to democratization since the 1950s was not poverty, underdevelopment or the existence of a predatory state apparatus but the institutionalization of racism and apartheid. Formally democratic, the vast majority of the population was in fact disenfranchised by the apartheid system, which was institutionalized after 1948 with the aim of preserving white cultural and economic supremacy. There was massive opposition to apartheid by the end of the 1950s. The state responded with terror and violence, culminating in the Sharpville massacre in 1960. The international outcry that followed discredited, but did not dislodge, the regime. Nevertheless opposition continued to build up, from strong social and civil movements as well as from the African National Congress (ANC), some trade unions, some church leaders and the Communist Party. State repression increased in the 1980s but was unable to eliminate opposition, especially when the tide of history seemed to be turning against the apartheid regime as US policy shifted towards open criticism. In 1990, under the Nationalist leadership of de Klerk, the apartheid regime was finally forced into negotiations. For the apartheid state, faced with the possibility of a total collapse, negotiations offered the chance of political reform in order to prevent a redistribution of economic resources and a corresponding loss of economic power from the white elite. For the ANC, entering the negotiations meant, inevitably, some degree of compromise and the risk of losing the support of the now radicalized black townships. The negotiations, therefore, did not symbolize, and were not able to create, consensus around the future of South Africa. Instead, both sides accepted that negotiations represented the best way to bring the violence and conflict to a close, but hoped to be able to press for deeper concessions. During the negotiations, it became clear that one-person-one-vote would be the only internationally acceptable outcome; but at the same time, that a radical redistribution of economic resources, such as land, would be impossible. In 1994, the first free elections in South Africa were won by the ANC's historic leader, Nelson Mandela, a prisoner of the apartheid regime for more than 27 years. Pact-making has meant that a (relatively) peaceful transition of power was achieved. But it has also tied the hands of the ANC in power, making reform difficult. Not surprisingly, then, democracy is proving disappointing for many; and economic problems, the need to reform the state and the security forces, the legacy of systematic human rights violations and rising violence and vigilantism constrain South Africa's democratic potential.

Theorizing Democratization in the Developing World

According to Karl (1990), 'the experience of Latin American countries in the 1980s challenged all ...presumptions about preconditions'. As a result, events in Latin America were largely interpreted from within agency-centred perspectives on democratization. The transitions have been seen as examples of democratization through elite negotiation and consensus-building (Burton, Gunther and Higley 1992) and have contributed to the idea that democratization is itself a process of sequential, and analytically distinct, 'stages' of political change (Schmitter, O'Donnell, and Whitehead 1986). The elite paradigm appeared to fit Latin America well, given the tight hold that relatively small elites have had over formal politics in the region. It also fed into the prevailing conservative assumption that the left, by overstating the chances for radical change in the 1960s, had actually brought about authoritarianism. Democracy, if it was to work this time, would require the moderation of the left; elite negotiation, by contributing to the re-creation of a cohesive political class that could include the left, could make a significant contribution to this process. Hence the influence of the elite paradigm spilled over into prescriptive policy advice.

Nevertheless, the assumption that elite-led democratization would produce functioning and effective democracies was questioned by the 1990s. Hagopian (1990) showed clearly how, in Brazil, democratization meant the restoration of civilian elites whose commitment to democracy was, at best, limited. It also preserved clientelism and prevented political parties from developing links with non-elite groups. Elitist democratization in Brazil was in some respects a continuity from the dictatorship, rather than a break with it. Elite-led transitions, in sum, tend to produce stable, but highly constrained, democracies.

As a result, contemporary research focuses by and large upon identifying the weaknesses of new democracies, the obstacles to democracy presented by traditions of excessive presidentialism (Phillip 1999) or the consequences of demobilization of civil society (Roberts 1998). Path dependency has become an important tool for explaining continuities between the authoritarian and democratic periods or the limitations of the new democracies. This has the effect of fragmenting studies of the 'region' into studies of nation-states, each with their distinct histories and development trajectories. And indeed, nearly twenty years after the onset of democratization in the region, it is the multiplicity of political models extant in Latin America that stands out: liberal democracy with democratic lacunae (Costa Rica); stable but limited democracy (Chile); delegative democracy (Argentina); military populism (Venezuela); disintegrating authoritarianism (Mexico) elitist democracy (Brazil); and facade democracy (Guatemala).

In contrast to Latin America, agency-centred approaches made little headway in terms of explaining events in Africa, with the notable exception of South Africa, where the transition was characterized by compromise, contingency and negotiation. Instead, scholars have drawn in particular on two distinct approaches:

● the globalization and governance approach, where democratization, in sub-Saharan Africa especially, is seen as the result of external

imposition and/or encouragement, with the aim of establishing conditions for order, development and market reform; and
● modernization-influenced approaches.

Modernization theory suggested that democracy was unlikely to emerge in developing countries because of high levels of poverty, the size of the rural economy, the small urban bourgeoisie and the persistence of ascriptive identities. While events in the 1980s and 1990s challenged that assumption to some degree, the African cases do seem to indicate that poverty – or, more properly, inequality – is an obstacle to substantive democratization. For Diamond (1988), it is quite clearly Africa's poor economic performance that undermines the chances of democratization. How far, then, can modernization explain the problems which beset democratization in the developing world generally? Modernization is useful in that it points to the importance of examining levels of development and their relationship with political processes. The Latin American cases suggest that economic difficulties, underdevelopment and poverty do not always make democratization impossible, though they may make it difficult. The impact of economic problems can be mediated by political institutions that create forms of inclusion or citizenship or act as a wall, protecting the most vulnerable groups from the worst effects of economic crisis or global integration. Remmer (1996) argues that 'the greater the competitive opportunities, the less important economic performance is to regime durablility' (see also Haggard and Kaufman 1995; Grindle 1996). In other words, an inclusive polity, even in a poor country, can insulate democracy from the consequences of economic instability. However, as numerous examples in Latin America and Africa show, exclusionary democracy/authoritarianism and extreme socio-economic inequality all too easily feed off each other.

The State

Democratization is an opportunity to reform the state. But institutions usually continue to operate after the transition within established cultural traditions and parameters. So democratization does not mean a clean slate or a new state. In this section, we examine how far legacies from the past impinge on the democratization project as well as examining how far reform has been possible. It should be remembered that democratization is only one of multiple pressures that states in developing countries have been under since the 1980s, and the exigencies of economic liberalization, for example, have impacted in a number of ways on the democratization of the state.

Legacies from the Past

The legacies of the past weigh to such an extent on the democratization project in Africa that they explain its failure. For Jackson and Roseberg (1982b), personal rule is a characteristic of most African states. Perhaps the greatest obstacle is the state's neopatrimonial or rent-seeking behaviour which makes it possible to block anything other than a formal process of electoralism. Bratton and van de Walle (1997) predict that neopatrimonial regimes, because of their institutional strength, will be able to resist full democratization.

Rent-seeking states tend to concentrate resources in the hands of a very restricted group of people, either family, friends or cronies. According to Peter Lewis (1996: 98) the neopatrimonial regimes in sub-Saharan Africa

> reflect the outward features of institutionalized administrative states while operating essentially along patrimonial lines. Though rooted in historical patterns of authority and social solidarity, neopatrimonial regimes emerged during the post indepedence era as African leaders consolidated their fledging regimes through an array of personal linkages and patron–client networks ... Power in such regimes is concentrated and personalized, entailing discretionary control over broad realms of public life.

According to Berman (1998), personalism emerged out of the colonial state, which was grounded in an alliance with local power-brokers. These emerged as the 'Big Men' of contemporary African politics. The patron–client networks that uphold the personalist state in Africa and that bedevil attempts to put the state on a rational and democratic footing, are therefore part of Africa's historical legacy. Nevertheless, it is also the case that neopatrimonialism has become more marked as a response to economic crisis.

Personalist states easily become predatory or monopoly states, as the example of Zaire (now Democratic Republic of Congo) under Mobutu shows (Evans 1992; Clapham 1996) The entire *raison d'être* of the Zairian state under Mobutu was that of private enrichment. Evans uses the example of Zaire to demonstrate that the predatory state actively impedes development, in contrast to a view that sees neopatrimonialism as stable and functional for economic growth, if undemocratic:

> Weakness at the center of the political-economic system undermines the predictability of policy required for private investment. The state fails to provide even the most basic prerequisites for the functioning of a modern economy: predictable enforcement of contract, provision, maintenance of infrastructure and public investment in health and education. (Evans 1992: 172)

The predatory state can prove particularly impermeable to democratic reform precisely because the state is so strong and enjoys a monopoly on political and economic resources.

In much of Latin America, the state was traditionally corporatist and the source of its power rested on the establishment of hierarchies of social incorporation. In this way, the state was able to constrain independent action on the part of civil society. Because it favoured business over labour, the corporatist state also acted as a brake on social and economic reform (see Box 8.1). The legacy of corporatism undoubtedly constitutes an impediment to democratic reform. But there are other long-standing state traditions that act as a barrier to democratization. Formal democracy has long served as a vehicle for elite domination in Latin America, creating states responsive principally to dominant interests. Parties have frequently served as instruments for a *caudillo* figure, rather than as representative channels for society. Even where parties have built up mass memberships, they tend to be dominated by a professional political caste. Oxhorn (1995) argues that in Chile the pre-1973 tradition of strong elite-led parties, with few connections to autonomous social movements and unresponsive to the party bases, closed the state off from civil society, making it difficult for the poor to have an effective voice in policy-making. Third-wave democratizations essentially reproduce this pattern of state–society relations. To make matters worse, there is now a generalized distrust in the state throughout Latin America. State services eroded considerably under the dictatorships and it is difficult now for states to deliver goods or design effective anti-poverty or governance strategies. At the same time, public distrust in the state has worsened as a result of the arbitrariness and terror that accompanied the dictatorship. Any policies now to strengthen the state are regarded with suspicion.

In general, then, embedded state practices and cultures undermine the chances for effective institutional change in both Latin America and

Box 8. 1   Corporatism and Populism in Latin America

Corporatism is 'a pattern of interest group politics that is monopolistic, hierarchically ordered, and structured by the state' (Collier 1995: 135). It was linked particularly to the populist regimes that emerged in the larger of the Latin American countries, especially in Brazil, Mexico and Argentina, although, in fact, corporatism represented a generic Latin American state formation during the period of industrialization and inward-oriented development, that is until around 1980. According to Wiarda (1981), Latin American corporatism draws on a long-standing Hispanic tradition of statism. This intensified in the 1940s and 1950s, with the onset of mass politics and the need to control the labour movement. Corporatism became a way of controlling the access of organized social and economic groups to the state. The state offered both inducements and constraints in return for control over organization and strategy. Corporatist regimes in theory created mechanisms to structure state–labour *and* state–business interactions. In practice, they controlled labour – and in some cases also the peasantry and the informal groups in the cities – more tightly than business. This has had a number of important consequences. First, labour became more dependent upon the state than business groups. This weakened labour organizations considerably because it diminished their policy and financial autonomy. As a result, labour and popular organizations suffered from state domination. Labour movements gained independence from the state (at the expense of exclusion) during the authoritarian period. But the turn to democracy has meant a reassertion of state control.

A number of post-transition countries have more recently experienced a resurgence of neopopulism. Argentina, Brazil, Peru and Venezuela have all elected populist presidents. However, neopopulism represents a new variant of the strong state and a break with past corporatist traditions where incorporation was rewarded with some minimal pay-offs. This time the state's control of labour is placed at the service of liberal economic modernization. In Argentina, for example, state control over labour prevented large-scale and organized protest against economic reforms that led to welfare cuts and rising unemployment. In other cases, such as Brazil or Venezuela, the resurgence of populism is an expression of popular frustration at the impenetrability of the state. Electing a *caudillo* into the presidency is a desperate attempt to put an independent in charge of government, with the aim of 'sorting out' the state.

Africa. They operate as a brake on distributional reform. They can lead to the reproduction of corporatism, clientelism and personalism. In this sense, they limit the chances for participation and a democratization of state–society relations.

Reform of the State

One of the problems that beset underdeveloped societies is state disorganization and inefficiency. As a result, democratization will almost inevitably be hindered by the inability of the state to deliver public goods. This diminishes the chances of either good government, or the development of successful anti-poverty strategies or social welfare programmes. This is well illustrated in the case of Brazil. For Weyland (1996), Brazil suffers such institutional fragmentation that the inefficiencies of the state have become an obstacle to redistribution. Social exclusion is reproduced by the state itself. The poor find it difficult to access the state; state bureaucracies are impenetrable and closed. Disorganized and inefficient states generate populism, for clientelism can work to secure immediate benefits. At the same time, however, clientelism prevents people from exercising citizenship rights because it locks them into structurally unequal exchange relationships (Weyland 1996). This of course contributes to decreasing the chances of building a substantive democracy: state inefficiency and populism constitute a vicious circle.

The chances of effective state reform have also been hindered in Latin America by the degradation of the state through corruption. Taking Brazil as an example again, Collor de Melo, the first directly elected president, was forced to resign following a corruption scandal, undermining the image of the Brazilian state internally, abroad, and within the international financial institutions. This was followed shortly by the arrest of the former president of Venezuela, Carlos Andres Perez, on charges of embezzlement of public funds. According to Little (1996), corruption is actually much more prevalent now, under civilian regimes, than when the military were in power. Elites are more unquestionably entrenched in power than under the authoritarian regimes. Moreover, corruption is ultimately paid for by the poor since it contributes to sealing off the state for private gain, distorts its patterns of accountability and reduces the resources available for social spending (Little 1992). Its long-term impact on the nature of democracy and the state is therefore considerable.

In view of this, it should not be surprising that the new institutions of democracy (parliaments, parties, local governments) in Latin America have only weak connections with the societies they are supposed to serve. In particular the state is failing the poor. A World Bank (1999b) survey of 60,000 of Latin America's poor revealed how very little trust they had in elected officials, politicians, the police and other state authorities. Because the formal institutions of democracy are regarded with suspicion, some countries, such as Bolivia and the Dominican Republic, have created parallel organizations to serve as channels between the state and society. In Bolivia, the government is using a 'National Dialogue' to promote policies of institutional reform, state modernization and anti-corruption drives (http:/www.imf.org/NP/prsp/2000/bol/01/index.htm). The state is attempting to strengthen grassroots associations and other informal institutions that have emerged in poor communities as a way of bypassing the formal institutions of the state. Consulting the organizations of civil society in this way could be said to be positive for democracy in that it creates channels for participation for groups unable to access the formal institutions. But it also raises a number of issues in terms of democratization. In particular, the lines of accountability and representativeness are not clear – Who decides, for example, which organizations can have representation? How are the policies that emerge legitimized? How can any policies that are proposed be implemented, if the official organizations of the state are excluded? It is no surprise that doubts have also been expressed about the value of these kind of ad-hoc consultations. In Bolivia, an important number of social movements and civil society groups regard the Dialogue as a performance staged for the international donor community, which stresses processes of consultation, rather than a serious attempt at reforming the state.

A different response is to encourage decentralization of services and policy-making. Decentralization has the advantage of breaking the monopoly of the central state and bringing decision-making closer to the people it is supposed to serve. But where decentralization of responsabilities goes unaccompanied by increased funding or powers of taxation, then it serves only to add another layer of inefficient bureaucracy. Nevertheless, in some parts of Brazil, decentralization has led to the introduction of a 'participative budget' where local communities are invited to discuss optimum ways of spending local resources. Championed by the Workers' Party, the participative budget seems to create a greater sense of owernship of local government and more efficient spending.

But increased participation in local decision-making cannot solve the greatest obstacles to democratizing the Latin American state which are a combination of lack of funds, an excess of social problems and no systematic or democratic channels for decision-making. The emphasis since the 1980s has been on the promotion of economic growth as a way out of this impasse. Economic reform has cut the formal responsibilities of the state, but has decreased its income and rendered it even less accessible and accountable because the introduction of economic reform has tended to depend on strong executive authority, alongside the 'technification' of the state, that is decision-making by 'experts', sealed off from popular pressures (Sola 1991). This is inevitably a barrier to democratization. It suggests that politics is too complex for 'ordinary people' and encourages demobilization and public apathy. Frequently, it is also a smokescreen for governments to avoid being held accountable since policies can be presented as the result of some impersonal and unavoidable law of economics or globalization. Consequently, economic reform has rarely led to leaner but more efficient states. In terms of social welfare, economic liberalization brought to a close the period in which the state, formally at least, assumed responsibility for social development. Instead the onus now rests with civil society, despite the fact that Latin American civil societies are not strong enough, or well-resourced enough, to take on these developmental tasks. The state is no longer required to engineer a 'better' society, merely to provide a safety-net. As a result, economic reform has gone hand in hand with successful poverty reduction in very few cases, although Chile stands as something of an exception in this respect (Weyland 1997).

In Africa, the crisis facing the state is less one of how to reform it but rather how to create it. The very existence of a 'state' in many countries, in the Weberian sense of an organization with a monopoly of force and a bureaucratic instrument for the administration of an uncontested geographic territory, is in crisis. In the most dramatic cases, the state has simply fallen apart or is a fictitious entity. Even where the boundaries of the state remain beyond contestation, its operations are under threat from a range of unelected, unaccountable, but nonetheless extremely powerful, networks, including illegal trade networks, local or transborder economic and social organizations and armed militia groups. The intensive de-territorialization of the state dates from the 1970s when

> the financial difficulties encountered by a growing number of African states meant that official circuits in large parts of the continent collapsed. The effect of the decline of state resources was compounded by the subsequent trend towards the privatization of the public sphere...Whole sections of society fell back on so-called 'parallel circuits'. (Bach 1999: 160)

Some states, such as Benin, Togo, the Gambia and Niger, actually encouraged the development of transborder exchanges and informal economic networks for rent-seeking purposes, even though, in the medium term to long term, this weakened the state. The result now is that democratization requires massive state-building rather than simply state reform. This is impossible to achieve, however, in a period of, *inter alia*, economic stringency, external dependence, public distrust and the defection of economic groups.

Civil Society and Democratization

Especially in Latin America, social movements of different kinds were involved in bringing down the authoritarian regimes. These were the most obvious manifestations of civil society dissent. Box 8.2 shows how community-based protest contributed to discrediting and delegitimizing the Pinochet regime in Chile.

Since democratization, social movements are generally less visible and their role is much smaller than the massive opposition movements before the start of transitions might have suggested. In Chile, the shanty-town organizations described in Box 8.2 were able to play a dynamic political role only until the Pinochet regime cracked. Thereafter, they declined in

---

Box 8.2 The Community Protests in Chile

In 1983, after ten years of dictatorship, protest erupted in the capital, Santiago. Economic crisis, a combination of the global debt crisis and collapse of the Chilean speculative boom, created an opportunity for mass dissent. A number of shanty towns in Santiago were the epicentre of the protests. Many of these communities, such as La Victoria or Conchali, drew on traditions of confrontation with the state over rights and services dating back to the 1960s or even 1950s. Before 1973, shanty-town activity was part of the spectrum of left-wing activity. Under Pinochet, some of these communities with a history of militancy, especially where the Communists had been strong, were able to offer effective resistance and turned their communities into no-go areas for the police and the security forces. According to Schneider (1995: 114–15), 'the Communist Party's work... had created a network of experienced activists, a language and framework to interpret injustice, and a shared belief in the efficiency of collective action'. The mass protests opened a space for opposition which the authoritarian regime was never able to close. Shortly afterwards, the political parties, except the Communist Party, were able to move from clandestinity to semi-openness. Tortuous and conflictual negotiations began within the opposition over how to present a common front to the military regime. This was to culminate eventually in Chile's pacted transition.

political significance. Similarly, community protest was important in Brazil until the establishment of elite-led democracy. This pattern was repeated in other transitions. Despite their rich tradition, then, these groups essentially met the same fate that befell community groups in Spain in the late 1970s. The transition changed the political structures in which they operated, allowed for the incorporation of some of their leadership and left community groups demobilized and disoriented.

The onset of democratization weakened social movements because it disrupted their cycles of protest. As the authoritarian regimes sought ways out of the impasse through negotiations with more acceptable civilian representatives, the community-based groups found themselves marginalized. Elite-led democratization divided the popular movements, the unity of which was always fragile. Some accepted the restrictive terms of transition, while others pressed for more the introduction of distributive policies. Furthermore, elite-led democratization drew support from bourgeois elements of civil society that also reorganized as the authoritarian project faltered. Business groups, some women's organizations, and cultural associations all provided the new democratic states with legitimate social linkages. At the same time, the introduction of liberal democratic procedures presents difficult strategic choices to popular social movements accustomed to combating the state, not working with it. In particular, it is not clear where they fit nor what their role should be. Are they post-materialist organizations, similar to those in some Western societies, or are they real alternatives to the formal political organizations? Do they articulate a different version of democracy? Is their aim to create new structures of democratic participation? And, just as crucially, in an era of electoral politics, where does their mandate come from? Or, put differently, are they even democratically legitimate (see Box 8.3)? Navarro (1993) shows, for example, how the Brazilian rural movements that expanded throughout the 1980s, and provided the only real opportunity for participation for many of the rural poor, have nonetheless generally low levels of internal democracy. This is a major weakness in many popular organizations and inevitably weakens them vis-à-vis the state and vis-à-vis more bourgeois social groups that understand the rules of the game much better.

There are, then, internal problems and dilemmas besetting popular social movements in Latin America that prevent them playing important roles in shaping the new democracies and lead to them being passed over as partners in policy-making in favour of 'more acceptable' civil society groups. Certainly, in terms of explaining the exclusion of the popular social movements it is important to pay attention to the role of the state

Box 8.3   The Civil Society Project

The state in the underdeveloped world lacks the resources to carry through democratic change or has been captured by special interests that have little commitment to substantive democratization or redistribution. Can civil society provide the resources from which to implement programmes of political and economic development? A significant number of pro-democracy activists and international donors think that it can. Even the World Bank now argues that democratization and development require the active participation of civil society (World Bank 2001). In some cases states have encouraged private organizations to take on previously public tasks, a move seen as a devolution of powers from the state to civil society. But there are problems with the idea that civil society organizations are the main structures on which to build a democracy or to deliver public services. First there are issues of accountability and representativeness. Attention has been drawn to the 'uncivil' side of civil society activism; they can be racist, sexist, violent and nationalist, as well as constructive and inclusive (Offe 1997). Perhaps even more significant, in relation to the developing world at any rate, civil society is simply not strong enough to challenge special interests or to serve as a channel for the incorporation of the very poor. In Brazil, civil society organizations are weakest precisely in the poorest parts of the country:

> Civil society in Brazil's north-east, where slavery was widespread until one hundred years ago, has historically been weak. The resources that sustain voluntary associations of all kinds in a rich country simply do not exist. Furthermore, the exigencies of survival make collective action extremely difficult. ... In 1979, when the union movement in other parts of Brazil was reaffirming its independent character, rural unions in [the north-east] also challenged employers and the state by conducting the first strike since 1963. This represents the rebirth of civil society in [the north-east] as far as rural labour is concerned. What has happened since that time, however, is salutary. It involves the partial and gradual re-subordination of civil society to political society and the state. (Pereira 1993: 366–7)

Finally, it is one thing to recognize that all of civil society, including the poor, should share the benefits of democracy; it is quite another thing to bring it about.

in determining which groups to work with and to listen to. The state in Latin America has been patterned over time to hear the voices of the rich and educated. Policy coalitions in Latin America have always excluded the poor, and they continue to do so. This divides already weak civil societies into opposing camps. These divisions are inevitably more marked now than under the dictatorships, when almost the whole of civil society, including elites, could unite against the dictatorships. Business carries a particular weight in Latin American politics as a result of the adoption of export-oriented models of capitalism. Roberts (1998: 160) suggests that the demobilization of social movements serves the interests of governments that find it difficult to deliver on their theoretical commitment of deepening participation.

In sum, new democracies in Latin America are generally insensitive to pressure from the poor. States have civil society partners, but they tend to be overwhelmingly pro-business or elite groups, even when leftist governments are in office. The poor are, at best, an *object* of government policy, not a partner in democracy. This is clear even in countries where sustained pro-poor policies have been introduced (Kurtz 1999). Policies have been designed *for* the poor, not *with* them. And, in any case, the bulk of these programmes seems directed not towards the very poor, but towards those groups that have some electoral significance for the government. The very poor lack even the voice to shout.

In Africa, economic crisis in the 1980s and 1990s represented an opportunity for urban-based civil society groups to separate themselves from the control of the state. A number of studies point to an increasing activism on the part of urban public sector workers in particular (Woods 1992; Bayart 1996). For Pankhurst (2000: 158), this research shows that 'the urban context ... is once again becoming a public space, in which there is a struggle to separate the private from the public, and to enforce political accountability on those in power'. But she questions the extent to which the findings from this research can be generalized. Her own work on Zimbabwe shows that while there is both a more active black associational life than in the 1970s and a more active white bourgeoisie, the state has been able to deal effectively, mainly through repression but also through cooptation, with pressure from the poor. As a result, she questions the utility of policies to support democratization through civil society and the extent to which strengthening civil society can be a strategy for empowerment of the poor. Certainly, any gains that have been made in sub-Saharan Africa have been confined to urban groups. It is difficult to find evidence that either democratization or economic crisis have allowed for the development of channels through which the rural poor can access the state. Harrison's (2000) work also reveals the systematic exclusion of the rural sectors from democratization in Mozambique.

Democratization and the Global Order

Democratization in Latin America and Africa began during a period of unprecedented economic crisis and continues at a time of a radical switch in the global political economy. The combined effect in Latin America and Africa is to shift the dominant economic model from state-led development to neoliberalism and to increase the penetration and influence of outside actors on domestic societies. The United States' over-arching presence in Latin America guaranteed it an important role in establishing the nature and timing of democratization in the region. Nevertheless, democratization in Africa has been even more profoundly shaped from the outside. In view of the intense pattern of external involvement in African politics through the 1990s, in fact, it is difficult to separate the external from the internal in African democratizations in anything other than a purely analytical way. Certainly it is not a question of outside forces aiding a principally domestic process, as in Southern Europe. According to Clapham (1996), Africa has witnessed the 'externalization' of both economic and political management in the 1990s to such an extent that the external has become a more significant variable for explaining policy formation in nation-states. The key question to be asked, from this, therefore, is how far genuine or substantive democratization can result from what is an essentially externally driven agenda. Box 8.4 examines this issue in more detail.

What accounted for the sudden interest in promoting democratization in Africa among Western donors in the 1990s? According to Harbeson (2000), external intervention was driven in the first place by the African economic crisis and international packages in support of economic restructuring(see Box 8.4). Support for democratization was a secondary spin-off from policies designed to encourage economic growth through market opening and liberalization. The World Bank was key in this respect. At the end of the 1980s, the World Bank endorsed a strategy for economic growth based on expanding the authority and productive capacity of small farmers, civil society and community organizations, in opposition to the state. It argued that economic development was hampered by the fact that the state in Africa fed off society. The state tended to close down civil society initiatives and entrepreneurship, in order to avoid political challenges and to allow rent-seeking elites to stay in control. The result was·to prevent economic growth taking place. The logic, therefore, was for international financial institutions to support democratization, meaning the introduction of a set of

Box 8.4   Externally Driven Democratization in Africa

Sub-Saharan Africa is extremely aid-dependent. Since the beginning of the 1990s, political conditionality policies have tied aid to the introduction of political reform. Typically, these policies focus on forms of election support. According to van Cranenburgh (1999), they include

- financial and technical assistance for the introduction of multi-party elections;
- the provision of election observation and monitoring teams;
- finance for voter education programmes;
- support for human rights groups and other NGOs;
- financial support for creation of a pluralistic media; and
- support for political parties

Most of this aid has been channelled into electoral assistance and observation. Additonally, multilateral organizations, principally the World Bank, have funded programmes of administrative and institutional reform, aimed at developing state capacity. By the end of the decade, the World Bank was also promoting policies to empower the state to carry out tasks to support entrepreneurialism and the private sector.

The intention of these programmes is to replace Africa's weak authoritarian, predatory or patronage states with democratic institutions. But results so far have been disappointing. In many countries, multi-party elections have been held despite the inability of the state to guarantee the rule of law. In some cases, the introduction of electoral politics has concentrated political resources in the hands of particular ethnic groups, leading to the exclusion of others from representation. This has sometimes led to outbreaks of ethnic violence. In general, political parties have not worked as independent channels of representation for society and have been grafted onto systems of patronage and clientelism. In the worst cases, elections have been forced on states in a period of armed rebellion and governmental collapse, as in the former Zaire under Mobutu. In cases such as this, externally funded programmes of democratization merely provide extra resources to be distributed between crony groups. Meanwhile programmes of administrative reform or 'good governance' have done little to address the severe economic problems in the region, although in some states (such as Benin, Zambia, Ethiopia and Mozambique) they have allowed for the implementation of economic liberalization. In sum, externally promoted democratization has yet to address the region's 'silent crisis' of economic marginalization and state collapse.

Sources: van Cranenburgh (1999); Chazan *et al.* (1999).

policies empowering civil society and rolling back the state, so as to encourage economic advancement. Thus 'the impetus for external encouragement for democratization was as much a recognition of democracy as a *means* to economic ends, as it was an *end* in itself. This relative underemphasis on democracy as an end in itself appears to have carried significant consequences ... among the most important of these ... has been an underemphasis on the political context within which democratization is to take place' (Harbeson 2000: 239; italics in the orginal).

Economic liberalization, and its spin-off, democratization, have been pushed through policies of political conditionality, which linked economic development aid to the introduction of political change. In some cases, international financial institutions have even been prepared to offer direct financial assistance for exclusively political reforms. Western governments have also linked aid to the introduction of packages of political reform. By the 1990s, a significant number of Western government-aided programmes for democratization were up and running in Africa. Nevertheless, the extent to which Western donors were fully committed to the introduction of democracy has been questioned. Olsen (1998) notes that the European commitment to democratization has been mediated by security concerns in Africa. This means, in practice, that European governments have placed the highest value on stability – whether democratic or authoritarian – in Africa.

In comparison, the role of direct external intervention in Latin America is considerably more muted. It is certainly true that the shift in US policy in the mid-1980s towards endorsing democracy over authoritarianism was positive for democratization. Less involved in the early transitions such as Argentina, the US pushed Chile and Central America towards electoral politics and has offered access to its internal market for regionally produced goods for states that comply. Training packages, aid and diplomatic support have also been available. Nevertheless, support for democracy from the US government has been forthcoming only in cases where the model of democracy remains strictly liberal and when it goes hand in hand with liberalization of markets and foreign investment regimes. And, in practice, the US offers only a qualified commitment to democracy; Mexico, for example, which is vital for US economic and security interests, is essentially excused from the obligation to become democratic.

Support for Latin American democratizations has also been forthcoming from a range of other international organizations. The European Union has programmes of support for civil society, European political parties have been active throughout the region and global NGOs have supported democracy programmes, especially in Brazil, the Andean countries, Central America and the Caribbean. But these kinds of activities sometimes have unintended consequences. Lambrou (1997) shows how the dependence on external finance has created a culture of reliance on external donors for fund-raising. And because local-based NGOs are frequently controlled by middle-class professionals, she questions the assumption that they automatically act as instruments for popular inclusion.

Conclusion

The results of democratization so far in Latin America are mixed. In some areas, the processes have been moderately successful. Electoral procedures are generally stable and hand-overs of government are peaceful and reasonably assured, although an intensification of populism is not completely out of the question. States have accommodated, partially at least, the new democratic norms, though the legal system, law enforcement and the police remain resistant to reform. On the debit side, however, democracy has done little to address the problems of poverty, marginalization and exclusion that prevent both economic and political development taking place. These failures account for a great deal of the political apathy that can currently be perceived in the region. Meanwhile, in Africa, the picture is much bleaker. Democratization in South Africa is relatively stable and resilient, but it is not underpinned by the introduction of policies of substantive democratization or economic redistribution to any degree. Elsewhere in the region, it is difficult to identify a clear process of democratization at all – only sets of policies aimed to make it happen. Democracy is not pushed firmly and decisively from either above or below.

What accounts for the limited success of democratization in Latin America and its near-failure in Africa? First of all, in Latin America, it is clear that democratization is either an elite-driven (South America) or externally driven (Central America) affair. This inevitably shapes the nature of the process. Of course, elite-driven democratization *can* become more receptive to pressure from below, but this takes time and effective political organization. In Africa, it is hardly likely that democratization would have become such a prominent part of the regional political agenda without pressure from international agencies and governments. Elites and states are resistant to change for the most part. Also, in both regions, democratization processes have inevitably been shaped by the processes of economic liberalization and export promotion that have been adopted through the 1980s and 1990s. The impact of these economic changes has generally, with only a very few and partial exceptions, been to shore up elite and external authority over local and popular groups, crossing substantive democratization off the agenda in the process.

9

Democratization in Post-Communist Countries

Perhaps more than any other region of the so-called 'third wave', the post-Communist world challenges the assumption that democracy is an automatic result of the collapse of authoritarian rule. For, while political change in *some* post-Communist countries fits the lens of democratization well, in others, the ex-Soviet Union and the Balkans most notably, the collapse of Communism has led to the implosion of the state, civil war and the rise of power contenders whose aim is state disintegration rather than state building. Explaining why that should be so is at the heart of this chapter. Has democratization in East and Central European countries fared better because these countries exhibit higher levels of capitalist development or more dynamic civil societies? Or can the difference be explained by the fact that East and Central European countries have greater state capacity or more unified states? Alternatively, can the distinct trajectories be explained by political leadership, statecraft or luck? Finally, can the different outcomes (different, at least, so far) be explained by geopolitics: is the relative success of countries such as Slovenia, the Czech Republic, Poland and Hungary a consequence of proximity to the democratic countries of the European Union (EU)?

This chapter presents an overview of political change following the collapse of Communism. The dominant theoretical approaches used to explain those changes are also discussed. The chapter then moves on to analyze post-Communist democratization in its three dimensions, namely: the role of the state; the significance of civil society and social organizations; and finally the impact of global change, geopolitics and external actors in determining the nature of post-Communist transformations.

Democratization in the Post-Communist World

Communism in Crisis

Communism was established in Russia after the October Revolution of 1917 when the Soviet Union was created. The Soviet system extended to the territories of East and Central Europe, which the Soviet Union liberated from the Nazis, after the Second World War. This meant the creation of Communist party-states across the part of Europe that was under the control of Moscow. An alliance system was established through the Warsaw Pact, which brought these countries together to ensure the defence of Communism against the capitalist West and which also created a hierarchy of domination in Eastern Europe under the aegis of the Soviet Union. Similarly, Soviet central planning was extended across Eastern Europe, with only partial exception being made for Poland. Yugoslavia and Albania also went on to establish some diplomatic and economic independence from Moscow.

The fall of Communism, symbolically at least, took place on 10 November 1989, when the Berlin Wall which divided Europe into East and West was forcibly torn down. But the disintegration of Soviet control over Eastern Europe had been signalled months earlier, by the Round Table negotiations established between the government and Solidarity, the independent trade union in Poland. Furthermore, the decision of the Hungarian government to do nothing to stem the flood of East Germans escaping to the West via Hungary during the summer months of 1989 was a clear indication that the Soviet Union was no longer in control of events in the region.

The collapse of Communism, then, was sudden. But it was the result of a long-drawn-out, multi-layered crisis, which was a combination of:

- severe and prolonged problems with centralized economic planning;
- profound political exhaustion, state decay and public apathy; and
- imperial overreach – that is, the increasing incapacity of the Soviet Union to rule legitimately outside the frontiers of the Russian heartland.

These three elements of crisis fed off each other. It is impossible to understand the economic crisis of Communism without reference to the political system. Communist political economy suppressed the market and was based on public ownership, the command economy and centralized planning. It was assumed that, together, these would unproblematically deliver a rational and efficient system of production and a just allocation of goods throughout the community. Communism's moral claim of superiority over capitalism rested ultimately on its promise to deliver more, and better, in material terms. To some extent, initially this seemed to be the case. Stalinism coincided with significant economic growth across the Soviet bloc. Industrialization, modernization and investment made economic expansion possible. The 1960s, however, witnessed serious problems with the planned economy inside the Soviet Union and also in the Eastern European countries. The emphasis on heavy industry, established during the 1950s, proved difficult to reorient towards the production of more consumer goods partly because of bureaucratization. Supplying and distributing goods was equally problematic. The situation worsened in the 1970s as consumer expectations increased. As a member of Solidarity strikingly put it, 'forty years of socialism and there's still no toilet paper' (Garton Ash 1999: 16).

'Politics in command' and the planned economy worked best in its initial phase in the Soviet Union, as Maravall (1997: 59) explains:

> [t]he economic efficiency of the model was greatest when the main task was accumulation, the level of development low and the priorities few and simple. In these circumstances it was possible to mobilize domestic resources, control popular consumption, generate high levels of savings and investment and transfer resources towards high priority objectives. But when the problem was no longer one of accumulation and investment rate but the productivity of these, the rationality of resource allocation and innovative activity, the model was inefficient.

Central planning travelled very badly to East and Central Europe, where it was applied almost in textbook form in the early 1950s. Its inefficiency in the more industrialized countries of Hungary, Germany (the German Democratic Republic) and Poland led to political dissatisfaction which, in Hungary and Poland at least, diminished the control Moscow exercised over national policies by the 1970s. The reforms did lead to some economic improvement in Hungary, but they also increased the spaces for dissent, as economic activities outside the state sector were tolerated and the party loosened its hold over social activities. As a result, the reforms led not to a re-legitimization of Communism but to the emergence of opposition and the development of an independent civil society (Lomax 1997).

In any case, partial reform such as that in Hungary and Poland was simply not enough. Ultimately, the emphasis on heavy industry was impossible to reform. Enormous investments had been made in immovable plants, machinery and production chains. Disrupting that system would have caused an unacceptable and severe dislocation of the economy. Furthermore, there were those who did not accept that there was a need to shift towards a more consumer-based economy. In particular, heavy industry was justified by the military and defence complex. In fact, a significant contribution to the structural economic crisis besetting Communism was the high cost to the Soviet Union of defence and security spending. Soviet economic problems were thus an integral result of East–West tension. Indeed, Gorbachev's foreign minister, Edward Shevardnadze, attributed the economic stagnation of the Soviet Union in the 1980s principally to the cost of defence. According to Linz and Stepan (1996: 240), Soviet military expenditure was three times that of the US and six times as great as the European Union average. In the light of all of this, it is not surprising that the partial reforms of the 1970s and the more radical attempts of Gorbachev in the 1980s were blocked. They were ambiguously received and there was little incentive for party officials to adopt them. As a result, they failed to halt economic stagnation. All this suggests that, from the very beginning of the Communist experiment until the 1980s, it is impossible to separate purely 'economic' problems of the command economy from the 'political' problems resulting from single party control, bureaucratization, central planning and the Cold War.

Nevertheless, despite these problems, the depth of the Communist crisis was only evident in hindsight. The implosion of Communism was unforeseen by either academics or policy-makers, in the East or West. Most believed that a reform of the Communist leviathan state was possible. This suggests that the Soviet Union had, in fact, been chiefly sustained by the bipolar antagonism that structured the international system between 1945 and 1989, allowing its faults to be hidden from view and encouraging the West to inflate its economic and political strength. Communism actually survived far beyond its 'natural' lifetime.

The Disintegration of the Soviet Union

The vast underlying structural crisis which beset the Soviet Union and its satellites was only revealed after Mikael Gorbachev became Secretary General of the Soviet Communist Party in 1985. Gorbachev is often credited with being the author of Communism's demise. His plan was to confront the economic crisis through reform (*perestroika*). Reforms aimed to increase the flow of investment in the public sector and in industry, expand external trade and introduce new forms of technology. He recognized, however, that economic reform would not succeed without some democratization of power. In the early 1980s, as a member of the Central Committee of the Communist Party, Gorbachev had advocated political opening (*glasnost*). Neither the economic reforms nor process of political liberalization were designed to bring about a liberal democracy; Gorbachev's intention was to introduce a programme of reforms in order to preserve the Communist system (Gill 1995). What happened was that in the process the reform movement gained its own momentum.

According to Sakwa (1996), the reforms can be divided into three distinct phases: rationalization (1985–6), reform (1987–90) and transformation (1990–1). Rationalization stopped short at identifying and acknowledging the economic problems affecting the Soviet Union. It promised moderate reform and some openness as solutions. This was not enough to rein in those radical members of the Communist Party who had taken heart from Gorbachev's initial statements, or to solve the material problems in the system, and more far-reaching reforms, political and economic, were attempted. In 1988, Gorbachev promised to reform the political institutions. As a result, the elections in March 1989 were freer than ever before and some non-Communists were elected to the new legislative chamber, the Congress of People's Deputies. This new agenda of reform changed the balance of power within the Communist Party. As more radical reforms were introduced, Soviet politics was caught in a struggle between radicals, committed to seizing the moment for reform, and conservatives, who wished to stop it completely. None of the party elite was, of course, committed to democratization in the sense of the introduction of liberal democracy. However, by 1990, a combination of popular pressure, from within Moscow especially, and events elsewhere in the Communist bloc began to drive the pace of events. In the course of this, a liberal parliamentary system emerged as an option for the first time. The governing elite, in attempting reform from above, found itself outpaced by pressures from inside the Communist bloc itself.

In particular, the tensions between centralization of decision-making and the demands for autonomy by the republics that made up the Soviet Union were the cause of the final dissolution. The first republics to demand greater autonomy, then independence, were the Baltic states. Meanwhile, Russian nationalism also re-emerged as a separate force. Boris Yeltsin was elected Chair of the important Russian Congress in 1990. Under Yelstin's leaderhsip, the Congress asserted Russian statehood by adopting a declaration of sovereignty in June 1990. This was followed by yet more nationalist demands from other parts of the Soviet Union. The Ukrainian declaration, the most radical of all, called for democracy and the creation of an Armed Forces under Ukrainian, not Soviet, control. It was thus pressure for self-determination, rather than democracy, which drove politics between 1990 and 1991. Increasingly, each component part of the nominally federal but in fact highly centralized Soviet Union was beginning to search for its own response to the disintegration of central control. Furthermore, as power shifted to the republics, it drained energy and authority from the centre and, crucially, from the Party itself. The shift was not orderly or controlled; nor was it clear which institutions or organizations of civil society would be empowered by the collapse of the centre. In the worst of cases, power leaked from the Communist Party to mafia networks and 'uncivil' nationalist groups; in almost all cases 'the media, the black economy and corrupt networks also became residual legatees of the declining system' (Sakwa 1996: 9–10).

Gorbachev accepted that reform had to go further and he offered a renegotiation of the terms of federation, as well as a series of economic reforms designed to increase the role of the market. But by this time, the Soviet Union was suffering a crisis of credibility and Gorbachev's promises were simply not enough either to halt the economic crisis, or to stem the collapse of the Communist Party. Consequently, the political crisis worsened. In August 1991 the opponents of reform attempted a coup while Gorbachev was away from Moscow. The August coup was a last-gasp attempt to save the Soviet Union from disintegration. Its aim was to turn the clock back. Yelstin, as President of Russian Federation, led a successful counter-coup, and, at the time, was hailed internationally as the saviour of the tentative process of democratization. The success of the counter-coup sealed the fate of the Soviet Union. It showed clearly that the forces of centralism did not have sufficient resources to resist the nationalist demands for autonomy. Rather belatedly, democratization was then grafted onto what was essentially a set of nationalist aspirations.

As the Soviet Union disintegrated, its component parts, the republics, found themselves effectively in a political vacuum. The way forward was not clear, either to society at large or to political elites. There was no clear political project beyond independence. Of course, in theory, the republics were free to attempt the transition both to statehood and to democracy. But there were – and are – considerable obstacles to democracy. In many independent territories of the ex-Soviet Union, there are neither social structures supportive of democracy nor a state tradition that can assist the process of political transformation. Democratization appears neither as a project from above nor from below. Furthermore, the way that new states emerged, by default almost, scarcely increases the chances for democratic outcomes. Indeed, it would be hard to disagree with Sakwa's assessment:

> the break-up of the Soviet Union fragmented the single large dictatorship into numerous small dictatorships, many worse than the decayed communist regime because of the energy with which they imposed themselves on the population, demanding conformity to communities defined by culture and ethnicity. (Sakwa 1996: 367)

Russia itself is struggling with severe economic restructuring, problems of political leadership, the difficulties of creating a democratic party system, the legacy of the strong state, revanchist nationalism and unresolved issues relating to where its legitimate borders should be – leading to a bloody war in Chechnya, which claims independence from Russia. Democratic institutions are only weakly legitimate, leaving a vacuum in politics that the Russian state, and the local elites who represent it, find all too easy to fill. Civil society is undeveloped, and the market is both contested ideologically *and* practically unrestrained. The conditions for democratization, at least in the short term, are poor.

East and Central Europe

The distinguishing feature of the collapse of authoritarianism in East and Central Europe, is its simultaneity: all the national communisms of 'the outer empire' collapsed at more or less the same time (Pravda 1996). This suggests a single common cause. The reforms introduced in the Soviet Union, and especially the beginning of *perestroika*, were important catalysts for change in East and Central Europe. The withdrawal of Soviet support was the most important of the multiple causes of the collapse of Communism in Eastern Europe (Waller 1993; Pravda 1996). Quite rapidly, however, the pace of change in East and Central Europe outstripped events in Moscow. According to Linz and Stepan (1996: 235) the 'domino-like collapse' of Communism in East and Central Europe was so swift that in some countries, such as Czechoslovakia, Romania and Bulgaria, there was no significant domestic pressure for change and transition was driven simply by the ripples from the regional wave.

Nevertheless, underlying the collapse of Communism in East and Central Europe lie popular and elite aspirations suppressed over generations – for economic reform, social freedoms and, most important of all, national self-determination. If democratization was driven in the first place by Gorbachev's reforms, then it was immediately nourished by deeply felt national demands to make nominal sovereignty real. The mode of transition, however, was principally determined by the extent to which even an embryonic opposition had existed prior to 1989 and the different national experiences of Communism. In Czechoslovakia and East Germany, some degree of material prosperity under Communism was able to mask mass discontent, preventing the development of strong opposition. Furthermore, in Czechoslovakia, the Soviet invasion in 1968 to crush 'socialism with a human face', froze the totalitarian system in place and the system largely was maintained through fear and mass disengagement with the public sphere. In the German Democratic Republic, in addition to relative prosperity, the trauma of division from West Germany, front-line status in the East–West conflict, a rigid surveillance state and a policy of allowing a few dissenters periodically to leave, together kept levels of opposition low. These options were not possible in Poland. Here, periodic economic crises had driven the leadership to seek closer collaboration with the West from the 1970s. And Poland, like Hungary, has incurred substantial foreign debts during the 1970s and 1980s, a result of their strategy of introducing market mechanisms into the production system. So, in Poland and Hungary, inroads had already been made into Communist domination before Gorbachev came to power. In short, the distinctly national post-Communist patterns were shaped by differing patterns of national history and culture, different levels of economic prosperity and degree of crisis, and patterns of state–society engagement opposition.

As the first of the East and Central European transitions, the Polish experience merits particular attention. Unlike some other post-Communist transitions, the Polish experience was not simply the result of the collapse of the Soviet empire. Democratization in Poland was, instead, the culmination of a process of sustained social opposition across the country through the 1980s. Its uniqueness, as it seemed at the time, brought the anti-Communist opposition unprecedented international support and media interest. Hence the Polish transition also benefited from the attention it received abroad. For the Western press, the leader of Solidarity, Lech Walesa, a Catholic, a nationalist and a trade unionist, came to embody in one person the differing strains of Polish opposition to Communism. International interest offered him a degree of protection. By the end of the 1980s, it was simply no longer possible for the Polish regime, dependent on external financing and weak internally, to break Solidarity up or to imprison Walesa.

Solidarity was born in 1980, under Walesa's charismatic leadership, and had a membership of 10 million. From the first, Solidarity was more than a trade union. It made political claims: for national self-determination, for freedom and for civil liberties. It received the blessing and support of Western politicians and of the Catholic Church and the Polish pope, John Paul II. Initially, the government attempted to suppress the organization through the introduction of martial law. This failed, however, and Solidarity survived. Unable to eradicate it, General Jaruzelski's government was eventually forced into negotiations in February 1989. The vitality of Solidarity had made the task of political and economic governance impossible. But even more surprising than the fact that negotiations took place at all was the outcome: the government agreed to the creation of a parliamentary democracy and to elections for June of that year. Quite incredibly for a social movement with no experience of electioneering, Solidarity won the elections. Just as significant was the fact that the Communist Party recognized that it had lost them (Garton Ash 1999). A few months later, a government was formed, led by Solidarity activists, supported by the Communist Party, which chose working with the new government as the best option for stability. Tadeusz Mazowiecki became Prime Minister. Walesa, meanwhile, was elected to the presidency a year later, in 1990. To all intents and purposes, then, the transition moved smoothly along the path laid down in the Round Table talks.

But there were important signs as early as 1990, that, despite the pact between Solidarity and the Communists, building democracy would not be an easy task. Some of the difficulties stemmed from the nature of the transition. Solidarity was a movement born in civil society, with a very loose structure, and it was ill-adapted to government. Furthermore, it rested overwhelmingly on the personal authority of Walesa, who, as far as it was possible to tell, was really more of a nationalist that a democrat. By 1990, competition between groups within Solidarity meant that it had effectively ceased to be a national movement. Thus, within a year, not only had Communism collapsed but Solidarity, which had shaped Polish politics through the 1980s, has disintegrated as a unified organization. At the same time, it became evident that civil society in Poland was not as strong or as dense as it had first appeared. Levels of electoral absentionism, for example, even in the key election of 1989, were also quite high. This was a worrying sign of public apathy. It was the first indication that perhaps the peak of civil society activism had passed; it seemed that Polish society had been prepared to mobilize against Communism but it was less sure that the new system was the solution. By the 1990s, civil society had been further weakened by the combined consequences of demobilization, the residual cultural and political effects of Communism and the social consequences of economic transformation (Bernhard 1996).

In fact, the economy had been moving towards a severe crisis at the time of the Round Table talks. Indeed, at the time even the Communists reportedly favoured the rapid introduction of market mechanisms in an effort to dynamize the economy (Gentleman and Zubek 1992) According to Zubek (1997) there was broad support for economic liberalization in Poland from the mid-1980s, mainly because it was interpreted as the key to unlocking Western support and to moving Poland out of the Soviet sphere. As a result, the first grand debate in post-1989 politics revolved around how to manage the economy and, in particular, who could manage the transition to a market economy more efficiently, the nationalists or the technocrats. Political debate, whether about how to deepen democratic culture or how to implement much-needed social reforms, was pushed into second place to these more urgent questions. To some extent, this was a reflection of the fact that the transition had been opened through elite negotiation. Space was not created during the transition for popular debate. At the same time, the outgoing regime was able to impose conditions for its withdrawal. These included amnesties for Communist misdeeds in the past; the unimpeded transformation of the Communist Party into a 'social democratic' party; the uncontested right of ex-Communists to participate in national politics; and protection for the state-created Communist labour union, which had been designed to sap strength away from Solidarity in the wake of the 1982 strikes. Together, these conditions guaranteed a presence in Polish politics for individuals associated with pre-1989 politics and a substantial Communist legacy for post-Communist politics.

As in Poland, the introduction of Western-style institutions in Hungary – democracy and the market – was part of a package to save the economy and secure Western aid. Affected by events in Poland and the Soviet Union, as well as by evidence of its loss of internal legitimacy, the Hungarian Communist Party dissolved itself in October 1989. The following month the Czechoslovak Communists, who had resisted liberalization, were brought down in a week by the hastily organized oppositional Civic Forum. In both countries, Round Table negotiations based on the Polish experience were arranged as a device to ensure some form of stable government. Party systems quickly emerged. Most parties were elite groupings of power contenders, with little real contact with the electorate. At the same time, the civil society option, which had seemed so vibrant during the early months of the transitions in both Hungary and Czechoslovakia began to fragment and weaken (Kopecky 2001). For the German Democratic Republic, the emergence of open opposition in the summer and autumn of 1989 was the signal for its unlamented demise. By November, half a million people felt confident enough to demonstrate against the regime in Leipzig. In the same month, the Party leadership resigned and the by now established formula was put to work: Round Table negotiations were held with the opposition. The end of East German Communism also meant the possibility of German reunification. As a result, East Germans re-entered the West, not as citizens of a post-Communist state, but as members of a new Germany.

The Balkans

The Balkan countries (Rumania, Bulgaria, Albania and the independent states of the ex-Yugoslavia) have followed different, and somewhat less successful, post-Communist paths. In all these countries, Communism had adapted more to local traditions than in East and Central Europe. At the same time, distance from Moscow and from the front-line of East–West conflict helped seal off these countries to some extent. Nevertheless the reverberations of events in East and Central Europe were also felt here: the Communist regime was removed in Bulgaria in November 1989 by reformists from within the governing party; in Rumania, the personalist Communist leader, Nicholai Ceauscescu, was forced to flee and was executed in December 1989; and Albania embarked upon a transition a year later. Unlike in East and Central Europe, these transitions were not the result of pacts between oppositions and governing elites; nor were they the result of unstoppable social pressure. So, although the new constitutions proclaimed a new era of liberal democracy, the terms of transition were unclear. In most countries, nationalism, or more properly conflicts between groups over who would successfully lay claim to representing the nation, initially defined the terms of democracy. Ethnic tensions shaped the new systems much less in Bulgaria or Slovenia, but elsewhere, politics became, to one degree or another, a fight for spoils between different groups.

The centrality of nationalism in contemporary Balkan politics is of course partly the result of its forcible suppression under Communism. It has become a tool for elites, through which they can create new bases of post-Communist legitimacy and ensure continued access to the state. Appeals to ethnic nationalism are possible, furthermore, because the terms of transition involved no inducements for elites to compromise (Gallagher 1995). But is also the result of the absence of failed state-building and in particular of the fact that the Communist states could never accept the development of civil society in the region. As a result, ethnic struggles slip easily into open conflict. In Yugoslavia, there were three wars following the collapse of Communism, between Serbia and Croatia, Serbia and Bosnia and Serbia and Kosovo, as well as thirteen years of dictatorship in Serbia by Communist-turned-nationalist Slobodan Milosevic who used the wars to stay in power. The bloody nature of these wars overshadowed ethnic and nationalist conflict elsewhere. But Gallagher (1996; 1998) shows how similar tensions dominate politics elsewhere in the region.

The national problem in the Balkans is, furthermore, intensified by the social and economic legacies of Communism. Stalinism had meant the introduction of heavy industry into what were mainly peasant economies. This created enormous social and economic change and has left a destabilizing legacy for transition politics:

> Stalinist heavy industry…left a class of ex-peasant factory workers in derelict industries lacking markets, who were ripe for populist mobilization just as landless peasants had been in the 1930s. (Gallagher 1995: 355)

These social problems tend to map, albeit unevenly, onto ethnic conflicts in the region, making liberalism and tolerance difficult to achieve and the creation of a national civil society almost impossible.

Theorizing Democratization in the Post-Communist World

The key questions for democratization in the post-Communist world are:

- Why did the transitions occur?
- What kinds of democracies are taking shape? and
- How can we explain the different post-Communist trajectories?

The starting point for answering these questions has, logically enough, been the frameworks inherited from studies of earlier transitions. Schmitter and Karl (1994) maintain that theories of democratization can be adapted to fit East and Central Europe. Higley, Kulberg and Pakulski (1996) advocate adopting the elite agency approach, developed for Southern Europe and Latin America, to explain the initiation of transition in East and Central Europe. They argue that in particular 'a desire among elites for greater security' was behind the turn towards democracy in post-Communist societies (Higley, Kulberg and Pakulski 1996: 134). It was not, then, simply a consequence of the Gorbachev effect. Different outcomes are attributed to different terms of transition. So, the persistence of 'semiauthoritarianism' in some new systems is due to 'the lack of turnover in top-level political positions' (Higley, Kulberg and Pakulski 1996: 138) and more successful outcomes, such as post-1989 Czechoslovakia, are the result of elite power-sharing (Higley, Kulberg and Pakulski 1996: 141–2).

But a number of studies have questioned the extent to which the transition framework constitutes an adequate lens through which to view post-Communism. It has been suggested that borrowed frameworks misrepresent the nature of the crisis which gripped the region in the late 1980s and which led to the collapse of Communism. Bunce (1995a; 1995b) argues that the nature of Communism means that comparisons with Southern Europe and Latin America are misleading. The role of society and the masses, she argues, was generally far more significant in Communist transitions than in Latin America. At the same time, the importance of geopolitics is certainly more immediately striking in post-Communism. The way out of this impasse is to adopt a middle position (see Sakwa 1996). This means that the differences between the post-Communist transitions and the earlier examples of Southern Europe and Latin America are important and are essentially ones of *context* (Gill 2000). In other words, understanding outcomes – or what kinds of new systems are being created – necessarily means paying attention to the economic, cultural, ideological and geopolitical legacies from Communism as well as to the behaviour of elites during the immediate transitional period.

Where democratization has been most successful, that is in East and Central Europe, theories of change borrow most heavily from the agency-centred perspectives. So there is a significant volume of research on pact-making and the terms of transition in East and Central Europe. Munck and Skalnik Leff (1997: 345), for example, argue that the degree to which the transition is the result of pacts 'affects the form of post transitional regime and politics through its influence on the pattern of elite competition, on the institutional rules crafted during the transition and on key actors acceptance or rejection of the new rules of the game'.

There is also a literature on institution building, parties and electoral systems (Lewis 1997; Kopecky and Mudde 2000). This literature sees the experiences of East and Central Europe as part of a data pool on democratization in general.

However, where the democratization project has run into problems, or where it hardly forms part of the political agenda, an array of competing perspectives has emerged, all of which assert the specificity of political, sociological and economic change in the region. Perhaps the most notable has been the political culture argument, an approach muted in studies on Southern Europe, Latin America and Africa. The legacies of Communist, Asian or an undeveloped mass culture have been used to explain the weak civil societies and low levels of independent political activity that can be found. A focus on culture also pays attention to the persistent or resurgent ethnic identities that split society and the state, and cause state and social crises or even ethnic violence and war in some parts of the region. Indeed, such are the problems posed by nationalism in the region that there have been calls to (re)introduce a focus on state-building into the literature on transition in post-Communist countries (Kopecky and Mudde 2000).

In terms of explaining outcomes, the culturalist approach should be complemented by a political economy focus, that explains the 'dual transition' problem – the impact of the establishment of markets alongside new political institutions. How has the need to restructure the economy created constraints or opportunities for democratization (see, for example, Stark 1992; Balcerowicz 1994; Bryant 1994; and Keman 1996)? Has the creation of markets made civil societies stronger? Are post-Communist states able to adapt to the very different functions they now have to carry out? In general, this research points to the vital importance of state capacity and social cohesion for successful democratization and those countries which are experiencing some success with democratization enjoy aspects of both.

The State

Democratization in ex-Communist countries implies a transformation of the role and competencies of the state. It is not simply a case of creating a more efficient state; democratization implies changing the rationale of state activity. This involves challenging cultures of secrecy and non-accountability and building a consensual relationship between state and society-based actors. But in the first place, of course, the post-Communist state must be able to claim uncontested sovereignty. A *sine qua non* of democratization, and one that cannot be taken for granted under post-Communism, is the legitimacy of the nation state.

The 'Stateness' Problem

Perhaps more than any other area of 'third wave' transitions, the question of nationalism and the stateness problem pose a question mark over democratization in post-Communist states. While some countries have coped strikingly well with this issue, more have been unable to do so. We analyzed above the extent to which nationalism has derailed democratization in the Balkans. But nationalism does not only affect democratization negatively when it leads to open war. The problem with any ethnic definition of the nation is that by creating insiders and outsiders within the same territorial unit, some groups are defined as beyond or outside citizenship, or at best as only having limited citizenship rights. In these cases, nationalism becomes a vehicle for policies of exclusion that are, at the same time, socially legitimized. This kind of nationalism is, in fact, far more endemic in post-Communism than is open warfare. Examples of this include ethnic Russians who suffer systemic discrimination in the Baltic states; and the growing numbers of Romany from the Czech and Slovak Republics who face social and political exclusion of such magnitude that they migrate in huge numbers.

The failure to challenge racist concepts of nationhood and to build societies based on tolerance and ethnic pluralism bodes ill for improving levels of participation, welfare and development in the long term. Moreover, the difficulties with the transition to market-based economies that many post-Communist countries have experienced have created communities who regard nationalism as the only way to express opposition to what are increasingly seen as policies of impoverishing Westernization. A defence of local traditions, the appeals to 'traditional' ways of life and the exclusion of 'the other' is the result. Western aid, even in defence of democracy, can actually provoke an even greater nationalist backlash in these circumstances. Of course, some of these problems are undoubtedly only short-term and it is possible to exaggerate the threat that ethnic nationalism presents. But it is also important to recognize that democracy requires communities to live together peacefully, even if it cannot force individuals to accept each other fully. This means that, in multi-ethnic states, policies and institutions must manage difference effectively. So far, however, post-Communist states have shown a real reluctance to create institutions that guarantee multi-cultural social and political rights.

State Capacity

The state tradition in Eastern Europe is very different from that of the West. These differences pre-date Communism (Anderson 1974) and are discussed in Box 9.1.

The Communist regimes used already existing state traditions to try and promote modernization, rationality and progress. The strong state was the means to carry through the Marxist project. It made the command economy possible. But Communist states also went to inordinate lengths to police the private sphere and to carry out policies of social control. They tried to shape beliefs through education and penetrated civil society by organizing leisure and cultural activities. Even family life was not immune from the reaches of the state. Surveillance was routinely carried out to ensure compliance, along with repression, information-gathering and the inculcation of fear. Indeed, Communist states depended on surveillance for their very survival. This has inevitably left an important and uncomfortable legacy in state traditions.

Box 9.1   The State Tradition in the East

Historically, the state in Eastern Europe was much stronger than in Western Europe. The state was important politically and economically, especially since alternative power contenders from within society were much weaker, mainly because economic development was slower, but also because of geographic fragmentation and poor communications. The idea that law enforcement should be independent of the executive, for example, was slow to develop. The boundaries of state activities were never clear and the state intervened in areas that by the end of the nineteenth century in the West were regarded as the private sphere. For Schopflin (1993: 11–12) 'the discretionary power of the state' in the East had its origins in 'the principle of the royal prerogative, [the idea] that the ruler has the right to take action in any area of politics unless he is expressly prevented from doing so by law. This principle enabled the state to retain and promote *its* autonomy in the crucial fields of taxation and military organization. Society was too weak to exercise control over these areas, whereby it could not sustain its autonomy *vis-à-vis* the state.' Communism drew on the established tradition of the strong state, not only in Russia and the territories of the former Soviet Union, but also in East and Central Europe.

Civil society is regarded with suspicion. The state apparatus remains primed for coercion, although in practice many post-Communist states no longer have the resources to repress effectively. Communist legacies such as these in Russia are discussed in Box 9.2.

Box 9.2   State Traditions in Russia

One of the characteristics of a democracy is an open and accountable state. The Russian state remains difficult to access and reluctant to offer information to its citizens. There is also evidence that state officials distrust the public and do not always tell the truth. The culture of the Russian state, then, is not radically different from that of the Soviet state. Government and officials have not caught up with changes made possible by the onset of democratization, such as the fact that the public can now access information from abroad. At the same time, the state, though it does not operate democratically, is no longer monolithic, so information leaks out quickly and incoherently. The events surrounding the sinking of the Russian nuclear submarine, the *Kursk*, in the Barents Sea in August 2000 reveal some of the pathologies of the Russian state.

The immediate government reaction to the accident was to lie. It claimed that many of the submarine's crew of 118 men had survived and that the Russian Navy would be able to rescue them. Offers of assistance from Britain and Norway were rejected. In fact, the Russian Navy did not have the equipment to mount a rescue. Finally, after a week, British and Norwegian teams were allowed in. This revealed what the government had always known – that the accident had been far worse than had been claimed and that most, if not all, of the men did not survive it. Meanwhile, the government treated the families of the sailors who died with contempt and disdain. No efforts were made to inform them before broadcasting news of the accident in the media, so the families learned that their fathers, sons and husbands had been in a serious accident from the television or the radio. Relatives were not offered assistance of any kind to enable them to travel to the naval base from where the rescue activities were supposed to be being organized and to where the submarine would, supposedly, be brought. They were given false hope that the men were alive, although they could see that little or no effort was being made to save them. Meanwhile, despite the crisis, President Putin remained on holiday, until it was officially announced that all the men were dead. There is, in all of this, little to mark out the responses of the Russian state from that of the Soviet state during the Chernobyl nuclear accident in 1986. Although traces of contamination were found as far away as the UK, the Soviet government denied that the accident was serious, restricted the flow of information to local inhabitants and effectively abandoned those affected to their fate.

Communist states were strong, but they were not efficient. Strength did not translate into capacity. The crisis of Communism, indeed, was rooted in the very inefficiency of the state. Economies were bedevilled by bottlenecks, shortages, under-production, antiquated machinery and weak distributional channels; and secretive, irrational and bureaucratic decision-making made by political elites who were out of touch with popular needs and demands. The lack of a capable bureaucracy now a real hindrance to the implementation of both political and economic reform. Equally, traditions of secrecy and of corruption create obstacles to the democratization and to mass support for the new systems. The World Bank (2000) has expressed concern that the problem of the state is at the heart of poor economic and political performance: 'in many countries, the public perceives corruption to be woven into the basic institutional framework, undermining governance and weakening the credibility of the state'. In particular, the Bank suggests that the post-Communist state is captured by special interests and that policies are shaped by restricted non-democratic networks.

Civil Society and Democratization in the Post-Soviet World

The impetus for democratization under Communism was national or regional (Przeworski 1991). In some countries, society clearly rejected Communism, sometimes via the formation of opposition organization and, in other cases, through the more passive route of simply by-passing the state. In East and Central Europe, in particular, the revolutions of 1989 were made in the name of 'the people'. In these cases, the transitions were taken to represent the triumph of the 'civil society project' (Smolar 1996). In contrast, in the ex-Soviet Union, the role of 'the people' in bringing down Communism was rather more ambiguous.

Labour unions, religious organizations and human rights movements emerged as signs of the development of civil society in East and Central Europe before 1989. But the cohesion and influence of these organizations declined after the immediate onset of transition. There are a number of reasons for this. First of all, the strength of civil society in 1989 was actually exaggerated. For Marata (2000) civil society was able to bring down authoritarian regimes but not strong or cohesive enough to offer an alternative political direction. By 1990 when the state reorganized following the Communist collapse there was already less space for social dissent than had been expected. Secondly, the process of economic reform fractured the civil society movements, making it difficult for them to engage effectively with the state. Drawing on research in Hungary, Miszlivetz (1997) attributes the loss of interest in participation after the first democratic breakthrough to the alienation that accompanied market reform. Thirdly, civil society withered with the eruption of revanchist nationalism. Nationalism not only offered an alternative site of mobilization, it represents the denial of the civil society project and the triumph of ascriptive identity (Seligman 1992). In Yugoslavia, civil society was simply crushed in the early 1990s by the forces of nationalism (see Box 9. 3).

Box 9.3   Civil Society and Nationalism in Yugoslavia

The collapse of the Eastern bloc led to the disintegration of Yugoslavia. A new, smaller, Yugoslavia emerged, based on Serbian hegemony. Because war broke out almost immediately, democratization in Yugoslavia lagged behind the rest of the region. Aggressive Serbian nationalism led to the wars that tore Bosnia and Kosovo apart in the 1990s. Milosevic was sustained in power in Serbia by nationalism, which effectively curtailed opposition. When NATO decided to intervene in 1999 to protect the Muslims in Kosovo, Milosevic's hold on power was strengthened. An intense wave of nationalism swept the country. Serbians constructed the NATO attacks as an attempt to destroy the country. Serbia suffered considerable material damage (it was estimated that 62 per cent of Serbia's transport system was destroyed, 70 per cent of its electrical power stations damaged and 80 per cent of oil refineries were affected by the bombing), but support for the government increased. Nationalism seemed to have eclipsed civil society and Milosevic remained in power.

Once the war was over, however, the political climate was very different. Forced to call presidential elections in September 2000 for reasons of domestic and international legitimacy, Milosevic hoped that nationalism, and electoral manipulation if necessary, would enable him to win. However, during the campaign, opposition from society erupted so strongly that it became clear he could only win by fraud. The opposition, with the support of the few independent observers who had been present at the elections, claimed outright victory in the first round. Milosevic tried to use force to quell the massive street demonstrations that erupted. A campaign of civil disobedience began. Children were kept off from school, a transport strike was organized in Belgrade and thousands of people took to the streets. Miners went on strike in the huge mining complex of Kolubara in an attempt to paralyze the economy as well. Journalists working for the state-controlled television and newspapers joined the opposition. As the opposition increased, so Milosevic's grip on the state weakened and the police refused to stop the strikers and the protesters. Milosevic was finally forced out of office.

More fundamentally, however, civil society was bound to weaken with the emergence of political society, as political parties coalesced around local and national elite figures and organized for the purpose of contesting elections and gaining power. Civil society was in effect drained by political society. According to Ost (1993), the intelligentsia in Eastern Europe had moved into the social movements as part of their project of revitalizing civil society in opposition to state. They were thus over-represented in the leadership of the 1980s social movements (Kopecky and Barnfield 1999). But when it became possible to join political parties or even the government, they chose to do so, leaving the social movements leaderless. At the same time, they had pushed the social movements towards adopting high moral and political agendas, rather than bread-and-butter questions of material improvement, making it difficult for the social movements to adapt to the new circumstances. Once democratization had begun, it was not clear, even to the members of the movements themselves, what further role they had to play. Disintegration was almost inevitable. For Lomax (1997) this failure to stay in civil society, rather than contributing to its demise, amounts almost to a betrayal of democratic ideals by the intelligentsia.

The weakness of civil society in post-Communism is therefore a considerable democratic fault line. Not only is it difficult to imagine participation and citizenship without vibrant social organizations, it is also difficult to imagine how pressures can be brought to bear to reform and change the state. At the same time, in view of the disintegration of the states and the collapse of state services in the former Soviet Union, civil society organizations are desperately needed to keep communities together and to provide the resources that allow people to survive physically and psychologically. Political parties, which have emerged strongly throughout the region, structure legislatures and elections but have relatively few social linkages. They cannot be substitutes for civil society.

Democratization and Globalization

The collapse of Communism in 1989 was a globalized event. In this sense, it was not the intentional result of conscious pro-democracy strategies planned over the long term. Rather it emerged out of the results of unforeseen actions and the unintended consequences of reform attempts, in a global context in which democratization was seen as the only possible alternative alternative to Communism. As protesters were pulling down the Wall in Berlin, they knew they were being watched in the world's media and this was one of the reasons they had the confidence to challenge the East German state. Without the international media, 1989 would simply not have happened. More properly, however, it was the proximity of the West, the penetration of Western social identities into the East and the pull of the capitalist economy which led to the Communist disintegration and which provided alternative social and economic models inside Communism. Put simply, it was no longer possible, in Europe at any rate, to sustain closed national systems, especially when they have long lost popular legitimacy.

How far post-Communism is shaped by its role within the global order is a question of a different order. After all, we argued above that state traditions in particular were important in understanding different post-Communist trajectories. Nevertheless, the globalization of the world economy is also a major determining factor, as Lewis (1997: 4) argues:

> the international context was of prime significance [for explaining democratization] and it was often through the combined effects of modernization and global economic and technological developments that the pattern of democratization has been determined.

In particular, joining Europe was a major driving force behind East and Central European transitions. But Europe was not really seen as an outside force in East and Central Europe. Democratization was about rejoining the West from which the region had been severed. From this perspective, democratization and Westernization, far from being global imposition, actually constituted a process of normalization. According to Milan Kundera (see Kearns 1996: 59), for the Poles, the Czechs and the Hungarians,

> their nations have belonged to a part of Europe rooted in Roman Christianity. For them the word 'Europe' does not represent a phenomenon of geography but a spiritual notion synonymous with the West. The moment Hungary is no longer European – that is, no longer Western – it is driven from its destiny, beyond its own history: it loses the essence of its identity.

For Kearns (1996: 62) this is precisely why European (or Western) advice was legitimate in post-Communist East and Central Europe, possessing 'an almost magical quality'. Glasman (1994) explains how the 'magic of the West' shaped events in Poland following Solidarity's electoral victories in 1989 and 1990. Before taking office, Solidarity's preference was for an industrial relations system which combined state regulation with a social market system. Once in power, however, concerns about the deteriorating economy, the need to create new channels of capital investment and a desire to join Europe combined to lead the government towards austerity measures, stabilization policies and a commitment to rapid marketization. For the Prime Minister, Mazowiecki, it was important that the transition to capitalism be validated by the experiences of Western Europe. Nevertheless, whatever magic the idea of Europe may have possessed, its role in the region was backed up by the resource dependency of the East. Europe possessed credits, investments, security, all of which were desperately needed.

Geopolitics and Democratic Promotion

It was partly as a result of globalization that democratization became a part of the political agenda under Communism. Furthermore, Western influences shaped domestic actors' identities and policy preferences, as the Polish example above reveals. In fact, after 1989, conscious policies undertaken by the West became a significant factor in post-Communist politics generally. For reasons of security, development and geopolitics, Western (and particularly Western European) actors have developed quite different agendas for East and Central Europe, the territories of the former Soviet Union and the Balkan states. Different Western actors have also focused on very different kinds of policies. Some are concerned with establishing a market economy, and others primarily support the creation of a democratic order.

The policies adopted by Western European governments and the European Union towards post-Communist countries can essentially be described as a mix of aid and advice. The option of rewarding favoured countries with closer trade links or even integration constitutes the backdrop that gives Western Europe a particular leverage. The PHARE programme was created in 1989 as the aid arm of EU's cooperation with the East (Pridham 1999). PHARE established firm political conditions for aid, relating especially to human rights and to the maintenance of formal democracy. The Trade and Cooperation agreements created shortly after gave way to the more complex Europe Agreements in the mid-1990s, and set up areas of political dialogue as well as economic and cultural cooperation (Hyde-Price 1994). Nevertheless, these programmes have come in for considerable criticism for tying aid (Kearns 1996), for their small budgets and hyped programmes (Nagle and Mahr

1999) and for mismanagement. According to some sources, up to two-thirds of the PHARE budget has gone in paying for consultancies rather than to the countries it is earmarked for (Ost 1997). In conclusion, while aid from the European Union aid has certainly been visible, its impact is questioned.

In contrast to the European Union, US aid has primarily been destined for the countries of the ex-Soviet Union and for Russia in particular. Much of this flows through the international financial institutions. Essentially it is economic aid, aimed at speeding up the transition to a market economy, but it comes with political conditionality attached. For Sharman and Kanet (2000), these policies actually hinder democratization. In particular, they encourage technocratic and undemocratic policymaking. Thus it is not only the social results of marketization in Russia – increased hardship and inequality – that are questioned but

> more…the manner in which decisions have been taken and implemented; in effect to avoid those institutions of democratic government that might slow, review or reject measures in line with societal interests and thereby stymie technocratic prescriptions. (Sharman and Kanet 2000: 236)

The limited success of these programmes is testimony to the 'technical' difficulties of supporting democracy from outside. But it also graphically illustrates the problems inherent in trying to impose liberal democracy as the only end-game in the messy and confused politics of post-Communism.

Given the difficulties that beset aid policies, then, why were they put in place and why do they continue? They are driven by a combination of a security logic – a hangover from the Cold War – and a view that the post-Communist countries represented almost virgin terrain for the development of capitalism. According to Nagle and Mahr (1999: 271): '"Western" influence in post-communist Europe is part of a larger emerging pattern of a liberated and adventurous global capitalism.' In other words, support for democratization is derived from the assumption that the new political order will create trade and investment opportunities which will benefit Western companies and governments. Ultimately, democratization programmes pull post-Communist countries into the mainstream of the global political economy. The result is an uneven subordination of the Eastern economies to Western Europe: the best-placed economies will achieve some integration with the European Union while the rest will become a hinterland. This pattern of integration into the West through economic discipline and subordination will make it difficult for the Eastern economies to close the gap with the West, leading to the institutionalization of dependency on the West. For Kearns (1996: 81), this dependency is maintained not only by the West itself but, crucially, by the new political elites of post-Communist countries who perceive short-term and personal benefits from the prestige and legitimation they are endowed with as a result of Western contacts.

Conclusion

This chapter has highlighted the complexities attaching to transition in post-Communist countries and discussed the extent to which a strong tendency towards democratization can be discerned. The varieties of post-Communist politics are greater even than in Latin America. Moreover, it is less possible to speak of a single regional pattern than in either Latin America or Southern Europe. Three basic patterns of post-Communism can be seen: stable, if limited, democracies in parts of East and Central Europe, sustained by bumpy economic development; unstable and contested democratization in Russia and the other territories of the former Soviet Union, where de-territorialization of the state and worsening poverty, this latter especially in Russia, undermine the chances for deepening democratization in the short term; and 'nationalism in command', that is the subordination of democratization in the Balkans by elites who are able to manipulate nationalist and ethnic tensions. The differences in regional experiences, then, are tremendous.

What accounts for these very different trajectories? We have drawn attention in particular to the legacies of the Communist state and the 'Eastern' state traditions and to the general weakness of civil society as factors constraining the democratization project. While civil society was able to contribute to the demise of communism in innumerable acts of resistance, great and small, it is presently weak, vis-à-vis both political society and the state. Statecraft, which might have been expected to be able to triumph over these unfavourable structural constraints, is, on the whole, proving to be less decisive in determining outcomes than was initially hoped. The very strong support the international community is lending to the democratization experiments in the region is an attempt to counter these obstacles. Indeed, generally, the processes of globalization are forces for change across the region. However, the extent to which they are supportive of democratization, especially in the sense of creating inclusive societies, based on some recognition of rights and citizenship, is rather more open to question. External assistance is tied, for the most part, to the development of trade and market linkages and citizenship programmes receive relatively low priority in funding terms. So, in the short term at least, the picture contradicts the excessive hopes expressed in 1989 for a rapid democratization of the entire region. Nevertheless, in some ways, the region has progressed towards democracy more than might have been hoped for. The electoral processes are for the most part stable, and international pressure, if nothing else, prevents a return to old-style dictatorships.

10
Democratization in Asia

The 1980s witnessed a surge of opposition movements and some progress towards electoral democracy in a number of Asian countries, such as Taiwan, South Korea and China. At the same time, the breakdown of the Communist bloc, the globalization of capitalism and the universalization of the discourse of democratization appeared to herald the end of the rigid cultural and economic divisions between East and West. The paradigm of democratization offers a novel interpretative focus for understanding change in Asia that draws attention to conflict between resistance from below and the state. For some scholars, however, the spread of democracy to Asia is more obviously part of a normative project of Westernization (Hurrell 1999). For Huntington (1996), the success of the third wave rests on its capacity to penetrate the previously closed and, for him, antagonistic, systems of the East.

Nevertheless, how far Asia is becoming more democratic, and, just as important, what kind of democracies are under construction, is a matter of heated debate. This chapter attempts to unravel that debate. It disentangles the processes of political change in the region, identifying first different national paths of political transformation. The chapter then analyzes the overarching frameworks applied to political change in the region. Finally, the chapter examines how far the transformation of Asia is due to globalization and examines the roles of the state and emerging civil society in democratization. It argues that while patterns of formal democratization can be discerned in some countries, in others, the state remains sufficiently strong and cohesive to resist pressure from below for change. Furthermore, Asia remains more able to resist global pressures to democratize. It is hard, therefore, to identify an assured pattern of democratization in the region.

Tentative Patterns of Regional Democratization

Before the 1980s, Asia was characterized by very different systems of government, styles of leadership, economic production and social values from those of the West. Not only was China socialist, but Asian capitalism was seen as very different from Anglo-American or European variants, with a strong role for the state in shaping and directing national markets and firms. Non-socialist Asian political systems were thought to exemplify 'Asian' values, even in countries such as Japan where the political systems were formally liberal democratic. This rigid ideological separation between East and West, however, was always exaggerated because of its utility to both governing elites in Asia and to Western policy-makers. Moreover, it became less and less tenable through the 1980s and 1990s. This was partly the result of the incorporation of Asia into global capitalism. In 1997, the Asian financial crisis contributed to the perception that Asian capitalism was less different from Western variants than had previously been thought. At the same time the sense of difference lessened with the emergence of pro-democracy movements across the region, from the Philippines to South Korea, Taiwan and China. As a result of both economic crisis and political agency, then, the picture of Asia as unchanging and fundamentally unsuited to democracy began to disintegrate.

Democratization has emerged most clearly as a trend in the Philippines, South Korea and Taiwan. More recently, there has been considerable pressure for democracy in Indonesia. In Singapore and China, in contrast, there is resistance on the part of the state and elites to change. We discuss below the contrasting experiences of democratization in four key regional countries, South Korea, Taiwan, the Philippines and China. In two (South Korea and Taiwan), transitions to democracy have begun. In another (the Philippines), a process of democratization opened abruptly and has since stalled. In the fourth (China), there have been substantial social and international pressures for democratization but the state and elites have so far been able to resist, through the application of a two-pronged strategy of economic growth and repression.

South Korea

South Korea's existence, as a result of the division of the country in 1948, is due to the Cold War. South Korean politics were therefore in a very fundamental way structured with reference to trends within the global order. Syngman Rhee's dictatorship (1948–60) was largely upheld through its legitimation by the US. In 1960, it was finally brought to an end by student protest. A short-lived democratic experiment followed under Jang Myeon, between 1960 and 1961. The political system fragmented, however, and the main opposition before 1960, the Liberty

Party, split into four distinct ideological factions. At the same time, there was uncertainty about how the changes inside South Korea would be received outside the country. In order to shore up the shaky regime, Myeon signed a new deal with the US, guaranteeing the US veto rights over national politics. This led to something of a nationalist backlash. It therefore came as no surprise when the government proved unable to resist takeover by the Armed Forces. President, formerly General, Park Chung Hee, remained in power from 1961 until 1979 and presided over a period of rapid economic growth. In some ways the dictatorship was similar to the bureaucratic-authoritarian regimes found in parts of Latin America at this time and saw its role as managing development, controlling dissent, closing down labour protest, and de-politicizing society. Elections, held in 1963, 1967 and 1971, were manipulated to favour Park's re-election, the National Assembly was tightly controlled and the judiciary was subject to executive intervention. Following Park's assassination, hard-liner General Chun Doo Hwan took over. After resigning from the Army, he was elected to the presidency for a fixed term of seven years in 1980.

Opposition to authoritarianism, which had never quite gone away, then resurfaced. Social protest, especially from the universities, increased steadily during the 1980s. The protests drew support from a range of social groups, including students, intellectuals, farmers and the urban poor. The state responded with severe repression and thousands of students were arrested in 1986 following a student sit-in in Konguk University. Reports of torture and human rights abuses increased after 1987. The protests intensified as Chun attempted to control the presidential elections in April 1987, so as to hand the presidency over to Roh Tae Woo, another hard-liner. Faced with widespread popular protest, Roh tried to make a deal with the opposition as an alternative to imposing martial law. Some liberalizing measures followed but the opposition was unable to take advantage of them because it remained divided. This allowed Roh Tae Woo to secure the presidency after all and the damage to the regime was confined to a loss of control of the National Assembly by the government-run ruling party, the Democratic Justice Party (DJP).

This period culminated in a transition of sorts. Political society has expanded beyond those tied directly to the government. But in fact, the opening created in 1987 has really led only to the formation of a grand conservative coalition (Lee 1994), rather than the introduction of democracy. The party system is based on cooperation within and between a narrow political elite. Although Roh and the DJP faced considerable popular opposition between 1987 and 1989, the opposition in

220   *Democratization*

the National Assembly led by the Kim Dae Jung, Kim Young Sam and Kim Jong Pil was based on regional, rather than class, social or ideological cleavages. The opposition in the Assembly did not connect easily with the protest movements in the streets. At the same time, regional-based rivalries meant that a unified opposition was difficult to achieve. As a result, Roh was able to push for the formation of a new Democratic Liberal Party, merging the DJP with two opposition parties, the Reunification Democratic Party, led by Kim Young Sam, and the New Democratic Republican Party, led by Kim Jong Pil. This represented the construction of a new conservative hegemony, incorporating elites previously active outside the regime. So, although the post-1989 regime has the legitimacy of the ballot box, it has not really led to a new era in Korean politics. The deal behind the creation of the new mega-party is unknown, although it is clear that opposition leaders had been coopted. It has brought stability to Korean politics at the expense of opening the system up and increasing participation.

As a result, democratization in Korea remains confined to the electoral and procedural levels. For Diamond and Myer (2000), it is really only an 'electoralist democracy'. A particularly disturbing feature of the system, from a democratic point of view, is the political power of the business community or the *chaebol,* the largest industrial conglomerates. These not only fund and control the political parties but are also 'direct participants' in the political process (Steinberg 1995: 390). At the same time, power remains highly concentrated in the executive, and pluralism is confined to an incorporation of regional elites. The legacies from the authoritarian period are important and legitimize a culture of respect for central authority, especially because the state managed the economy well – in the eyes of the middles classes, at least (Shin 1999: 248). Nevertheless, there are pressures from below and civil society remains an important site of conflict, generating pressures for further democratization.

Taiwan

Like South Korea, Taiwan is a product of the Cold War. After the Chinese Revolution of 1949, the defeated Chinese Nationalists withdrew to the island of Formosa, thereby creating a new state, Taiwan or the Republic of China. Taiwan won recognition from the West as a way of trying to isolate mainland Communist China. The governing Kuomintang (KMT) established a monopoly of political power on the island and martial law was in force until 1987. The KMT retained some legitimacy because it represented nationalist aspirations to a 'free' China. At the same time, it encouraged participation through corporatist organization. According to Rigger (1996), the result was 'a state and society fused in ... "mobilizational authoritarianism"'. By encouraging organization in a way that it could control, the state was able to close civil society as an alternative space for dissent – in a fashion remarkably similar, in fact, to the political style of the Chinese Communist Party. Opposition did surface during the 1950s and 1960s, especially from Taiwanese-born citizens who resented the dominance of the mainland Chinese, but it was very quickly repressed.

By the 1970s, the KMT's capacity to control the political system was under threat. Successful industrialization had produced a generation of independent professionals, as well as public officials and entrepreneurs. Unlike South Korea, industrialization was not dominated exclusively by large corporations. The small to medium-sized companies made an important contribution to the country's economy, although they enjoyed far fewer privileges from the state. They were also difficult for the state to coopt. Furthermore, because development was aimed at the export market, many entrepreneurs had regular and repeated contact with the West. Around the same time, Taiwan lost its seat at the UN as Communist China sought rehabilitation with the West. The result was a rise in serious political opposition for the first time.

However, a distinctive feature of the opposition movement was that it was generally structured around ethnic, rather than class, conflict. The opposition's main grievance focused on the need to 'nationalize' politics, that is to reform the KMT so that it reflected more accurately the ethnic composition of the country. Democratization, then, came to mean a reversal of the trend of domination of the mainland Chinese to the exclusion of those born in Taiwan and the end of an the economy organized on the basis of a rigid ethnic stratification. While politics and public employment were the preserve of mainland Chinese, business and agriculture were in the hands of the ethnic Taiwanese.

Initially, the KMT responded to opposition with violence. Nevertheless, social organizations continued to press for political rights, reform and ethnic justice. The opposition Democratic Progressive Party (DPP) was established in 1986. Accepting that reform was inevitable, the KMT lifted martial law and tried to reshape the political order so as to allow for some political change while maintaining KMT control over the process of political decompression. A series of political reforms were introduced, culminating in the first direct presidential elections in 1996. The KMT has, so far, managed to stay in power. How far all of this can be said to represent a process of democratization is the subject of some debate. Taiwan's elections are relatively fair, but the degree of consolidation of the new institutions is low (Chu and Diamond 1999). At the same time, while levels of liberty are formally considerable, expectations of social and political conformity are high. Just as worrying, corruption is widespread – vote-buying is common, for example – and attitudes to the state reflect the idea that public office is a source for personal enrichment. It is hard, in fact, to identify much that has changed within the state.

The Philippines

Philippine history is a mosaic of cross-cultural traditions . As well as indigenous and regional influences, Spanish colonialism has left a history of Catholicism and the US occupation between 1899 and 1945 transformed the culture, language and outlook of the political elites. The US withdrawal led to the creation of a presidential system. Limited democracy survived until Ferdinand Marcos came into office. Elected President in 1965, he introduced martial law in 1972. He was able to remain in office until 1986, when he was ousted by mass demonstrations against the regime. The Marcos dictatorship was almost a prototype of the kleptomania state and public funds were pillaged by Marcos's family and cronies. It stands in sharp contrast to the developmental dictatorships of South Korea, Taiwan or Singapore. In order to remain in power, Marcos consistently manipulated elections, changed the nature of the governing institutions and bought off the business community.

Opposition to the dictatorship increased in the 1970s, as the state became more repressive and the Catholic Church called for Marcos to step down. In 1983, the assassination of the moderate opposition leader, Begnino Aquino, was the catalyst for massive popular opposition and elite defections from the Marcos camp. In an attempt to reassure his most important allies abroad, the US, and to show the military hardliners that he could still be trusted to control the country, Marcos brought the presidential elections forward to 1986. Corazon Aquino, the murdered opposition leader's widow, stood against Marcos. The elections were held despite increasing public disorder. The Army, which had decided to abandon Marcos, began organizing a coup. Meanwhile, Marcos claimed victory in the elections. Such was the popular outcry that he was forced to flee the country, as people took to the streets in their thousands, eliminating at the same time the military's chance of seizing power. As a result, Corazon Aquino was sworn in as president.

Democratization began following the collapse of the authoritarian regime. But the new system was not really the result either of sustained popular opposition or of elite pressure for change. The movement on the streets, though massive, was spontaneous and unorganized. Civil society was actually much weaker than it initially appeared. Meanwhile elite commitment to democracy was low. The military, which tried to come forward as heirs to the dictatorship, was really only sidelined because of the sudden eruption of popular opposition to Marcos. As a result, despite a clear popular preference for democracy, the process of creating a functioning democracy in the Philippines has been problematic and conflictual. Aquino could not count upon an organized and democratic political class. Although she was able to hand power over in elections in 1992, her main concern throughout her period in office was simply to survive. The Army, which only reluctantly accepted the transition, was an active opponent of change and democracy and staged six coup attempts between 1986 and 1989. As a result, Aquino and governments that followed have had a very reduced capacity to introduce reforms. Little progress has been made, either, to reform the institutions of the state. With ineffectual state institutions and weak civil society organizations, the only channel for public criticism is through street protest. In January 2001, mass protests in the streets were once again used to force the resignation of President Estrada. He was later found guilty of corruption and embezzlement of public funds. Nevertheless, while he was in office, there were no institutionalized mechanisms that were effective channels to question his abuse of power.

Meanwhile, the failure to address either questions of the state or the urgent social problems in the country has progressively eroded popular faith in democracy and led to a surge in radical activism, including the development of a Muslim guerrilla force in the countryside. In short, then, an opportunity for democracy opened rapidly but moving beyond a mere electoral democracy is difficult and the democratic order is contested and unstable. Furthermore, democratization is blocked by problems of corruption and state inefficiency. As such, it stands in sharp contrast to the incremental and controlled political openings of South Korea or Taiwan.

China

In 1949, the Chinese Communists seized power, defeating the Chinese Nationalists (the KMT) and bringing to an end decades of political instability and foreign occupation. The new state set about creating a largely self-sufficient national economy, privileging production in collectives. By the 1960s, the Chinese had developed a distinctive version of Communism, based on large-scale mobilization and terror. As in other Communist countries, the legacies of a single party state and a centrally planned economy create significant material and cultural obstacles to democracy. However, in the Chinese case, pre-Communist political culture and long-standing Chinese power structures – the imperial tradition and Confucianism – have also been identified as antithetical to liberal democratic values (Randall 1997). In fact, the success of the Chinese revolution lay not only in its capacity for control and the imposition of order after anarchy, but also in its manipulation of long-standing cultural traditions of unquestioning loyalty to the state and of the independence of the bureaucracy. This gave rise to the populist cult of Chairman Mao, the founder of the Communist state. The result is a strong state, nervous of civil society, a weak and underdeveloped tradition of independent activity outside the state and low levels of individual autonomy.

Following a timid rapprochement with the West in the early 1970s under Mao, Deng Xioping began the process of economic reform, including opening the economy to the West. China has experienced considerable economic growth as a result. The economic reforms have led to dramatic social upheaval, including migration to the cities, an increase in the number of employed in factories and an overall rise in living standards. But development is uneven and consumption depends on region, with the coastal cities and in particular Shanghai consistently enjoying the highest levels of growth, in contrast to the millions of Chinese still employed in the countryside or in the failing state enterprises. Pei (1994) has deemed these changes a 'capitalist revolution'. Certainly, the Communist Party now seeks legitimacy through economic growth and modernization (He 1996).

Some political change has followed the opening up of the economy. But the reforms have mainly been aimed at rationalizing the state and eliminating bureaucratic inefficiency, rather than starting a controlled democratization. There is now a greater role for the National People's Congress as a check on government. Village elections, the lowest level of the political system, have also been the site of greater freedom of choice, although they are still subject to tight control. But none of these reforms have been enough to satisfy the demands of Chinese dissidents or the Democracy Movement which emerged in Beijing and other cities from the late 1970s onwards. In fact pro-democracy movements have been quite severely repressed. Between 1979 and 1980, the Democracy

Wall movement was closed down and its leaders imprisoned. Nevertheless, democratic pressures built up again after 1985. Students demonstrated in growing numbers through 1986 for political change, focusing on the right to freedom of expression as well as a relaxation of social control in universities. These protests were to lead ultimately to the Tiananmen Square occupation in 1989 (see Box 10.1) and a wave of state repression which has not yet come to an end. According to the organization Human Rights in China (HRIC): 'human rights abuses have reached such alarming proportions since late 1998 that HRIC believes that the Government of China is currently conducting the most ruthless suppression of dissent since the crackdown on the 1989 demonstrations' (WWW.publications.parliament.uk/pa/c1999900/cmselect/cmfaff/574/5 7406.htm). Any demonstration of dissent can now earn harsh penal sentences. Moreover, repression is not confined to intellectuals. Independent workers' organizations have become a particular target since 1989. Many of those found guilty are subject to re-education through labour, a policy dating back to the Cultural Revolution in the

---

Box 10.1   The Tiananmen Square Massacre

More than a million demonstrators gathered in Tiananmen Square in the centre of Beijing to demand political reform in April 1989. The protests lasted almost six weeks and coincided with a visit to China of Mikael Gorbachev, thus ensuring widespread coverage in the international press. What happened in Tiananmen has come to symbolize the events of 1989 as much as the tearing down of the Wall in Berlin. In the Chinese case, however, the outcome was much less felicitous.

Initially the students gathered to demand the rehabilitation of Communist leader, Hu Yaobang, purged for excessive sympathy to student protests in 1986. As more students joined in, however, the demands radicalized. Changes to the government were demanded, as Deng was regarded as too corrupt and too tied to the past to implement reform. Initially reluctant to move against the demonstrators, the government tried to persuade the students to trust the Party. Martial law was declared when this strategy failed. Nevertheless, it seemed that the Army would not move against the students, although they did surround the Square with troops. But on 4 June the Army moved in and violently cleared the Square. The immediate repression was followed by arrests and executions. The government has since chosen to repress dissent and presents pro-democracy activists as disloyal and unpatriotic. So far, the Chinese government has weathered all Western criticism for the repression it has unleashed.

1960s. It is hard, therefore, to escape the conclusion that despite pressures for change, democratization is at present blocked in China. Meanwhile, stagnant authoritarianism in China also limits the democratization process in Hong Kong, which reverted to the Chinese mainland in 1999. With few checks on executive authority, weak parties and poorly organized interest groups, Hong Kong can only really be described as a 'pseudodemocracy' (Diamond and Myers 2000).

Theorizing Democratization in Asia

The most important perspectives through which to view the processes of democratization in Asia are the modernizationist view and the culturalist perspective. Asia is, in fact, taken to both constitute proof of the modernization paradigm – that economic development eventually culminates in democracy – and to provide evidence for its refutation. Bell *et al.* (1995) argues that it is the persistence of 'Asian values' that has allowed the region to resist full democracy – or even democracy at all, in some cases – economic growth notwithstanding; and that economic growth drives the region towards a culturally specific form of political development which mixes, at best, some of the principles of democracy – elections, for example – with authoritarianism. They term this 'illiberal democracy' (Bell *et al.* 1995). In effect, they suggest that non-democratic cultural patterns are so deeply embedded in state and society that Asia can buck the trend and resist the global pressures to democratize. Instead, authoritarian elites draw on a coherent regional project, which borrows enough from democracy to satisfy external critics but which is in fact a reworking of the authoritarian status quo. Box 10.2 examines in more detail the debate about Asian values and democratization. However, others have resisted culturalist arguments as a way of explaining the failure of substantive democracy. Jones (1998), for example, suggests that the weight of the state is more important. We return to this argument below.

Work on Asia has also been influenced by the development of more recent paradigms explaining democratization. For example, the agency perspective has been applied to the process of rule-making, bargaining and elite negotiations that took place in South Korea, (for example, Cheng and Kim 1994). Similarly, the impact of globalization has also been the focus of research, especially since democratization pressures appear to be generated following integration into the global political economy. Youngs (2000) identifies democratization in Hong Kong as a

---

Box 10.2   Asian Values: An Obstacle to Democratization?

The relatively peaceful process of industrialization in South Korea, Taiwan, Singapore and Malaysia has sometimes been attributed to the prevalence of a value system of deference, consensus, respect, social harmony, bureaucracy and order in the region. This builds on the work of Lucien Pye (1966; Pye and Pye 1985) who claimed to have identified distinct cultural and psychological patterns in Asia that shape its political practices and social relationships. These values were identified as part of the Confuscian legacy. Because they encourage devotion to political leaders and give importance to the community over the individual, they are seen as inimicable to the liberal tradition of individualism and to the development of a critical civil society. However, the notion that such disparate countries share completely similar value systems is overly simplistic and should be questioned. Similarly, there is no intrinsic reason why democracy is impossible in Asia. In fact, according to Freeman (1996), the values that are now described as somehow exclusively 'Asian' are actually very similar to those held by Western conservatives, especially the emphasis on social order, hierarchy and the importance of an uncritical respect for authority. In terms of the view of the state and the importance of social harmony, Asian values could even be said to be akin to Christian Democratic culture. Moreover, the tensions between conservatism and democracy have not prevented the emergence of democratic traditions and values in Europe, and there is no reason to suppose that they inevitably will in Asia. Furthermore, values and cultures are complex, dynamic and fluid. This means that Asian politics is not permanently encased in a given set of inherited traditions, if indeed it ever was.

---

consequence of the global political economy. She argues that the process was driven by the fact that democracy appeared as the most secure route through which the West could retain a capitalist Hong Kong. In short, democracy was imposed by the needs of global capitalism, without any significant pro-democratization struggles actually taking place. Finally, the growing importance of the distinction between electoralist and substantive democratization is important in studies of Asia because it allows for a more nuanced depiction of the processes of political change occurring in the region. For Diamond and Myers (2000), the distinction between the introduction of elections and democratization is particularly important in Asia. So, even in South Korea and Taiwan, regarded as the most successful of the Asian transitions, where elections routinely take place, the quality of democracy is actually very low. The mass of the population is exceptionally deferential towards elites and the state, and levels of citizenship are low.

The State

Most Asian countries are usually described as having 'strong states'. State strength is held to have accounted for economic development and a number of Asian countries experienced rapid capitalist development under the direction and control of the state. The success of East Asian capitalism was attributed primarily to states with the capacity to establish enabling legal frameworks for capitalism, implement pro-business policies, create powerful bureaucracies to watch over the economy and oversee policy implementation. Governments were able to rely on a range of policy tools to promote industrialization and development, ensure a favourable environment for private investment and control the social consequences of that process. South Korea, Taiwan, Singapore, Malaysia, and to a lesser extent, Indonesia and Thailand are examples of states that were able to promote rapid industrialization in the 1950s and 1960s. Economic development took place without massive social dislocation, although the extent to which there is social harmony in the region has sometimes been overestimated. Nevertheless, strategies of consensus-formation, the cooptation of import-substituting groups who were granted a say in making economic policy and policies of welfare management prevented the eruption of large-scale social problems in Taiwan and Malaysia and South Korea. As the state took on the function of improving living standards for the burgeoning working classes in the cities, wealth creation seemed actually to lead to trickle-down. But in Indonesia and to some extent Thailand, strength has meant the capacity to repress social dissent as well as the capacity to articulate a programme of national economic development. In China, a latecomer to the global economy in the 1980s, the state clearly aims to be both developmental and repressive.

The strong state is legitimized in Korea, Indonesia, Malaysia, Taiwan and China because of its appeals not only to developmentalism but also to nationalism. This has been built up over time through the creation of national norms and cultures, inculcated through the education system, for example. It is worth remembering that the values we now identify as Asian were, in fact, 'selectively reinvented' by ruling elites concerned with nation building and meeting economic targets during the 1960s, 1970s and 1980s (Jones 1998: 149). This now enables these states to counter Western human rights and pro-democracy activism with a coherent discourse of their own. A discourse of protecting national values from dissolution is therefore part of the repertoire of the strong state in the region. It serves, furthermore, as a justification for the repression of dissent. So, as a result, nationalism and the strong state tradition have together created as a wall, rendering Western criticism for the slow progress of democracy and human rights violations relatively ineffectual. How hard it is for Western governments to make an impact on the human rights issue in Asia is illustrated in Box 10.3.

Democratization in the region, then, is constrained by the existence of strong states that have a much greater capacity to resist pressures from below than developing states in Latin America or Africa, for example. The strong state is particularly effective as a source of labour

---

Box 10.3   The Chinese State and Human Rights

In 1999, representatives from the British Parliamentary Select Committee on Foreign Affairs visited China. They were keen to raise the issue of human rights and indicated that they wished to meet with Chinese human rights activists. They were told by Chinese government officials that this was an 'inappropriate demand'. It was implied that they were engaging in an act of cultural imperialism. The report of the Select Committee at the end of the visit describes how their desire to meet with opposition members was continually frustrated:

> In the event, we reluctantly decided not to hold the meetings which we had planned because of advice that we received that there would be considerable personal dangers for any Chinese national who might have the audacity to criticize the Chinese Government to us or generally to discuss human rights. ... We challenged Vice Minister Ma Canrong on his government's stance. He told us that we should respect the wishes of our hosts ... and not do what our hosts disliked. In his view, dissidents were hostile to the Chinese Government, and friendship would be prejudiced if the Committee met such people. ... [E]stablishing relations with people who were hostile to the Chinese Government was not a way of fostering goodwill. We found this explanation chilling. We concluded that the way we were prevented from meeting human rights activists during our visit was a graphic illustration for us personally of the absence of human rights in China.

(WWW.publications.parliament.uk/pa/c1999900/cmselect/cmfaff/574/57406.htm)

and popular repression (Hewison and Rodan 1996), at the same time as it is able to mobilize intellectual support around projects of national resistance to Westernization.

The success of the strong state in East Asia rested on the symbiotic relationship fostered by the developmental state with national business groups. For Johnson (1987) the East Asian state regulated growth by favouring, but also disciplining, national capital. This was thought to allow the state a significant degree of autonomy in policy-making terms, despite its pro-business bias. In fact, it has emerged that the ties between business and the state have not led to rational and efficient policy-making. Errors in industrial policy and poor management are, in fact, now regarded as integral causal components of the 1997 economic crisis in Korea, for example (Haggard 2000a). Economic policies emerged out of the closed and institutionalized relationship between government and business. This led, in turn, to 'the socialization of private risk taking' as the government sought to minimize risks to business groups, partly motivated by the web of financial, economic and political relationships that has developed between the public and the private sector. In the end, the state, rather than regulating business, had been captured by it (Haggard 2000a: 199).

It is not surprising, then, that the state itself is seen as the principal obstacle to democratization. As a result, for Haggard (2000a), and Gills (2000), the chances for democratization depend upon a transformation of the overdeveloped state. The first step towards this came with the Asian financial crisis (see Box 10.4). Even more than internal opposition, it is the crisis of the very model of state-led capitalism which they claim opens the possibility of democratization in the long term. Nevertheless, in some countries, the financial crash actually provoked a crisis of faith in democracy. In South Korea, public support for democracy slipped considerably in 1997 (Diamond and Kim 2000:5). Moreover, reform since 1997 has been slow. Although the relationship between business and government has altered somewhat in the wake of the financial crisis of 1997, the legacy of close collaboration and a pro-business bias in state policy hinder the chances for successful democratization (Jongryn and Chung-in 1999). The state remains overly tied to business and unreceptive to demands from labour.

Within our case studies, the existence of overdeveloped pro-business states hinders democratization in South Korea and Taiwan especially. The process of democratization in the Philippines, in contrast, suffers from problems of state incapacity. According to Caspar (1995), the main achievements of Philippine democracy so far lie in the area of social

Box 10.4   The 1997 Financial Crisis and Democratization

The Asian financial crisis of 1997, affecting Korea, Thailand, Malaysia, the Philippines and Indonesia, took the world unawares. Until then, international investors and financial agencies thought that the Asian model of capitalism was resistant to cyclical downturns. The worst of the economic consequences of the crisis were over by 1999. But the political impact is more long-term. In particular, it opened up fissures in the model of authoritarian capitalism, especially in terms of capital–labour relations and elite–mass relations. The developmental state was weakened in terms of its capacity to control society and to deliver for it. As a result, democratization pressures are now greater. For Gills (2000: 401), 'the fundamental axis of change lies ... in the social, ideological and political change [the crisis] sets in motion'.

One major consequence of the crisis is that it has opened a debate about the relationship between business and the state in the region. Openness to business on the part of the state was regarded as an essential component of the successful development model, even though it clearly privileged business over the rest of society in terms of access to government. But according to Haggard (2000b), the relationship between business and the state was never as positive for growth as had been imagined. The crisis revealed that the relationship between business and government officials had led to rent-seeking, corruption and cronyism. Furthermore, it is now clear that the least democratic states experienced the highest levels of corruption. More corruption scandals have been revealed in Indonesia and Thailand than in South Korea. As a result, the crisis has generated greater levels of opposition and calls for transparency in the affected countries, as well as fatally weakening illegitimate governments such as that of Indonesia.

reconciliation rather than in terms of a reform of the state. The weakness of the Philippine state is also revealed in its inability either to suppress or to negotiate successfully with the rebel guerrilla movements. In China, meanwhile, bureaucratic single party control, a capacity for repression and a dynamic process of economic growth are, together, responsible for maintaining the regime in power. Consequently, for Bernstein (1994), democratization can only begin with change within the ruling party. But while party elites are committed to economic modernization they view democracy as a threat to stability, development and order. After Tiananmen the party took care to reinforce its control over the Army. So economic liberalization is not, at least in the short run, leading to greater openness within the ruling party or a greater receptiveness to civil society demands. Nor has it sufficiently strengthened autonomous social forces to be able to confront the state successfully enough to win concessions.

Civil Society

The strong state could be said to rest on traditional Asian values of deference towards leaders and the communal, rather than the individual, good. Clearly, Asian values constitute an obstacle to the development of active and critical civil societies. But Asian values are by no means the only ones that can be traced in the region. Indeed, given the tradition of resistance from below, it is possible to argue that their importance has been overemphasized. There is, in fact, a tradition of opposition in countries such as Singapore, Malaysia, Thailand, Indonesia and the Philippines dating back to the 1920s. The revolutionary movements of this period were defeated, but they have left an important legacy and created a public space within which it is possible to criticize the state and the capitalist order (Hewison and Rodan 1996). For different reasons, opposition increased in a number of countries such as Thailand, Indonesia, South Korea and China in the 1980s that drew on this tradition of critical opposition. Hewison (1999) argues that the political space available to the opposition increased mainly because exceptional economic growth in the 1980s led to industrial expansion and more organized working-class activities. In Thailand, Indonesia and to a lesser extent the Philippines, opposition movements emphasized their links with the anti-colonial agitation of the past.

Opposition from within civil society has pushed democratization in Indonesia, Thailand and the Philippines. Popular protest and 'people's power' had been sufficient to force Marcos to flee the country in 1983. Fifteen years later, in 1998, the Indonesian dictator Suharto was overthrown by a sudden eruption of sustained social protest. Behind the protests in Indonesia lay several years of expanding civil society activism. This encompassed NGOs, students, intellectuals and, by the 1970s, workers' organizations. The financial crisis of 1997 revealed deep and embedded patterns of corruption in government. The state under Suharto was revealed as rent-seeking, cynical and incapable. As a result, the long-standing opposition to the regime was strengthened. Increasingly abandoned by the tame official opposition and the Armed Forces, Suharto resigned in order to try and promote a peaceful transition that would ensure legal protection for his family and cronies. But democratization has stalled at this point, as the opposition movements, though strong enough to oust Suharto, have so far been unable to push a real opening of the political system. Meanwhile international governance institutions such as the World Bank, though formally concerned with deepening the space for civil society, prefer to insist on short-term policies of order and financial retrenchment, rather than political reform. The international financial agencies fear the short-term disruption that opening up the system any further might cause.

In China, deepening civil society is perhaps the only route to democracy, given the strength of the party-state. According to White, Howell and Xiaoyuan (1996), the liberalization of the Chinese economy in the 1980s led to an explosion of organizations beyond the party-state. The first real signs of an open critique of the system was the Democracy Wall movement in 1978. Wall-posters near the residences of Chinese officials identified errors in the political system and called for change. New journals emerged, edited by intellectuals, which called for reform of the system but also rejected Western liberalism in China. By the end of the 1980s civil society had expanded. It was no longer confined to intellectuals but had spread to encompass other groups, especially after the introduction of economic reforms and the development of a more marketized economy. The protest movements of the 1980s drew strength from a variety of sources. The massive demonstrations in April and May 1989 in Beijing and other cities united teachers, factory workers, writers, journalists, public officials, entrepreneurs and ordinary urban dwellers as well as intellectuals and students. But this 'civil society' occupies a restricted space, geographically as well as politically. In practice it is confined to the eastern and coastal areas which have been the site of most rapid economic growth. At the same time, it is not always clear precisely what the 'democracy' movement in China encompasses. For some, the preferred option is reform of the present system rather than its overthrow. At the same time, the state remains very strong. There is some tolerance of discussion, greater than in the past, within the party-state. But pressures from outside the state remain liable to sudden and potentially violent repression. In sum, we can identify growing pressure from society, but as yet there is no real pluralism in political society and no legitimized space for civil society. And despite the growing space that non-state organizations occupy, it is important to remember that opposition is really only articulated by elites; civil society has yet to broaden to workers, or gender groups. For these reasons, He (1996) suggests that there is really only a semi-civil society. Civil society organizations have not yet generated a set of autonomous and non-state values (Pei 1994:

208). Furthermore, they are not strong enough to act as a bulwark against the encroachment of the state.

The growing confidence and size of civil society movements throughout the region and the expansion of political space for opposition are mainly a result of rapid economic change. This process has transformed class structures, communities, networks and belief systems. But the real strength of civil society movements is difficult to gauge. On the one hand, civil society movements are certainly more visible than fifteen years ago. But, on the other, the state remains strong enough to determine the pace of change, in most regional states. Where civil society has been able to force political change, as in the Philippines, Thailand or Indonesia, political society has generally regrouped in defence of elitism and closed down the spaces for popular opposition. For these reasons, the extent to which civil society movements are an immediate source of pressure for democratization is uncertain. Rodan (1996: 40) sees opposition movements as having a number of possible end-games of which democracy is only one. It is not at all clear that elites or the state will compromise with emerging civil and social movements. Even where civil society has proved relatively strong, as in South Korea in the 1980s, democratization was conceived of as a strategy for by-passing society.

Globalization and Democracy

Perhaps more than in any other region, democratization in Asia has to be linked to processes of globalization. Integration into the global political economy has created a range of pro-democracy pressures, both direct and diffuse. Economic pressures, generating increasing social tensions and pressures for change from below, have expanded as the Asian economies have integrated into global, rather than simply national or regional, trade and production chains since the 1980s. As Foot (1997) points out, 'globalization weakens family and traditional structures leaving a vacuum at the societal level unless these structures are replaced with new associational ties'. These new ties have operated as mechanisms to open society up. At the same time, the region has become increasingly subject to influence from the global media, with the result that there has been a sudden influx of images that present consumption and popular control as part of the democratic West, in contrast to pictures of Asia trapped within its own antiquated cultural universe. Of course how these images filter through national societies and are interpreted varies considerably from country to country. So, in China, 'democracy' became a way of expressing opposition to Communist control in the wake of events in 1989 elsewhere, the visit of Gorbachev to China, and the growing links between the Chinese middle class and the outside world. In Malaysia, Western democracy is constructed as selfishness and licentiousness by the government-controlled media, in contrast to the order and austerity that are said to characterize development in that country.

Increasingly complex interactions between the West and Asian countries have thrown into relief the extent to which policies of democratization are, in fact, built upon the normative principles of liberal human rights and individualism. Because only South Korea and Taiwan are regarded as having established even electoralist democracy, most Western pressure is, essentially, pressure to respect human rights. For the West, a commitment to democracy implies an *a priori* commitment to respect for human rights, defined as freedom of speech, of assembly and of religion. Asian governments have generally resisted this liberal position on rights, in favour of an 'Asian' version that stresses communal rights, arguing, in addition, that the West is guilty of attempting to impose its own culture across the world. Prime Minister Mathathir in Singapore and the Chinese leadership have adopted this view especially energetically. Nevertheless, Western ideas about human rights can now penetrate Asian societies easily, with the result that Chinese opposition movements are increasingly using the notion of liberal universalist rights as a tool to criticize the Chinese authorities and to win support abroad.

The human rights issue has led to Asia becoming an important site of what Hurrell (1999: 277) describes as the 'normative ambitions of international society'. This led, in the first instance, to pressure being brought to bear on some non-democratic governments in the region. Because economic links were rapidly developing between China and the West especially, China became the target of considerable pro-democracy pressure by the European Union (EU) after the Tiananmen Square massacre. Cultural links were broken between EU governments and China, for example. But the policy garnered no immediate results and full relations were restored six months later. This was due principally to the fact that EU member states feared that the Chinese would reply with sanctions against European investors. As a result, the policy was abandoned in favour of one of dialogue. In effect, in contrast to Western policies towards smaller developing countries, the option of conditionality – of applying economic sanctions to bring about political change – was abandoned. Instead the West now has a policy of encouraging reform through aid and persuasion. Examples of the kind of policies undertaken by the West to encourage democratization in China are discussed in Box 10. 5.

Box 10.5   British Aid to China: Democratization by Dialogue?

British aid to China, like that of other EU states, is based on the notion of constructive engagement and positive support for change. These policies have come to be termed a 'dialogue' with China. The policy of dialogue developed in response to the difficulties EU governments encountered in tabling motions criticizing China's human rights record in the UN after Tiananmen Square. Between 1990 and 1996, the EU countries tabled annually a motion condemning Chinese abuse of human rights. It was consistently blocked by the Chinese government. In 1997, the EU abandoned that strategy. In that year, without support from the rest of the EU, Denmark tabled a resolution on Chinese human rights. It was backed by the UK. Although the resolution was blocked as in the past, the Chinese government imposed trade sanctions on Denmark. Fear of similar sanctions – in effect excluding particular countries from participating in China's growing economy – meant that no further motions were tabled. In 1998, EU countries agreed to open a dialogue with China instead.

Britain now tries to encourage human rights through selective aid policies, including the promotion of legal reform. In 1999 alone, more than half a million pounds was spent on a programme of legal cooperation. According to the Foreign Office, its aim is to encourage greater respect for human rights in Chinese institutions. Nevertheless, the utility of programmes of this sort has been questioned. At best, their effect is cumulative, partial and long-term. It may also be that policies such as the legal reform programme are really about creating a climate of certainty and mutual understanding between the Chinese and foreign investors by creating clear and shared norms of behaviour. Furthermore, the British aid programme has failed to include NGOs in anything other than a formalist way. This stands in marked contrast to the way European human rights policies are normally formulated. The NGOs are excluded partly at the insistence of the Chinese government. But it is also because the Western agenda with China is primarily constructed around trade and investment and, as a result, the NGOs themselves have dropped out of a dialogue which they feel is not working to promote human rights. For the NGOs, the dialogue serves the interests of the Chinese government which is seeking to maintain the status quo.

Conclusion

Authoritarianism is on the retreat in Asia. But it not clear how far democratization is an established trend. For Chan, Triakerkvliet and Unger (1999), the region is converging around a project of 'soft' authoritarianism rather than democracy. Where transitions have taken place, as in South Korea and Taiwan, democracy is controlled and the state remains dominant. Even in Thailand, where elections have been held consistently since 1992, governments are elitist and vote-buying and electoral manipulations are widespread practices (Hewison and Masrikrod 1997). At the same time, it is by no means certain that democratization, however slow, is a trend across the whole of the region. China, the largest and now the most rapidly developing country, has so far been able to resist national and international pressures for democracy.

In terms of explaining the complex series of changes in the region in the 1980s and 1990s, it is important to look at interactions between the global level and changes within nation states. Asia is in the throes of global incorporation, cultural shifts and an increasing interdependence with the West. The pressures to democratize generated by globalization are intense. At the same time, a gradual unpicking of the established national models of politics is slowly taking place, due primarily to the sweeping economic changes that the region has experienced. So, in Asia, as much as in post-Communist countries, there are complex linkages between economic and political change and between the internationalization of politics and cultural transformation. Political change in Asia is driven by economic reorganization and by global example, as well as by local and indigenous pressures on elites and masses. Nevertheless, the legacy of the strong state, both in a developmental and a political sense, is such that democracy is by no means guaranteed. For this reason, the pace of change has generally been hastened by the financial crisis of 1997 which revealed tremendous problems with state-led development. The crisis shook the foundations of authoritarian regimes, most notably in Indonesia. But on the positive side, it should be remembered that years of growth and development make democracy possible in Asia, in the sense, at least, that the state is equipped for and capable of dealing with distribution and welfare (Haggard 2000b). This makes democratization an option in the future, even it has, so far, failed to live up to the expectations that were generated after 1989.

Conclusion

Democracy is a way of making decisions collectively and establishing rules and policies through popular decision-making. It is a form of government over which the people exercise control and which operates in the people's interest. Democratic citizenship is inclusive and political institutions aim to translate citizen preferences into policy. In spite of globalization, which has led to a view that there is a need for global democratic governance, democracy still remains resolutely tied to the national polity. In Chapter 1, following Iris Marion Young (1999), it was argued that creating and maintaining democracy requires both an active state to regulate society and organize the distribution of public goods, including welfare programmes, and participatory and critical civil society organizations. As a result, this book has suggested that democratization can best be understood as the introduction and extension of citizenship rights, alongside the creation of a democratic state. Democratic consolidation comprises the routinization and deepening of these democratic practices.

How far democracy is being achieved through the recent trend towards democratization has been analyzed through a review of five major regions of the world, namely Southern Europe, Latin America, Africa, the post-Communist countries and Asia. In these chapters, we have analyzed the sources of democratization, and examined the extent to which the new regimes deepen social citizenship and create democratic states. The evidence presented suggests a mixed picture. Of contemporary attempts at democracy, Southern Europe has fared best of all while parts of East and Central Europe have achieved considerable progress in a relatively short period of time, especially in terms of creating a democratic political society. Latin American democracies remain highly problematic, though they are less contested than in the past. Nevertheless, states are excessively influenced by elites and undemocratic practices and low levels of citizenship are sustained by the absence of social, economic and cultural equity. Meanwhile, democracy remains elusive in Russia and in many part of Africa and Asia. In much of sub-Saharan Africa, the formal structures of democratic politics in no way reflect the distribution of power in society and the processes of decision-making. In short, whilst there is greater commitment to

238

building democracy than even before, it is still only partially established outside Europe and North America. Theoretically, the book has addressed two questions. The first concerns the *causes* of democratization. The second is why the *outcomes* of contemporary attempts at democratization have varied so much. What factors make for successful democratization and, by implication, what are the causes of stalled or failed experiments in democratization? This concluding chapter summarizes the answers to these questions, drawing together what has been learned from the case studies.

The Causes of Democratization

Traditional theories of democratization focused either on national structures or national actors in producing the conditions for the emergence of democracy or in engineering the deals that make it possible. Modernization theory identifies capitalism, education and consumption as the benchmarks of modernity and the signposts for an emerging democratic order. Historical sociology emphasizes the centrality of the invisible structures of class for understanding any political order. The emergence of democracy correlates in particular with the development of an articulate, self-conscious and organized working class or other subaltern social movements. Agency scholarship, meanwhile, rejected the idea that democracy is an exceptional political order and viewed it as a possible outcome after authoritarian regimes break down, if elites and leaders are able to engage constructively, rationally and with a view to achieving compromise. Democracy becomes possible when institutions can be crafted in such a way as to guarantee the vital interests of elites. These frameworks provide important insights into democratization. They were applied to studies of regimes change and democracy-building in Southern Europe and Latin America especially.

However, by the 1990s, it was obvious that more than simply national forces were at work. Democratization was becoming a genuinely global aspiration. Huntington (1991) argued that significant change in patterns of global communications and global consumption created the conditions for the spread of democratic values, while the loss of legitimacy of the various forms of authoritarianism by the end of the 1980s, the liberalization of trannsnational organizations such as the Catholic Church and the transformation of US and European global policies, all made democracy a potential outcome in ways that had not been possible before. As Chapter 2 argued, Huntington's innovative thesis was flawed in that it did not specify chains of causality or mechanisms for the transmission of democracy through the global order. He also failed to recognize the ambiguity that lies that the heart of globalization. He simply assumed that democracy has become the present norm, rather than the exceptional creation that it had been deemed in the past, and, as a result, no deeper explanations were required.

It is important, however, to ask questions that Huntington ignores, such as how, exactly, globalization might favour democracy and whether it is an unambiguous force for democracy in countries beyond the capitalist core. In fact, globalization, understood as a combination of the creation of a global political economy and the tentative creation of forms of global governance, both of which rely and draw strength from the formation of global networks in media, culture and consumption, can only be said definitively to favour the deepening of globalized capitalism. Even for organizations of global governance that are reflexively pro-democratic, the new democratic political order is seen essentially as functional for capitalism. Democratization has become part of the agenda of international agencies that seek either to promote development through the intensification of capitalism or to establish conditions of global stability for the benefit of Western capitalism. For this reason, Gills (2000) sees globalization as merely ' a new political architecture for capitalism'. It is a mechanism for global integration through the generation of capitalist linkages and hierarchies of production. At the same time, because it is socially and economically polarizing, new forms of global inequalities are generated and embedded.

Can this scenario be said to be a stimulant or a cause of democratization? In the first place, globalized production networks could contribute to democratization because they are part of a deepening of capitalism. Economic development may lead to rises in living standards and makes the provision of services and public goods possible. In turn, this creates the circumstances in which the whole community can have a stake in the political and economic order. Economic development also makes possible the creation of a complex and dense civil society. However, capitalism does not, in itself, guarantee the emergence of democracy. Capitalism exists independently of democracy and the one does not follow automatically from the other. In fact, democracy also creates tensions with the capitalist order, because it has the potential to empower socially and economically subordinated groups who find space to challenge the status quo. Indeed, for many democracy activists, the attraction of democracy is precisely that it has the potential to reform and limit the capitalist order.

By opting for integration into global capitalist markets and intensifying capitalist relations of production, newly democratizing countries choose policies that do not provoke the hostility of either Western powers or the governance institutions. In so doing, they may limit the chances of incurring external hostility. This may be beneficial for democratizing governments but strategies of global integration also imply risks for the democratic order. The global political economy tends to favour the interests of business over labour and to reduce the possibilities of governments embarking on large-scale policies of economic or social redistribution. Globalized capitalism, in other words, no longer necessarily creates or empowers large pools of organized working people, as national capitalism did in Europe in the nineteenth and twentieth centuries. Moreover, the global political economy is build upon the deepening divisions between 'core' and 'marginalized' states (Hurrell and Woods 1995). The result is that most developing countries find their margin for political manoeuvre and autonomy substantially reduced. Under these conditions of extreme dependence, imitative and superficial projects of democracy perhaps become more likely. But substantive democracy becomes increasingly difficult because neither the state nor social forces are capable of defending – in some cases, not even of defining – national goals and interests. The creation of a global political economy is, then, ambiguous in terms of its relationship with democratization. On the one hand, it contributes to democratization via the extension of markets and capitalism; on the other, it leads to the development of restrictive capitalism subordinated to the core, limiting the autonomy of the state and stunting the development of democratic social forces.

Nevertheless, globalization is more than simply the creation of global capitalism. It also comprises the gradual creation of global norms and cultures. As a result, democracy, respect for human rights and the importance of the rule of law, at least at the level of rhetoric, have been elevated to the position of ordering principles in the international system in the post-Cold War period for the first time. Extending democracy beyond its Western homeland is now the stated project of important and powerful global actors. Significant resources are committed to pro-democracy activities. Furthermore, the end of the Cold War led to a transformation of the rhetoric and the justification for interventions by outside forces inside sovereign states. Interventions are now carried out in the name of democracy. It is easy to be cynical about Western interventions, such as NATO's involvement in the Balkans or the British involvement in Sierra Leone, which Western governments claim are aimed at establishing democracy and protecting human rights. They are, very obviously, concerned at least as much with establishing the conditions for Western stability and security. Once in place, however, democratization policies have sometimes developed a life of their own and democratization has become an autonomous discourse. Western policymakers are slowly being forced to scrutinize their actions and their choice of allies in the light of their stated aims by their own civil societies, as well as by transnationally active groups. At the same time, adopting policies of democratization has created expectations outside the West. Democratization is no longer a term used exclusively by academics and policy-makers. It has become the *lingua franca* for local struggles over land, community rights, and environmental protection, for example, as well as being grafted on to long established North–South issues such as debt and development. It may be, therefore, that democratization policies, conceived of as a way of regulating the international order after the fall of Communism, actually have a potential for contributing to real change on the ground because of the unintended consequences that can flow from them.

Trasnationally active civil society groups have been particularly keen to take advantage of the ambiguities of globalization which have been created by the adoption of a Western discourse of democratization and human rights. These groups are pressurizing Western governments and global institutions to take their claims to support democracy seriously, to flesh out precisely what a commitment to global democracy means and to separate democratization from its current position as third fiddle to the West's commitment to economic liberalization and its own security interests. Whilst these groups have the potential to become enormously significant in defining international norms, they cannot be said yet to have been prime movers in the wave of democratization. Nevertheless they are working hard to fill the currently rather vacuous commitment to democracy with meaning.

Globalization, then, in all its ambiguities, ultimately lies behind the contemporary appeal of democracy. Governance institutions are concerned primarily with stability or market-led development and liberal democracy is seen as the political arrangement most likely to favour both these outcomes. Nevertheless, globalization, on its own, cannot explain democratization. Just as important as the development of global capitalism and the technological revolution in shaping this opportunity has been the breakdown of the Cold War order and its reformation as a result of the end of bipolarity. This has required international elites to reformulate the ideological bases of their dominance. For global institutions and Western governments, this meant an openness to democracy outside the West for the first time.

Explaining Outcomes

We have established that globalization can provide an opportunity for democracy. But it cannot explain differential outcomes from democratization. Contemporary experiments in democratization encompass a considerable number of countries where democratization is limited to the introduction of elections. In others, much more institutional change has taken place and it is possible to identify the establishment of a democratic political society, although little has been done to democratize civil society, the state, and the policy-making process or to create cultures of participation and citizenship. In these cases, democratization is, at least so far, limited to the formal institutions of government; substantive democracy, resting on citizenship and participation, is largely absent. But there are also a few examples of stable and substantive democracy, and others where we can identify as yet unresolved struggles to turn a limited experiment in democracy into one that has real meaning for society at large. What accounts for these very different outcomes?

The answer lies in the framework, culture and opportunities furnished by national politics. Political opportunity is subject to interpretation by actors (Keck 1992: 5). Actors in national civil societies need to seize on the opportunities presented by globalization, in other words, to engage in pro-democracy struggles. Moreover: these actors must then have sufficient resources to transform the state. Consequently, the two key factors that explain differing outcomes are the nature of the state and the density, thickness and composition of civil society. Successful democratization requires:

- an active civil society, or at least strong and well-organized social organizations, that pre-dates the transition or, minimally, are established during the course of it (Perez Diaz 1993: 40);
- a complex civil society, made up of a range of different groups, that is able to engage in processes of sustained collective action based on assuring the extension of citizenship rights throughout society;
- a transformation of the state, so that it can claim to represent democratically, and to be accountable to, the entire national community

though the extension of citizenship to all, or at least most, adults who live within its boundaries; and

● a state able to mediate conflict, set national goals, deliver public goods and extract the resources required to carry out these functions from society.

Few democratizing countries meet these rigorous standards. Even if democratization is not imposed from outside, it may be that a developed state and a complex civil society are only partially in place as democratization begins. After all, the opportunity for democratization may be created by the collapse of the authoritarian regime; the onset of democratization does not, therefore, imply the full maturity of the forces that are needed to sustain a democratic project over the long term. Of course, democratization itself can stimulate the development of civil society; and there are numerous examples of civil society groups emerging during the very transition itself. The state is more problematic. States are notoriously resistant to change. Reform of state cultures and practices and of the patterns of access to the state generally takes place incrementally. In previous chapters, we have analyzed the problems of elitism and non-democratic cultures that are embedded in the state and the difficulties that diminished or contested sovereignty and the persistent lack of state capacity present to the democratic project. Furthermore, elitism and privileged access to the state are frequently encoded in the very foundations in the state and are difficult to eliminate without a complete rupture with the past. Certainly, changes to the state of this sort will not even form part of the agenda if democratization is merely a cosmetic set of changes introduced to please international observers. But even where democratization has its origins, at least partly, in national social and political changes, it may be that it cannot be fully carried through because of the scale of obstacles in the way. Moreover, the sort of compromises needed to keep democratization a possibility may mean, ironically, that only a limited democratization is possible.

One of the most important lessons from the case studies the book brings together, therefore, is the extent to which experiments in democratization are path-dependent. History matters. As Tarrow (1998) points out, the 'repertoires of contention' of civil society are conditioned to an important extent by the actions and the myths embedded in national politics over time. Democratization does not – indeed cannot – represent a complete rupture in terms of state-society interactions. Nor does it automatically transform state behaviour, the interests the state represents and the cultures it embodies.

With this in mind, then, it is remarkable quite how far some democratizing experiments have come. The most obvious successes lie in Southern Europe. Here democratization began at a time when states possessed greater autonomy and could embark on policies of taxation and redistribution, allowing Spain and Portugal to provide services under democracy that had not been available beforehand. Secondly, in Spain especially, the transition marked the culmination of civil society activism that had been maturing for a number years under the dictatorship, contributing, in fact, to the crisis of authoritarianism and to the transition itself. But there are other examples where, despite constraints, democracy is slowly being built. A few Latin American examples stand out – Chile and Uruguay, where new governments build to some extent on state traditions of plural representation and the active provision of public goods, and Brazil, where despite the limitations and failures of the state, civil society groups have not abandoned activism and organization. In South Africa too, despite rising violence and social problems such as the provision of health and education, significant advances have been made towards the institutionalization of democracy. Even in parts of Asia, especially South Korea and Taiwan, where democratization arrived late, the technical capacity of the state is a support for political reform, even though civil society is weak.

Contemporary democratization brings together countries that are more geographically dispersed, with widely different levels of development and with different cultural and religious traditions, than in either of the two earlier waves. Until now, the majority of countries where democracy has been attempted have been either European or Latin American, the latter a region where Western religious, cultural and ideological norms predominate. The contemporary movement, by contrast, encompasses countries where religious and cultural norms are non-Western. Of course, proximity to the West implies certain advantages. In the post-Communist countries, it is striking that the most successful examples of democratization are to be found closest to the countries of the European Union. But there is no reason to suppose that democratization in the Czech Republic, Hungary and Poland is stronger than in Estonia or Russia simply because of this proximity. Equally, the slow progress of democratization in Russia and Estonia could be attributed to unresolved questions of nation-building or poor state capacity. Belonging to the West, or closeness to the Western heartland, is no guarantee of democracy, as the years of dictatorship in Latin America in the 1960s and 1970s attest to.

Nevertheless, the argument persists that it is easier for liberal democracy to take root in Western cultures because of its emphasis on individualism. Individualism is the result of the model of capitalism which developed in Europe and the US, as well as being an embedded idea within liberal Western philosophy and a fundamental part of Christian thought. Asian values and traditions are thought to lay greater stress on the community and the well-being of the nation, rather than the individual. As a result, non-democratic regimes in Asia have sometimes justified themselves in terms of 'Asian democracy', meaning that the state claims to have the development and welfare of the community as its guiding philosophy. Furthermore, the democratization debate can seem an uncomfortable 'fit' in Asia because concept like 'civil society' have less resonance or a different meaning altogether outside the West. This should not be taken to imply that democratization is not possible in Asia. It may suggest, however, that *liberal* democracy is not the automatic outcome of struggles for representation and rights in the region. A more cosmopolitan and less ethnocentric understanding of what constitutes democracy may ultimately be the result (Freeman 1996).

The Future of Democratization

In the years immediately after 1989, it was confidently predicted that democratization would successfully sweep across the globe. Certainly, democratization has had dramatic effects on the international system, on the foreign policies of major Western states and on the way civil society organizations have acted. The significance of democratization is such that there can be no return to a pre-1989 world. It is no longer possible for the West to accept authoritarianism and human rights abuses without a murmur of criticism. Furthermore, the fact that democratization has become an issue of global concern has led to change in non-democratic countries. Authoritarian elites have been forced to hide under a cover of democracy and to seek new ideological bases for domination. Furthermore, pro-democracy and human rights activists are now empowered to some extent to push for reform.

Nevertheless, this book has expressed a qualified pessimism about the state of new democracies. Few have achieved democratic consolidation. The extent to which opportunities for genuine democratization were created after 1989 was undoubtedly exaggerated. Does this mean that the opportunities for democratization that opened in the 1980s and 1990s have now come to an end? That is unlikely. The international climate is not favourable to overt authoritarian rule; consequently reversals are difficult to imagine. Nevertheless, it is possible for current authoritarian regimes to survive, especially if they are important to the West in security or trade terms, provided they show some willingness to engage with the West over the issue of rights and democratization. A more likely scenario is that democracy will remain embryonic and unconsolidated in much of the developing world, at least until the national structures that can sustain democracy develop sufficiently to make further progress possible. It may be, even, that new forms of authoritarianism are generated beneath a cloak of democratic rule. Taking the long view, however, new and stronger democracies may also emerge. Attempts at democratization, even when they fail or only partially succeed, form part of history and, as such, part of the collective memory of communities. In this sense, all attempts at democracy, even if they fail, can contribute to democratization in the long term. However, the present global order is sufficient only to offer partial or limited democracy for the most part to countries outside the capitalist core. Deeper democracy in developing and peripheral countries will depend not only on a change in the terms of global engagement, but also on a transformation of state structures and power relations within nation states. Creating democracies, in other words, requires not just a favourable global order; it demands collective action from below and radical processes of social transformation within nation states.

Bibliography

Agh, A. (1996) 'The End of the Beginning: The Partial Consolidation of East Central Parties and Party Systems', Budapest Papers on Democratic Transition No. 156, Budapest University of Economics.

Allen, C. (1995) 'Understanding African Politics', *Review of African Political Economy*, 65.

Almond, G. A. and S. Verba (1963) *The Civic Culture: Political Attitudes and Democracy in Five Nations* (Princeton, NJ: Princeton University Press).

Alvarez, S. (1990) *Engendering Democracy: The Women's Movement in Brazil* (Princeton, NJ: Princeton University Press).

Anderson, P. (1974) *Lineages of the Absolutist State* (London: New Left Books).

Arblaster, A. (1994) *Democracy* 2nd edn (Milton Keynes: Open University Press).

Archibugi, D., D. Held and M. Kohler (1998) *Re-imagining Political Community* (Cambridge: Polity Press).

Areilza, J. A. (1983) *Cronica de la Libertad* (Barcelona: Anagrama).

Arnson, C. and J. Mendelson (1992) 'Projecting Democracy in Central America: Old Wine, New Bottles', in W. Leogrande, L. Goodman and J. Mendelson (eds), *Political Parties in Central America* (Boulder, CO: Westview Press).

Bach, D. (1998) 'Regionalism Versus Regional Integration', in J. Grugel and W. Hout (eds), *Regionalism Across the North South Divide* (London: Routledge)

Baker, G. (1999) 'The Taming of the Idea of Civil Society', *Democratization*, 6, 3, 1–29.

Balcerowicz, L. (1994) 'Understanding Postcommunist Transitions', *Journal of Democracy*, 5, 4, 75–89.

Bartell, E. and L. Payne (eds) (1995) *Business and Democracy in Latin America* (London: University of Pittsburgh Press).

Barton, J. R. A. (1997) *Political Geography of Latin America* (London: Routledge).

Bauman, Z. (1994) 'After the Patronage State A Model in Search of Class Interests', in C. Bryant and E. Mokrzycki, *The New Great Transformation? Change and Continuity in East-Central Europe* (London: Routledge).

Bayart, J. F. (1996) 'Civil Society in Africa', in P. Chabal (ed.), *Political Domination in Africa*: *Reflections on the Limitations of Power* (Cambridge: Cambridge University Press).

Baylies, C. (1995) 'Political Conditionality and Democratisation', *Review of African Political Economy*, 65.

Beard, G. (2001) 'Regionalism and Social Movements in the Caribbean: Social Organization in the Dominican Republic in a Global Perspective' (unpublished paper, Society for Latin American Studies (SLAS), Birmingham, April 2001).

Beetham, D. (1992) 'Liberal Democracy and the Limits of Democratization', *Political Studies*, special issue, vol. 40.

Beetham, D. (1997) 'Market Forces and Democratic Polity', *Democratization*, 4, 1.

Bell, D., D. Brown, K. Jayasuriyia and D. Jones (1995) *Towards Illiberal Democracy in Pacific Asia* (New York: St Martin's Press).

Berman, B. (1998) 'Ethnicity, Patronage and the African State: The Politics of Uncivil Nationalism', *African Affairs*, 97.

Bermeo, N. (1978) 'Redemocratization and Transition Elections', *Comparative Politics*, 19, 2.

Bermeo, N. (1992) 'Democracy and the Lessons of Dictatorship', *Comparative Politics*, 24, 3.

Bernhard, M. (1996) 'Civil Society After the First Transition: Dilemmas of Post-Communist Democratization in Poland and Beyond', *Communist and Post-Communist Studies,* 29, 3.

Bernstein, C. (1994) 'Democratization in China', in R. Slater, B. Schultz and S. Dorr (eds), *Global Transformation and the Third World* (Boulder, CO: Lynne Rienner).

Bessel, R. (1997) 'The Crisis of Modern Democracies', in D. Potter, D. Goldblatt, M. Kiloh, and P. Lewis (eds), *Democratization* (Cambridge: Open University/Polity Press).

Black, A. (1997) 'Communal Democracy and its History', *Political Studies*, 45.

Blakeley, G. (2000) 'Democratisation and Participation in Spain: The Case of Barcelona' (unpublished Ph.D. thesis, Department of Peace Studies, University of Bradford).

Bobbio, N. (1989) *Democracy and Dictatorship* (Cambridge: Polity Press).

Bogdan, D. (1996) *Ethnic Nationalism: The Tragic Death of Yugoslavia* (University of Minnesota Press).

'Bolivia Interim Poverty Reduction Strategy Paper' (2000) http:/www. imf.org/NP/prsp/2000/bol/01/index.htm, retrieved on 13 Jan. 2000.

Bratton, M. (1998) 'Second Elections in Africa', *Journal of Democracy*, 9, 3.

Bratton, M. and N. van de Walle (1997) *Democratic Experiments in Africa: Regime Transitions in Comparative Perspective* (Cambridge: Cambridge University Press).

Bryant, C. (1994) 'Economic Utopianism and Sociological Realism: Strategies for Transformation in East-Central Europe', in C. Bryant and E. Mokrzycki, *Change and Continuity in East-Central Europe* (London: Routledge).

Brysk, A. (1993) 'From Above and Below. Social Movements, the International System and Human Rights in Argentina', *Comparative Political Studies,* 26, 3.

Bulletin of Latin American Research (2000) Special Issue, 'Old and New Populism in Latin America' 19, 2.

Bunce, V. (1995a) 'Comparing East and South', *Journal of Democracy*, 6, 3.

Bunce, V. (1995b) 'Should Transitologists be Grounded?', *Slavic Review*, 54.

Burnell, P. (1997) *Foreign Aid in a Changing World* (Buckingham: Open University Press).

Burton, M., R. Gunther and J. Higley (1992) 'Elites and Democratic Consolidation in Latin America and Southern Europe: An Overview', in J. Higley and R. Gunther (eds), *Elites and Democratic Consolidation in Latin America and Southern Europe* (Cambridge: Cambridge University Press).

Callaghy, T. (1993) 'Vision and Politics in the Transformation of the Global Political Economy: Lessons from the Second and Third Worlds', in R. Slater, B. Schultz and S. Dorr (eds), *Global Transformation and the Third World* (Boulder, CO: Lynne Rienner) pp. 161–258.

Callinicos, A. (1991) *The Revenge of History* (Cambridge:Polity Press).

Cammack, P. (1994) 'Political Development Theory and the Dissemination of Democracy', *Democratization* 1, 3.

Cammack, P. (1997) 'Democracy and Dictatorship in Latin America, 1930–80', in D. Potter, D. Goldblatt, M. Kiloh, and P. Lewis (eds), *Democratization* (Cambridge: Open University/Polity Press).

Cardoso, F. H. and E. Faletto, (1979) *Dependency and Development in Latin America* (Berkeley, CA: University of California Press).

Carothers, T. (1991) *In the Name of Democracy: US Policy Toward Latin America in the Reagan Years* (Berkeley, CA: University of California Press).

Carothers, T. (1994) 'The NED at 10', *Foreign Affairs*, 95.

Carothers, T. (1996) *Assessing Democratic Assistance: The Case of Romania* (Washington, DC: Carnegie Endowment).

Caspar, G. (1995) *Fragile Democracies: The Legacies of Authoritarian Rule* (Pittsburgh: University of Pittsburgh Press).

Castells, M. (1983) *The City and the Grassroots* (Berkeley, CA: University of California Press).

Castells, M. (1996) *The Rise of the Network Society* (Oxford: Blackwell).

Cerny, P. G. (1990) *The Changing Architecture of Politics: Structure, Agency, and the Future of the State* (London: Sage).

Chalmers, D., S. B. Martin and K. Piester (1997) 'Associative Networks: New Structures of Representation for the Popular Sectors?', in D. Chalmers, C. Vilas, K. Hite, S. B. Martin, K. Piester and M. Segarra, *The New Politics of Inequality in Latin America* (Oxford: Oxford University Press).

Chan, A. B. J. Triakerkvliet and J. Unger (1999) *Transforming Asian Socialism :China and Vietnam Compared* (St. Leonards, New South Wales: Allen & Unwin).

Chazan, N., P. Lewis, R. Mortimer, J. Ravenhill, D. Rothchild and S. Stedman (1999) *Politics and Society in Contemporary Africa*, 3rd edn (Boulder, CO; Lynne Rienner).

Cheng, T. J. and Eun Mee Kim (1994) 'Making Democracy; Generalizing from the South Korean Experiences', in E Friedman (ed.), *The Politics of Democratization* (Boulder, CO: Westview Press) pp. 125–47.

Chibber, P. and M. Torcal, (1997) 'Elite Strategy, Social Cleavages and Party Systems in a New Democracy: Spain', *Comparative Political Studies*, 30, 1.

Chu, Y. H. and L. Diamond (1999) 'Taiwan's 1988 Elections', *Asian Survey*, 39, 5, 808–22.

Clapham, C. (1996) *Africa and the International System* (Cambridge: Cambridge University Press).

Clark, A. M., E. Friedman and K. Hochstetler (1998) 'The Sovereign Limits of Global Civil Society', *World Politics*, 51, 4.

Cohen, J. and A. Arato (1992) *Civil Society and Political Theory* (Cambridge, MA: MIT Press).

Colas, A. (1997) 'The Promises of International Civil Society', *Global Society*, 11, 3.

Collier, D. (1995) 'Corporatism', in P. Smith, (ed.), *Latin America in Comparative Perspective: New Approaches to Methods and Analysis* (Boulder, CO: Westview Press).

Collier, D. and S. Levitsky (1997) 'Democracy with Adjectives: Conceptual Innovation in Comparative Research', *World Politics*, 49, 4.

Collier, P. (1991) 'Africa's External Economic Relations 1960–90', *African Affairs*, 90.
Collier, R. B. and J. Mahoney (1997) 'Adding Collective Actors to Collective Outcomes Labor and Recent Democratization in South America and Southern Europe', *Comparative Politics*, 29, 3.
Collins, R. (1991) *Macrohistory: Essays in Sociology of the Long Run* (Stanford, CA: Stanford University Press).
Cook, M. L. (1997) 'Regional Integration and Transnational Politics: Popular Sector Strategies in the NAFTA Era', in D. Chalmers, C. Vilas, K. Hite, S. B. Martin, K. Piester and M. Segarra, *The New Politics of Inequality in Latin America* (Oxford: Oxford University Press).
Cox, R. W. (1987) *Production, Power, and World Order: Social Forces in the Making of History* (New York: Columbia University Press).
Cox, R. W. (1997) 'Democracy in Hard Times: Economic Globalization and the Limits to Liberal Democracy', in A. McGrew (ed.), *The Transformation of Democracy? Globalization and Territorial Democracy* (Cambridge: Polity Press).
Cranenburgh, O. Van (1999) 'International Policies to Promote African Democratization', in J. Grugel (ed.), *Democracy without Borders: Transnationalization and Conditionality in New Democracies* (London: Routledge).
Craske, N. (1999) *Women and Politics in Latin America* (Cambridge: Polity Press).
Crawford, B. (1997) 'Foreign Aid and Political Conditionality', *Democratization*, 4, 3.
Crisp, B. (1998) 'Lessons from Economic Reform in Venezuelan Democracy', *Latin American Research Review*, 33, 1.
Cruise O'Brien, D. B. (1991) 'The Show of State in Neo-Colonial Twilight: Francophone Africa', in J. Manor (ed.), *Rethinking Third World Politics* (London: Longman).
Curtis, G. L. (1997) 'The East Asian Prospect: A Recipe for Democratic Development', *Journal of Democracy*, 8, 3.
Dahl, R. (1961) *Who Governs?* (New Haven, Conn: Yale University Press).
Dahl, R. A. (1985) *Preface to Economic Democracy* (Cambridge: Polity Press) 1st pub. 1956.
Dahl, R. (1989) *Democracy and its Critics* (London: Yale University Press).
Dawisha, K. and B. Parrott (1997) *Politics, Power and the Struggle for Democracy in South-East Europe* (Cambridge: Cambridge University Press).
Dentich B. (1994) *Ethnic Nationalism: The Tragic Death of Yugoslavia* (Minneapolis: University of Minnesota Press).
Desfor Edles, L. (1998) *Symbol and Ritual in the New Spain* (Cambridge: Cambridge University Press).
Di Palma, G. (1990) *To Craft Democracies: An Essay on Democratic Transition* (Berkeley, CA: University of California Press).
Diamandouros, P. N. (1986) 'Regime Change and the Prospects for Democracy in Greece: 1974–1983', in G. O'Donnell, P. Schmitter and L. Whitehead, *Transitions from Authoritarian Rule: Southern Europe* (London: Johns Hopkins University Press)
Diamond, L. (1988) 'Introduction: Roots of Failure, Seeds of Hope', in J. Linz and L. Diamond (eds), *Democracy in Developing Countries, Vol. 2: Africa* (Boulder, CO: Lynne Rienner).

252   *Bibliography*

Diamond, L. (1992) 'Economic Development and Democracy Reconsidered', *American Behavioral Scientist*, 35, 4/5.

Diamond, L. (1994) 'Rethinking Civil Society Towards Democratic Consolidation', *Journal of Democracy*, 5, 3.

Diamond, L. (1996) 'Is the Third Wave Over?', *Journal of Democracy*, 7, 3.

Diamond, L. (1999) *Developing Democracy: Toward Consolidation* (London: Johns Hopkins University Press).

Diamond, L. and Byung-Kook Kim (2000) *Consolidating Democracy in South Korea* (Boulder, CO: Lynne Rienner).

Diamond, L. and R. Myers (2000) 'Introduction Elections and Democracy in Greater China', *China Quarterly*, June.

Dunkerely, J. (1998) *Power in the Isthmus* (London: Verso)

Dunn, J. (1992) *Democracy: The Unfinished Journey: From 508 BC to AD 1993* (Cambridge: Cambridge University Press).

Ekiert, G. and J. Kubick (1998) 'Contentious Politics in New Democracies: East Germany, Hungary, Poland and Slovakia 1989–1993', *World Politics*, 50, 4 (July).

Escobar, A. and S. Alvarez (eds) (1992) *The Making of Social Movements in Latin America* (Boulder, CO: Westview Press).

Esping-Anderson, G. (1992) 'Budgets and Democracy: Towards a Welfare State in Spain and Portugal, 1960–1986', in I. Budge and D. Mackay (eds), *Developing Democracy* (London: Sage).

Evans, P. (1992) 'The State as Problem and Solution: Predation, Embedded Autonomy, and Structural Change', in S. Haggard and R. Kaufman (eds), *The Politics of Adjustment: International Constraints, Distributive Conflicts, and the State* (Princeton, NJ: Princeton University Press).

Evans, P. (1997) 'The Eclipse of the State? Reflections on Stateness in an Era of Globalization', *World Politics*, 50, 1.

Evans, P., D. Rueschmeyer and T. Skocpol (eds), (1985) *Bringing the State Back In* (Cambridge: Cambridge University Press).

Featherstone, K. (1994) 'The Challenge of Liberalization: Parties and the State in Greece After the 1993 Elections', *Democratization*, 1, 2.

Fine, R (1997) 'Civil Society Theory, Enlightenment and Critique', *Democratization* 4, 1.

Finer, S. E. (1966) *Anonymous Empire* (London: Pall Mall).

Fishman, R. M. (1990) *Working Class Organization and the Return to Democracy in Spain* (Ithaca: Cornell University Press).

Foot, R. (1997) 'Human Rights, Democracy and Development: The Debate', *East Asia*, 4, 2.

Fowraker, J. (1989) *Making Democracy in Spain: Grassroots Struggle in the South 1955–1975* (Cambridge: Cambridge University Press).

Frank, A. G. (1971) *Capitalism and Underdevelopment in Latin America: Historical Studies of Chile and Brazil* (Harmondsworth: Penguin).

Freeman, M. (1996) 'Human Rights, Democracy and "Asian Values"', *The Pacific Review*, 9, 3.

Fukuyama, F. (1992) *The End of History and the Last Man* (London: Hamish Hamilton).

Gallagher, T. *Portugal: A Twentieth Century Interpretation* (Manchester: Manchester University Press).

Gallagher, T. (1989) 'The Portuguese Socialist Party: The Pitfalls of Being First', in T. Gallagher and Williams, (eds), *Southern European Socialism* (Manchester, Manchester University Press).

Gallagher, T. (1995) 'Democratization in the Balkans: Challenges and Prospects', *Democratization*, 2, 3.

Gallagher, T. (1996) 'A Feeble Embrace: Romania's Engagement with Democracy, 1989–1994', *Journal of Communist Studies and Transition Politics*, 12, 2.

Gallagher, T. (1998) 'Conflicts Between East European States and Minorities in an Age of Democracy', *Democratization*, 5, 3.

Gallie, W. B. (1964) *Philosophy and Historical Understanding* (London: Chatto & Windus).

Garcia Marquez, G. (1976) *The Autumn of the Patriarch* (London: Picador).

Gariorowski, M. J. and T. J. Power (1998) 'The Structural Determinants of Democratic Consolidation: Evidence from the Third World', *Comparative Political Studies* 31, 6.

Garton Ash, T. (1999) *We the People* (London: Penguin).

Gentleman, J. and V. Zubek (1992) 'International Integration and Democratic Development: The Cases of Poland and Mexico', *Journal of Interamerican Studies and World Affairs*, 43, 1.

Giddens, A. (1990) *The Consequences of Modernity* (Cambridge: Polity Press).

Gill, G. (1995) 'Liberalization and Democratization in the Soviet Union and Russia', *Democratization*, 2, 3.

Gill, G. (2000) *The Dynamics of Democratization* (London: Macmillan – now Palgrave).

Gills, B. (2000) 'The Crisis of Postwar East Asian Capitalism: American Power, Democracy and the Vicissitudes of Globalization', *Review of International Studies* 26.

Giner, S. (1986) 'Political Economy, Legitimation and the State in Southern Europe', in G. O'Donnell, P. Schmitter and L. Whitehead (eds), *Transitions from Authoritarian Rule: Southern Europe* (Baltimore: Johns Hopkins University Press).

Gladdish, K. (1993) 'Portugal: An Open Verdict', in G. Pridham (ed.) *Securing Democracy: Party Politics and Democratic Consolidation in Southern Europe* (London: Routledge).

Glasman, D. (1994) 'The Great Deformation: Polyani, Poland and the Terrors of Planned Spontaneity', in C. Bryant and E. Mokrzycki, (eds.), *The New Great Transformation? Change and Continuity in East-Central Europe* (London: Routledge).

Goverde, H. P. Cerny, M. Haugaard and H. Lentner (2000) *Power in Contemporary Politics* (London: Sage).

Grabendorff, W. (1992) 'The Party Internationals and Democracy in Central America', in L. W. Goodman, W. M. Leogrande and J. Mendelson (eds), *Political Parties and Democracy in Central America* (Boulder, CO: Westview Press).

Grabendorff, W. (1996) 'International Support for Democracy in Contemporary Latin America', in L. Whitehead (ed), *The International Dimensions of Democratization: Europe and the Americas* (Oxford: Oxford University Press).

Grindle, M. (1996) *Challenging the State* (Cambridge: Cambridge University Press).

Grugel, J. (1996) 'Democratisation in Latin America: The European View, *European Review of Latin American and Caribbean Studies*, 60 (June).

Grugel, J. (1998) 'State and Business in Neo-Liberal Democracies in Latin America', *Global Society*, 12 , 2.

Grugel, J. (ed.) (1999) *Democracy Without Borders: Transnational and Non-State Actors in Eastern Europe, Africa and Latin America* (London: Routledge).

Grugel, J. (2000) 'Romancing Civil Society: European NGOs in Latin America', *Journal of Interamerican Studies and World Affairs*, 42, 2.

Grugel, J. and T. Rees (1997) *Franco's Spain* (London: Edward Arnold).

Guehenno, J. M. (1993) *La fin de la democratie* (Paris: Flamarion).

Haggard, S. (2000a) 'Political Economy of the Korean Financial Crisis', *Review of International Political Economy*, 7, 2.

Haggard, S. (2000b) 'The Politics of the Asian Financial Crisis', *Journal of Democracy*, 11, 2.

Haggard, S. and R. Kaufman (1995) *The Political Economy of Democratic Transitions* (Princeton, NJ: Princeton University Press).

Haggard, S. and R. Kaufman (1997) 'The Political Economy of Democratic Transitions', *Comparative Politics*, 29, 3.

Hagopian, F. (1990) 'Democracy by Undemocratic Means?: Elites, Political Pacts and Regime Transition in Brazil', *Comparative Political Studies*, 23, 2.

Hagopian, F. (1992) 'The Compromised Consolidation: The Political Class in the Brazilian Transition', in S. Mainwaring, G. O'Donnell and J. S. Valenzuela (eds), *Issues in Democratic Consolidation* (University of Notre Dame Press).

Hall, J. (1995) 'In Search of Civil Society', in J. Hall (ed.), *Civil Society: Theory, History and Comparison* (Cambridge: Polity Press).

Hadenius, A. (1992) *Democracy and Development* (Cambridge: Cambridge University Press).

Harbeson, J. (2000) 'Externally Assisted Democratization: Theoretical Issues and African Realities', in J. Harbeson and D. Rothchild (eds), *Africa in World Politics: The African State System in Flux* (Boulder, CO: Westview).

Harrison, G. (1994) 'Mozambique: An Unsustainable Democracy', *Review of African Political Economy*, 61.

Harrison, G. (2000) *The Politics of Democratization in Rural Mozambique* (London: Edward Mellen Press).

Harvey, N. (1999) *The Chiapas Rebellion: The Struggle for Land and Democracy* (Duke University Press).

Havel, V., V. Klaus and P. Pithart (1996) 'Civil Society after Communism: Rival Visions', *Journal of Democracy*, 7, 1.

Hawthorne, G. (1991) 'Waiting for a Text? Comparing Third World Politics', in J. Manor (ed.), *Rethinking Third World Politics* (London: Longman).

He, B. (1996) Dilemmas of Pluralist Development and Democratization in China', *Democratization*, 3, 3.

Held, D. (1992) 'Democracy: From City-State to a Cosmopolitan Order?', *Political Studies*, Special Issue, Vol. 40.

Held, D. (1995) *Democracy and Global Order: From the Modern State to Cosmopolitan Governance* (Cambridge: Polity Press).

Held, D. (1996) *Models of Democracy*, 2nd edn (Cambridge: Polity Press).

Held, D. (1999) 'The Transformation of Political Community', in I. Shapiro and C. Hacker-Cordon, *Democracy's Edges* (Cambridge: Cambridge University Press).

Held, D., A. McGrew, D. Goldblatt, and J. Perraton, (1999) *Global Transformations: Politics, Economics and Culture* (Cambridge: Polity Press).

Hellinger, D. (1992) 'US Aid in Africa: No Room for Democracy', *Review of African Political Economy*, 55.

Herbst, J. (2000) 'Understanding Ambiguity During Democratization in Africa', in J. Hollifield and C. Jillson (eds), *Pathways to Democracy: The Political Economy of Democratic Transitions* (London: Routledge).

Hershberg, E. (1997) 'Market-Oriented Development Strategies and State–Society Relations in New Democracies: Lessons from Contemporary Chile and Spain', in D. Chalmers, C. Vilas, K. Hite, S. B. Martin, K. Piester and M. Segarra, *The New Politics of Inequality in Latin America* (Oxford: Oxford University Press).

Hewison, K. (1999) 'Political Space in South East Asia: "Asian Style" and Other Democracies', *Democratization*, 6, 1.

Hewison, K. and G. Rodan (1996) 'The Ebb and Flow of Civil Society and the Decline of the Left in South East Asia', in G. Rodan, *Political Oppositions in Industrializing Asia* (London: Routledge).

Hewison, K. and S. Masrikrod (1997) 'Thailand's 1996 Election: A Cheer for Democracy?', *Australian Quarterly*, 69.

Heywood, P. (1995) *The Government and Politics of Spain* (London: Macmillan).

Heywood, P. (1998) 'Sleaze in Spain', *Parliamentary Affairs*, 48, 4.

Higley, J. and R. Gunther (eds) (1992) *Elites and Democratic Consolidation in Latin America and Southern Europe* (Cambridge: Cambridge University Press).

Higley, J., S. Kulberg and J. Pakulski (1996) 'The Persistence of Postcommunist Elites', *Journal of Democracy* 7, 2.

Hipsher, P. (1996) 'Democratization and the Decline of Urban Social Movements in Chile and Spain', *Comparative Politics*, 28, 3.

Hirshmann, D. (1995) 'Democracy, Gender and US Foreign Assistance: Guidelines and Lessons', *World Development*, 23, 8.

Hirst, P. (1989) *The Pluralist Theory of the State* (London: Routledge).

Hirst, P. (1997) *From Statism to Pluralism* (London: UCL Press).

Hirst, P. and G. Thompson (1996) *Globalization in Question: The International Economy and the Possibilities of Governance* (Cambridge: Polity Press).

Hochstetler, K. (1997) 'Democratizing Pressures from Below? Social Movements in New Brazilian Democracy', Latin American Studies Association (LASA) XX Annual Congress, Guadalajara, 1997.

Holden, B. (1993) *Understanding Liberal Democracy*, 2nd edn (London: Harvester/Wheatsheaf).

Holm, H. and G. Sorensen (1995) *Whose World Order? Uneven Globalization and the End of the Cold War* (Boulder, CO: Lynne Rienner).

Hoogvelt, A. (1997) *Globalisation and the Postcolonial World* (London: Macmillan – now Palgrave).

Hoskin, G. (1997) 'Democratization in Latin America', *Latin American Research Review*, 32, 3.

Huber, E. (1995) 'Assessments of State Strength', in P. Smith, (ed.), *Latin America in Comparative Perspective: New Approaches to Methods and Analysis* (Boulder, CO: Westview Press).

Huber, E. and F. Stafford (eds) (1995) *Agrarian Structure and Political Power: Landlord and Peasant in the Making of Modern Latin America* (Pittsburgh,: Pittsburgh University Press).

Huntington, S. P. (1991) *The Third Wave: Democratization in the Late Twentieth Century* (Norman: University of Oklahoma Press).

Huntington, S. P. (1996) *The Clash of Civilizations and the Remaking of World Order* (New York: Simon & Schuster).

Hurrell, A. (1999) 'Power, Principles and Prudence: Protecting Human Rights in a Deeply Divided World', in T. Dunne and N. Wheeler, *Human Rights in Global Politics* (Cambridge: Cambridge University Press).

Hurrell, A. and N. Woods (1995) 'Globalisation and Inequality', *Millennium: Journal of International Studie,* 24, 3.

Hyde-Price, A. (1994) 'Democratisation in Eastern Europe: The External Dimension', in G. Pridham and T. Vanhanen (eds), *Democratisation in Eastern Europe: Domestic and International Perspective* (London: Routledge).

Jackson, R. and C. Roseberg (1982a) 'Why Africa's Weak States Persist: The Empirical and the Juridical in Statehood', *World Politics,* 35, 1.

Jackson, R. and C. Roseberg (1982b) *Personal Rule in Africa* (Berkeley, CA: University of California Press).

Jelin, E. (1996) 'Citizenship Revisited: Solidarity, Responsibility and Rights', in E. Jelin and E. Hersberg (eds), *Constructing Democracy: Human Rights, Citizenship and Society in Latin America* (Boulder, CO; Westview Press).

Jessop, R. (1990) *State Theory: Putting the Capitalist State in its Place* (Cambridge: Polity Press).

Johnson, C. (1987) 'Political Institutions and Economic Performance: The Government–Business Relationship in Japan, South Korea and Taiwan', in F. Deyo (ed.), *The Political Economy of the New Asia* (Ithaca: Cornell University Press).

Jones, D. M. (1998) 'Democratization, Civil Society and Illiberal Middle Class Culture in Pacific Asia', *Comparative Politics,* 30, 2.

Jongryn, M. and Moon Chung-in (eds) (1999) *Democracy and the Korean Economy* (Stanford, California: Hoover Institution Press).

Judge, D. (1999) *Representation Theory and Practice in Britain* (London: Routledge).

Kaldor, M. and I. Vejvoda (1997) 'Democratization in Central and East European Countries', *International Affairs,* 73, 1.

Kaplan, C. (1998) 'Ethnicity and Sovereignty: Insights from Russian Negotiations with Estonia and Tartartan', in Lane and Rothschild (eds), *The International Spread of Ethnic Conflict* (Princeton,NJ: Princeton University Press).

Karl, T. L. (1986) 'Imposing Consent? Electoralism vs Democratization in El Salvador', in P. Drake and E. Silva (eds), *Elections and Democratization in Latin America, 1980–1985* (San Diego: University of California Press).

Karl, T. L. (1990) 'Dilemma of Democratization', *Comparative Politics,* 23, 1.

Karl, T. L. (1995) 'The Hybrid Regimes of Central America', *Journal of Democracy,* 6, 3.

Keane, J. (ed.) (1988) *Civil Society and the State* (London: Verso).

Kearns, I. (1996) 'Eastern Europe in the Transition into the New Europe', in A. Gamble and A. J. Payne (eds), *Regionalism and World Order* (London: Macmillan – now Palgrave).

Keck, M. (1992) *The Workers Party and Democratization in Brazil* (London: Yale University Press).

Keck, M. (1995) 'Social Equity and Environmental Politics in Brazil: Lessons from the Rubber Tappers of Acre', *Comparative Politics*, 27, 4.

Keck, M. and K. Sikkink (1998) *Activists Beyond Borders* (Ithaca, NY: Cornell University Press).

Keman, H. (1996) 'Managing the Mixed Economy in Central and Eastern Europe: Democratic Politics and the Role of the Public Sector', *Democratization*, 3, 2.

Kitschelt, H. (1992) 'Political Regime Change: Structure and Process-Driven Explanations', *American Political Science Review*, 86, 4.

Kopecky, P. (2001) *Parliaments in the Czech and Slovak Republics: Party Competition and Parliamentary Institutionalization* (Aldershot: Ashgate).

Kopecky, P. and E. Barnfield (1999) 'Charting the Decline of Civil Society: Explaining the Changing Roles and Conceptions of Civil Society in East and Central Europe', in J. Grugel (ed.), *Democracy without Borders: Transnationalization and Conditionality in New Democracies* (London: Routledge).

Kopecky, P. and C. Mudde (2000) 'What Has Eastern Europe Taught Us About the Democratization Literature (and vice-versa)?', *European Journal of Political Research*, 37, 4.

Kopstein, J. S. (1996) 'Chipping Away at the State: Workers' Resistance and the Demise of East Germany', *World Politics*, 48, 3.

Kuron, Z. (1990) 'Overcoming Totalitarianism', *Journal of Democracy*, 1, 1.

Kurtz, M. (1999) 'The Political Economy of Pro-Poor Policies in Chile and Mexico', Paper prepared for the World Development Report Meetings 2001, 16–17 August, Castle Donnington, UK.

Lambrou, Y. (1997) 'The Changing Role of NGOs in Rural Chile after Democracy', *Bulletin of Latin American Research*, 16, 1.

Lee, H. (1994) 'Uncertain Promise: Democratic Consolidation in South Korea', in E. Friedman (ed.), *The Politics of Democratization* (Boulder, CO: Westview Press).

Leftwich, A. (1996) 'Two Cheers for Democracy?', *Political Quarterly*, 67, 4.

Lewis, P. (1996) 'Economic Reform and Political Transition in Africa: The Quest for a Politics of Development', *World Politics*, 49, 1.

Lewis, P. (1997) 'Theories of Democratization and Patterns of Regime Change in Eastern Europe', *Journal of Communist Studies and Transition Politics*, 13, 1.

Lijphart, A. (1984) *Democracies: Patterns of Majoritarian and Consensus Government in Twenty-One Countries* (Yale University Press).

Lijphart, A. (1994) 'Presidentialism and Majority Democracy', in J. Linz and A. Valenzuela (eds), *The Failure of Presidential Democracy: Comparative Perspectives* (Baltimore: Johns Hopkins University Press).

Lindblom, C. (1977) *Politics and Markets* (New York: Basic Books).

Linz, J. (1994) 'Presidential or Parliamentary Democracy: Does it Make a Difference?', in J. Linz and Valenzuela (eds) *The Failure of Presidential Democracy: Comparative Perspectives* (Baltimore: Johns Hopkins University Press).

Linz, J. and A. Stepan (1996) *Problems of Democratic Transition and Consolidation: South Europe, South America, and Post-Communist Europe* (Baltimore: Johns Hopkins University Press).

Lipset, S. M. (1959) 'Some Social Requisites of Democracy: Economic Development and Political Legitimacy', *American Political Science Review*, 53, 1.

Little, W. (1992) 'Political Corruption in Latin America', *Corruption and Reform*, 7.

Little, W. (1996) 'Corruption and Democracy in Latin America', *IDS Bulletin*, 27, 2.

Lomax, B. (1997) 'The Strange Death of "Civil Society" in Post-Communist Hungary', *Journal of Communist Studies and Transition Politics*, 13, 1.

Lukes, S. (1974) *Power: A Radical View* (London: Macmillan – now Palgrave).

Lyrintzis, C. (1989) 'PASOK in Power: The Loss of the "Third Road to Socialism"', in T. Gallagher and A. Williams (eds), *Southern European Socialism Parties, Elections and the Challenge of Government* (Manchester: Manchester University Press).

Macias, R. S. (1996) 'Executive Legislative Relations and the Institutionalization of Democracy', in R. Seider (ed.), *Central America: Fragile Transitions* (London: Macmillan).

MacKensie, I. (1994) 'Introduction: The Arena of Ideology', in R. Ecleshall, V. Geoghegan, R. Jay, M. Kenny, I. Mackensie and R. Wilford, *Political Ideologies* (London: Routledge).

Macpherson, C. B. (1977) *The Life and Times of Liberal Democracy* (Oxford: Oxford University Press).

Mainwaring, S. (1999) *Rethinking Party Systems in the Third Wave of Democratization:The Case of Brazil* (Stanford: Stanford University Press).

Mair, P. (1997) *Party System Change: Approaches and Interpretations* (Oxford: Oxford University Press).

Mann, M. (1993) *The Sources of Social Power, Volume 2, The Rise of Classes and Nation States, 1760–1914* (Cambridge: Cambridge University Press).

Marais, H. (1998) *South Africa Limits to Change: The Political Economy of Transition* (London: Zed Books).

Marata, A. (2000) 'Labour Movements, Democratic Transitions and Economic Reforms: The Cases of Spain, Argentina and Poland' (unpublished MA Dissertation, Department of Politics, University of Sheffield, Sheffield, 2000).

Maravall, J. M. (1982) *The Transition to Democracy in Spain* (London: Croom Helm).

Maravall, J. M. (1995) 'The Myth of the Authoritarian Advantage', in L. Diamond and M. Plattner, (eds), *Economic Reform and Democracy* (Baltimore: Johns Hopkins University Press).

Maravall, J. M. (1997) *Regimes, Politics and Markets Democratization and Economic Change in Southern and Eastern Europe* (Oxford: Oxford University Press).

Marshall, T. H. (1973) *Class, Citizenship and Social Development* (Westport, Conn: Greenwood Press).

Martin, L. and K. Sikkink (1993) 'US Policy and Human Rights in Argentina and Guatemala', in P. Evans, H. Jacobson and R. Putnam (eds), *Double-Edged Diplomacy: International Bargaining and Domestic Politics* (Berkeley, CA: University of California Press).

Maxwell, K. (1986) 'Regime Overthrow and the Prospects for Democratic Transitions in Portugal', in G. O'Donnell, P. Schmitt and L. Whilehead (eds),

Transitions from Authoritarian Rule Southern Europe (Baltimore: Johns Hopkins University Press).

Maxwell, K. (1995) *The Making of Portuguese Democracy* (Cambridge: Cambridge University Press).

Mbembe, A. (1991) 'Power and Obscenity in the Post-Colonial Period: The Case of Cameroon', in J. Manor (ed.), *Rethinking Third World Politics* (London: Longman).

McGrew, A. (1997) *The Transformation of Democracy?* (Cambridge: Polity Press).

Mendus, S. (1992) 'Losing the Faith: Feminism and Democracy', in J. Dunn (ed.), *Democracy: The Unfinished Journey 508BC to AD 1993* (Cambridge: Cambridge University Press).

Middlemas, K. (1979) *Politics in Industrial Society* (London: Andre Deutsch).

Miszlivetz, F. (1997) 'Participation and Transition: Can the Civil Society Project Survive in Hungary?', *Journal of Communist Studies and Transition Politics*, 13, 1.

Moore, B. (1966) *Social Origins of Democracy and Dictatorship* (Boston, MA: Beacon Press).

Mouzelis, N. (1978) *Modern Greece: Facets of Underdevelopment* (London: Macmillan – now Palgrave).

Mujal-Leon, E. (1989) *European Socialism and the Conflict in Central America* (London: Praeger).

Munck, G. and L. S. Leff (1997) 'Modes of Transition and Democratization in South America and Eastern Europe in Comparative Perspective', *Comparative Politics*, 29, 3.

Nagle, J. D. and A. (1999) Mahr *Democracy and Democratization: Post Communist Europe in Comparative Perspective* (London: Sage).

Nash, K. (1998) 'Beyond Liberalism? Feminist Theories of Democracy', in G. Waylen and V. Randall, *Gender, Politics and the State* (London: Routledge).

Navarro, Z. (1993) 'Democracy, Citizenship and Representation: Rural Social Movements in Southern Brazil 1978–1990', *Bulletin of Latin America Research*, 13, 2.

Ndegwa, S. (1996) *The Two Faces of Civil Society: NGOs and Politics in Africa* (West Hartford, Conn: Kumarian Press).

Nef, J. (1994) 'The Political Economy of Inter-American Relations: A Structural and Historical Overview', in R. Stubbs and G. R. D. Underhill (eds), *Political Economy and the Changing Global Order* (London: Macmillan – now Palgrave).

Nelson, J. (1989) 'The Politics of Long-Haul Economic Reform', in J. Nelson (ed.), *Fragile Coalitions: The Politics of Adjustment* (New Brunswick: Transaction Books).

O'Brien, R., A. Goetz, J. A. Scholte and M. Williams (2000) *Contesting Global Governance: Multilateral Economic Institutions and Global Social Movements* (Cambridge: Cambridge University Press).

O'Donnell, G. (1973) *Modernization and Bureaucratic Authoritarianism: Studies in South American Politics* (Berkeley, CA: University of California Press).

O'Donnell, G. (1992) 'Transition, Continuities and Paradoxes', in S. Mainwaring (ed.), *Issues in Democratic Consolidation* (Bloomington: Indiana University Press).

O'Donnell, G. (1993) 'On the State, Democratization, and Some Conceptual Problems: A Latin American View with Glances at Some Post-Communist Countries', *World Development*, 21, 8.

O'Donnell, G. (1994) 'Delegative Democracy', *Journal of Democracy*, 5, 1.

O'Donnell, G. (2000) 'The Judiciary and the Rule of Law', *Journal of Democracy*, 11, 1.

O'Donnell, G. and P. Schmitter (1986) 'Negotiating (and Renegotiating) Pacts', in G. O'Donnell and P. Schmitter, *Transitions from Authoritarian Rule: Tentative Conclusions from Uncertain Democracies* (Baltimore: Johns Hopkins University Press).

Offe, C. (1997) 'Micro-Aspects of Democratic Theory: What Makes For the Deliberative Competence of Citizens?', in A. Hadenius (ed.), *Democracy's Victory and Crisis* (Cambridge: Cambridge University Press).

Olsen, G. R. (1998) 'Europe and the Promotion of Democracy in Post-Cold War Africa: How Serious in Europe and for What Reason', *African Affairs*, 97.

Ost, D. (1993) 'The Politics of Interest in Post Communist East Europe', *Theory and Society*, 22.

Ost, D. (1997) 'East-Central Europe in Transition', in B. Crawford (ed.), *Markets, States, and Democracy* (Boulder, CO: Westview).

Oxhorn, P. (1995) 'From Controlled Inclusion to Coerced Marginalization: The Struggle for Civil Society in Latin America', in J. Hall (ed.), *Civil Society, Theory History and Comparison* (Cambridge: Polity Press).

Pankhurst, D. (2000) 'Striving for "Real" Democracy in Africa: The Roles of International Donors and Civil Society in Zimbabwe', in H. Smith (ed.), *Democracy and International Relations* (London: Macmillan – now Palgrave).

Parrott, B. (1997) 'Perspectives on Postcommnist Democratization', in K. Dawisha and B. Parrott (eds), *Politics, Power and the Struggle for Democracy in South-East Europe* (Cambridge: Cambridge University Press).

Parsons, T. (1951) *The Social System* (London: Routledge & Kegan Paul).

Pateman, C. (1970) *Participation and Democratic Theory* (Cambridge: Cambridge University Press).

Pateman, C. (1988) *The Sexual Contract* (Cambridge: Polity Press).

Pateman, C. (1989) *The Disorder of Women* (Cambridge: Polity Press).

Payne, A. J. (1991) 'Westminster Adapted: The Political Order of the Commonwealth Caribbean', in J. I. Dominguez, R. A. Pastor and R. D. Worrell (eds), *Democracy in the Caribbean: Political, Economic and Social Perspectives* (London: Johns Hopkins University Press).

Pearce, J. (1997) 'Civil Society, the Market and Democracy in Latin America', *Democratization*, 4, 2.

Pearce, J. (2000) 'Building Civil Society from the Outside: The Problematic Consolidation of Central America', in H. Smith (ed.), *Democracy and International Relations* (London: Macmillan – now Palgrave).

Peden, G. C. (1991) *British Economic and Social Policy: Lloyd George to Margaret Thatcher* (London: Phillip Allan).

Pei, M. (1994) *From Reform to Revolution: The Demise of Communism in China and the Soviet Union* (Cambridge, MA: Harvard University Press).

Pereira, A. (1993) 'Economic Underdevelopment, Democracy and Civil Society: The North-East Brazilian Case', *Third World Quarterly*, 14, 2.

Perez Diaz, V. (1993) *The Return of Civil Society: The Emergence of Democracy in Spain* (London: Harvard University Press).

Philip, G. (1999)'Institutions and Democratic Consolidation in Latin America in', J. Buxton and N. Phillips (eds), *Developments in Latin American Political Economy* (Manchester: Manchester University Press).

Phillips, A. (1991) *Engendering Democracy* (Cambridge: Polity Press).

Phillips, A. (1993) *Democracy and Difference* (Cambridge: Polity Press).

Phillips, A. (1999) *Which Equalities Matter?* (Cambridge: Polity Press).

Powell, C. (1996) 'International Aspects of Democratization: The Case of Spain', in L. Whitehead (ed.), The International Dimension of Democratization: Europe and the Americas (Oxford University Press).

Power, T. J. and M. J. Gasiorowski (1997) 'Institutional Design and Democratic Consolidation in the Third World', *Comparative Political Studies*, 30, 2.

Pravda, A. (ed.) (1996) *The End of the Outer Empire* (London: Sage/Royal Institute for International Affairs).

Preston, P. (1986) The Triumph of Democracy in Spain (London: Methuen).

Pridham, G. (1991) 'International Influences and Democratic Transition: Problems of Theory and Practice in Linkage Politics', in G. Pridham (ed.), *Encouraging Democracy: The International Context of Regime Transition in Southern Europe* (London: University of Leicester Press).

Pridham, G. (1993) 'Southern European Parties: Democracies on the Road to Consolidation: A Comparative Assessment of the Role of Political Parties', in G. Pridham (ed.), *Securing Democracy: Party Politics and Democratic Consolidation in Southern Europe* (London: Routledge).

Pridham, G. (1999) 'The European Union, Democratic Conditionality and Transnational Party Linkages: The Case of Eastern Europe', in J. Grugel (ed.) *Democracy without Borders: Transnationalization and Conditionality in New Democracies* (London: Routledge).

Przeworski, A. (1986) 'Some Problems in the Study of Transition to Democracy', in G. O'Donnell, P. Schmitter and L. Whitehead (eds), *Transitions from Authoritarian Rule: Comparative Perspectives* (Baltimore: Johns Hopkins University Press).

Przeworski, A. (1991) *Democracy and the Market: Political and Economic Reforms in Eastern Europe and Latin America* (Cambridge: Cambridge University Press).

Przeworski, A. (1995) *Sustainable Democracy* (Cambridge: Cambridge University Press).

Przeworski, A. (1999) 'Minimalist Conception of Democracy: A Defense', in I. Schapiro and C. Hacker Cordon (eds), *Democracy's Value* (Cambridge: Cambridge University Press).

Przeworski, A. and F. Limongi (1997) 'Modernization: Theories and Facts', *World Politics* 49, 2.

Putnam, R. (1993) *Making Democracy Work: Civic Traditions in Modern Italy* (Princeton NJ: Princeton University Press).

Pye, L. (1996) *Aspects of Political Development* (Boston: Little, Brown).

Pye, L. and S. Verba (eds) (1965) *Political Culture and Political Development* (Princeton, NJ: Princeton University Press).

Pye, L. and M. Pye (1985) *Asian Power and Politics: The Cultural Dimensions of Authority* (Cambridge, Mass.: The Belknap Press).

Radcliffe, S. and S. Westwood (1996) *Remaking the Nation: Place, Identity, and Politics in Latin America* (London: Routledge).

Rai, S. (1996) 'Gender and Democratization in the South', in R. Lucknam and G. White, (eds), *The Jagged Wave* (Manchester University Press).

Ramirez, R. (1993) 'LA OEA, los paises latinoamericanos y la democracia en el hemisferio', *Sintesis*, 21.

Randall, V. (1997) 'Why Have the Political Trajectories of India and China Been So Different?', in D. Potter, D. Goldblatt, M. Kiloh and P. Lewis (eds), *Democratization* (Cambridge: Open University/Polity Press).

Remmer, K. (1991) 'New Wine or Old Bottlenecks?', *Comparative Politics*, 23, 4.

Remmer, K. (1996) 'The Sustainablility of Political Democracy: Lessons from South America', *Comparative Political Studies*, 29, 6.

Remmer, K. (1997) 'Theoretical Development and Theoretical Decay: The Resurgence of Institutional Analysis', World Politics, 50,1.

Rhodes, R. and D. Marsh (1992) *Policy Networks in British Government* (Oxford: Oxford University Press).

Rigger, S. (1996) 'Mobilisational Authoritarianism and Political Opposition in Taiwan', in G. Rodan (ed.), *Political Opposition in Industrializing Asia* (London: Routledge).

Roberts, K. (1998) *Deepening Democracy? The Modern Left and Social Movements in Chile and Peru* (Stanford: Stanford University).

Robertson, R. (1992) *Globalization: Social Theory and Global Culture* (London: Sage).

Robinson, M. (1995) 'Strengthening Civil Society in Africa: The Role of Foreign Political Aid', *IDS Bulletin*, 26, 2.

Robinson, W. I. (1996) *Promoting Polyarchy: Globalization, US. Intervention, and Hegemony* (Cambridge: Cambridge University Press).

Rodan, G. (ed.) (1996) *Political Opposition in Industrializing Asia* (London: Routledge).

Rosenau, J. N. (1992) 'Governance Order and Change in World Politics', in J. N. Rosenau and E. O. Czempiel (eds) *Governance Without Government* (Cambridge: Cambridge University Press).

Rostow, W. W. (1960) *The Process of Economic Growth* (Oxford: Clarendon Press).

Roxborough, I. (1979) *Theories of Development* (London: Macmillan – now Palgrave).

Rueschemeyer, D., E. Stephens and J. Stephens (1992) *Capitalist Development and Democracy* (Cambridge: Cambridge University Press).

Rustow, D. (1970) 'Transition to Democracy: Toward a Dynamic Model', *Comparative Politics*, 2, 3.

Sakwa, R. (1996) *Russian Politics and Society*, 2nd edn (London: Routledge).

Sandbrook, R. (1996) 'Transition without Consolidation: Democratization in Six African Cases', *Third World Quarterly*, 17, 1.

Sartori, G. (1987) *A Theory of Democracy Revisited* (London: Chatham House).

Schmitter, P. (1995) 'Transitology: The Science or the Art of Democratization', in J. Tulchin and B. Romero (eds), *The Consolidation of Democracy* (Boulder, CO: Woodrow Wilson Center/Lynne Rienner).

Schmitter, P. (1996) 'The Influence of the International Context upon the Choice of National Institutions and Policies in Neo-Democracies', in L. Whitehead (ed.), *The International Dimensions of Democratization: Europe and the Americas* (Oxford: Oxford University Press).

Schmitter, P. and T. L. Karl (1993) 'What Democracy Is ... and Is Not', in L. Diamond and M. Plattner (eds), *The Global Resurgence of Democracy* (Baltimore: Johns Hopkins University Press).

Schmitter, P. and T. L. Karl (1994) 'The Conceptual Travels of Transitologists and Consolidologists: How Far to the East Should They Go?', *Slavic Review*, 53.

Schmitter, P. and G. O'Donnell (1986) *Transformations from Authoritarian Rule: Tenative conclusions from Uncertain Democracies* (Baltimore: Johns Hopkins University Press).

Schmitter, P., G. O'Donnell and L. Whitehead (1986) *Transitions from Authoritarian Rule* (Baltimore: Johns Hopkins University Press).

Schmitz, H. P. and K. Sell (1999) 'International Factors in Processes of Political Democratization: Towards a Theoretical Integration', in J. Grugel (ed.), *Democracy without Borders: Transnationalization and Conditionality in New Democracies* (London: Routledge).

Schneider, C. (1995) *Shanty Town Protests in Pinochet's Chile* (Temple, Texas: Temple University Press).

Scholte, J. A. (2000) *Globalization: A Critical Introduction* (London: Macmillan).

Schopflin, G. (1993) *Politics in Eastern Europe, 1945–1992* (Oxford: Blackwell).

Schumpeter, J. (1976) *Capitalism, Socialism and Democracy* (London: George Allen & Unwin).

Seligman, A. (1992) *The Idea of Civil Society* (Princeton, NJ: Princeton University Press).

Shapiro, I. and C. Hacker-Cordon (1999) 'Promises and Disappointments: Reconsidering Democracy's Value', in I. Shapiro and C. Hacker-Cordon (eds), *Democracy's Value* (Cambridge: Cambridge University Press).

Share, D. (1986) *The Making of Spanish Democracy* (New York: Praeger).

Sharman, J. C. and R. E. Kanet (2000) 'International Influences on Democratization in Postcommunist Europe', in J. Hollifield and C. Jillson (eds), *Pathways to Democracy: The Political Economy of Democratic Transitions* (London: Routledge).

Shaw, M. (1994) 'Civil Society and Global Politics: Beyond a Social Movement Approach', *Millennium: Journal of International Studies*, 32, 3.

Shevtsova, L. (2000) 'The Problems of Executive Power in Russia', *Journal of Democracy*, 11, 1.

Shin, D. C. (1999) *Mass Politics and Culture in Democratizing Korea* (Cambridge: Cambridge University Press).

Shugart, M. and S. Mainwaring (1997) *Presidentialism and Democracy in Latin America* (Cambridge: Cambridge University Press).

Sieder, R. (1996) 'Elections and Democratization in Honduras Since 1980', *Democratization*, 3, 2.

Sikkink, K. (1993) 'Human Rights, Principle Issue Networks and Sovereignty in Latin America', *International Organization*, 43, 3.

Sikkink, K. (1996) 'The Emergence, Evolution and Effectiveness of the Latin American Human Rights Network', in E. Jelin and E. Hershberg, *Constructing Democracy: Human Rights, Citizenship and Society in Latin America* (Boulder, CO: Westview Press).

Silva, E. (1999) 'The New Political Order in Latin America: Towards Technocratic Democracies?', in R. G. Gwynne and C. Kay (eds), *Latin America Transformed: Globalization and Modernity* (London: Edward Arnold).

Skocpol, T. (1979) *States and Social Revolutions* (Cambridge: Cambridge University Press).

Skocpol, T. (1985) 'Bringing the State Back In: Strategies of Analysis in Current Research', in P. B. Evans, D. Rueschmeyer and T. Skocpol, *Bring the State Back In* (Cambridge: Cambridge University Press).

Smith, M. (1993) *Pressure, Power and Policy; State Autonomy and Policy Networks in Britain and the US* (London: University of Pittsburgh Press).

Smolar, A. (1996) 'From Opposition to Atomization', *Journal of Democracy*, 7, 1.

Sola, L. (1991) 'Heterdox Shock in Brazil: Tecnicos, Politicians and Democracy', *Journal of Latin America Studies*, 23, 1.

Sole Tura, J. (1985) 'Socialist Governments in Southern Europe between Reformism and Adaptation to State Structures', paper presented to the European consortium for Political Research.

Sorensen, G. (1993) *Democracy and Democratization: Processes and Prospects in a Changing World* (Boulder, CO: Westview).

Sorensen, G. (1999) 'Rethinking Sovereignty and Development', *Journal of International Relations and Development*, 2, 4.

Stark, J. (1992) 'Path Dependence and Privatization Strategies in East Central Europe', *Eastern European Politics and Societies*, 6.

Steinberg, D. I. (1995) 'The Republic of Korea: Pluralizing Politics', in L. Diamond, J. Linz and S. M. Lipset (eds), *Politics in Developing Countries* (Boulder, CO: Lynne Rienner).

Stepan, A. (1986) 'Paths toward Redemocratization: Theoretical and Comparative Considerations', in G. O'Donnell, P. Schmitter and L. Whitehead, *Transitions from Authoritarian Rule: Comparative Perspective* (London: Johns Hopkins University Press).

Stiglitz, S. (2000) 'The Insider: What I Learned … World Economic Crisis', *The New Republic*, 17 April.

Strange, S. (1992) 'States, Firms, and Diplomacy', *International Affairs*, 68, 1.

Strange, S. (1995) 'The Defective State', *Daedelus*, 124 (Spring 1995).

Sum, N.-L. (1995) 'More Than a "War of Words": Identity Politics and the Struggle for Dominance during the Recent "Political Reform" Period in Hong Kong', *Economy and Society*, 24, 1.

Sum, N.-L. (1999) 'Politics of Identities and the Making of the "Greater China" Subregion in the Post-Cold War Era', in G. Hook and I. Kearns (eds), *Subregionalism and World Order* (London: Macmillan – now Palgrave).

Tarrow, S. (1995) 'Mass Mobilization and Regime Change: Pacts, Reform and Popular Power in Italy (1918–1922) and Spain (1975–1978)', in R. Gunther, P. Diamandouros and H. J. Puhle (eds), *The Politics of Democratic Consolidation* (Baltimore: Johns Hopkins University Press).

Tarrow, S. (1998) *Power in Movement: Social Movements and Contentious Politics*, 2nd edn (Cambridge: Cambridge University Press).

Taylor, L. (1998) *Citizenship, Participation and Democracy: Changing Dynamics in Chile and Argentina* (London: Macmillan – now Palgrave).

Taylor, L. (1999) 'Globalization and Civil Society – Continuities, Ambiguities and Realities in Latin America', *Indiana Journal of Global Legal Studies*, 7.

Therborn, G. (1978) 'The Rule of Capital and the Rise of Democracy', *New Left Review*, 103.

Tilly, C. (1978) *From Mobilization to Revolution* (Reading, MA: Addison-Wesley).

Tilly, C. (1984) 'Social Movements and National Politics', in C. Bright and S. Harding (eds), *Statemaking and Social Movements: Essays in History and Theory* (Ann Arbor: University of Michigan Press).

Tilly, C. (1990) *Coercion, Capital and European States 900–1990* (London: Blackwell).

Tilly, C. (1995) *Popular Contention in Britain* (Cambridge, MA: University of Harvard Press).

Tilly, C. (1997) 'The Top-Down and Bottom-Up Construction of Democracy', in E. Etzioni-Halevy, *Classes and Elites in Democracy and Democratization* (New York: Garland Publishers).

Trudeau, R. (1993) *Guatemala Politics: The Popular Struggle for Democracy* (Boulder, CO: Lynne Rienner).

Tsingos, B. (1996) 'Underwriting Democracy: The European Community and Greece', in L. Whitehead (ed.), *The International Dimension of Democratization* (Oxford : Oxford University Press).

Van Rooy, A. and M. Robinson (1998) 'Out of the Ivory Tower: Civil Society and the Aid System', in A. Van Rooy, *Civil Society and the Aid Industry* (London: Earthscan).

Vanhanen, T. (1990) *The Process of Democratization: A comparative Study of 147 States 1980–1988* (London: Crane Russak).

Waller, M. (1993) *The End of the Communist Power Monopoly* (Manchester: Manchester University Press).

Walzer, M. (1992) 'The Civil Society Argument', in C. Mouffe (ed.), *Dimensions of Radical Democracy: Pluralism, Citizenship and Community* (London: Verso).

Waylen, G. (1996) 'Democratisation, Feminism and the State in Chile: The Establishment of SERNAM', in S. M. Rai and G. Lievesley (eds), *Women and the State: International Perspectives* (London: Taylor & Francis).

Waylen, G. (1998) Gender, Feminism and the State', in G. Waylen and V. Randall (eds), *Gender, Politics and the State* (London: Routledge).

Waylen, G. (2000) 'Gender and Democratic Politics: A Comparative Analysis of Consolidation in Argentina and Chile', *Journal of Latin American Studies*, 32, 3.

Weale, A. (1999) Democracy (London: Macmillan – now Palgrave).

Weir, S. and D. Beetham (1999) *Political Power and Democratic Control in Britain* (London: Routledge).

Weiss, L. (1998) *The Myth of the Powerless State: Governing the Economy in a Global Era* (Cambridge: Polity Press).

Weyland, K. (1996) 'Obstacles to Social Reform in Brazil's New Democracy', *Comparative Politics*, 29, 1.

Weyland, K. (1997) 'Growth with Equity in Chile's New Democracy', *Latin American Research Review*, 32, 1.

White, G., J. Howell and S. Xiaoyuan (1996) *In Search of Civil Society: Market Reform and Social Change in Contemporary China* (New York: Clarendon Press).

White, S. (2000) 'Russia, Elections, Democracy', *Government and Opposition*, 35, 3.

White, S., R. Rose and I. McAllister (1997) *How Russia Votes* (London: Chatham House).

Whitehead, L. (1986) 'International Aspects of Democratization', in G. O'Donnell, P. Schmitter and L. Whitehead (eds), *Transitions from Authoritarian Rule: Comparative Perspective* (Baltimore: Johns Hopkins University Press).

Whitehead, L. (1991) 'Democracy by convergence and Southern Europe', in G. Pridham (ed.), *Encouraging Democracy: The International Context of Regime Transition in Southern Europe* (London: Leicester University Press).

Whitehead, L. (1996) 'Three International Dimensions of Democratization', in L. Whitehead (ed.), *The International Dimension of Democratization* (Oxford: Oxford University Press).

Whitehead, L. and G. Gray-Molina (1999) 'The Long Term Politics of Pro-Poor Policies', paper prepared for the World Development Report 2001, Castle Donnington, 16–17 August 1999.

Wiarda, H. (1981) *Corporatism and National Development in Latin America* (Boulder, CO: Westview Press).

Wiseman, J. (1997) 'The Rise and Fall and Rise (and Fall?) of Democracy in Sub-Saharan Africa' in D. Potter, D. Goldblatt, M. Kiloh, and P. Lewis (eds), *Democratization* (Cambridge Open University/Polity Press).

Woods, D. (1992) 'Civil Society in Europe and Africa: Limiting State Power through a Public Sphere', *African Studies Review*, 35, 2.

World Bank (1999a) *World Bank Development Report 1999* (Washington: World Bank).

World Bank (1999b) *Voices of the Poor* (Washington: World Bank).

World Bank (2000) 'Anti-Corruption in Transition: A Contribution to the Policy Debate', wbweek@worldbank.org, 2–6 October 2000.

World Bank (2001) *World Bank Development Report* (Washington: World Bank).

Yashar, D. (1997) *Demanding Democracy Reform and Reaction in Costa Rica and Guatemala, 1870s–1950s* (Stanford: Stanford University Press).

Yashar, D. (1998) 'Contesting Citizenship: Indigenous Movements and Democracy in Latin America', *Comparative Politics*, 31, 1.

Young, I. M. (1999) 'State, Civil Society and Social Justice', in I. Shapiro and C. Hacker-Cordon, (eds), *Democracy's Value* (Cambridge: Cambridge University Press).

Young, T. (1995) 'A Project to be Realised: Global Liberalism and Contemporary Africa', *Millennium: Journal of International Studies*, 24, 3.

Youngs, G. (2000) 'Political Economy, Democracy and Transition: The Case of Hong Kong', in H. Smith (ed.), *Democracy and International Relations* (London: Macmillan – now Palgrave).

Zartman, I. W. (1995) 'Posing the Problem of State Collapse', in I. W. Zartman (ed.), *Collapsed State – The Disintegration and Restoration of Legitimate Authority* (Boulder, CO: Lynne Rienner).

Zubek, V. (1997) 'The End of Liberalism? Economic Liberalization and the Transformation of Post-Communist Poland', *Communist and Post Communist Studies*, 30, 2.

Index